AQA (B)

Advanced

General
Studies

AQA (B)

Advanced
General
Studies

Colin Swatridge

Editor: Eric Magee

Philip Allan Updates, an imprint of Hodder Education, part of Hachette Livre UK, Market Place, Deddington, Oxfordshire OX15 0SE

Orders

Bookpoint Ltd, 130 Milton Park, Abingdon, Oxfordshire OX14 4SB
tel: 01235 827720
fax: 01235 400454
e-mail: uk.orders@bookpoint.co.uk
Lines are open 9.00 a.m.–5.00 p.m., Monday to Saturday, with a 24-hour message answering service. You can also order through the Philip Allan Updates website: www.philipallan.co.uk

© Philip Allan Updates 2008

ISBN 978-1-84489-610-3

First printed 2008
Impression number   5   4   3   2
Year   2012   2011   2010   2009   2008

Some of the websites referenced in this textbook may no longer be available.

Design by Gary Kilpatrick
Printed in Italy

Contents

Example 3

Example 4

Example 5

Introduction

What this book is for

This book is for students of General Studies who are following AQA specification B. It is both:

- a coursebook providing subject content, and suggestions for discussion and writing
- a guide to ways of preparing for the unit tests (or examination papers)

You should be familiar with the specification: that is, with the two units at AS and (if you are taking the full A-level) the two further units at A2:

AS	A2
Conflict	Power
Space	Change

You should know that each unit is divided into five *areas of study*. These are:
- Science and technology
- Society and politics
- Arts and media
- Business and industry
- Beliefs and values

For the AS units, each area of study is then divided into two topics. For example, under the unit title **Conflict**, the 'Science and technology' area is divided into these two topics:
- A Human aggression
- B Controversy in science and technology

Conflict is the theme that runs through all the topics in Unit 1. The same applies to **Space**, **Power** and **Change** for units 2, 3 and 4 respectively.

There is material on all these topics, in all these areas of study, under all four themes, in this book. There are also plenty of examples of the type of questions that appear in the specification, and that will appear in unit tests. Answers to these questions are given in the Teacher Guide that accompanies this book.

You will find the AQA General Studies specification B, specimen assessment units, and mark schemes on the AQA website: www.aqa.org.uk.

The information on the AQA website and the material in this book should be all that you need to equip yourself with the content and skills needed for this specification and for the unit tests that are based on it. Much of what you read online, or in print (in newspapers, for example), and much of what you watch on television, in live or recorded form, might also be relevant to General Studies. You should also feel free, in this subject, to draw on your own experience (whether this is of foreign travel or of stacking shelves in a supermarket), in a way that you may not be able to in other subjects.

What you will find here

There are ten topics in Unit 1 and ten topics in Unit 2. There are 15 topics in each of the A2 units, Units 3 and 4. There is material on all 50 topics in this book.

Each topic is dealt with under two headings:
- Content
- Skills

Under 'Content', you will find sources and texts, usually in the form of prose extracts, but sometimes they will be tables of data, and sometimes (in Unit 2: **Space**) they will be images. In Units 1 and 2 (the AS units) the word 'sources' is used, but in Units 3 and 4 (the A2 units) we have used the term 'texts', as an indicator that you will need to call upon your own knowledge, as well as that provided in the extracts, in order to answer the questions adequately.

Under each topic heading in the specification, you will find a set of four questions. Thus for Unit 1 (Conflict), under 'Science and technology: Human aggression', you will find the questions:
- What are the causes of aggression?
- How and why should we attack others and defend ourselves?
- Are sports and games an effective channel for aggression?
- How does technology change the nature of warfare?

These questions are designed to *open up* the topic — to explain what it means in practice. (They are not a sample of the sorts of question that will be asked in unit tests.) The sources and texts in the 'Content' sections have been selected and adapted so as to address these questions.

Under 'Skills', you will find the type of questions that will be asked in unit tests, and guidance as to how they might best be answered. In the main, they will be *Why...?, How...?, How far...?* and *To what extent...?* questions, rather than *What...?* or *When...?* questions. You may be asked to think about questions of a *What...?* kind, and perhaps to jot something down in writing, for example:

What do you understand by the term: 'the media'?

However, such a question will only be asked to prepare you for tackling larger *Why.../How...?* questions.

Questions will not usually be of the sort that expect a particular answer — never mind a 'right' answer. You will need some *knowledge* in order to answer questions, but how you use that knowledge to support a *point of view* is just as important.

How you might answer questions

It is suggested that any answer to a question — be it a long answer or a short one — should consist of three components. These might be best represented by the following letters:

S

Ex

C

A 'sexy' answer is one that is enlivened by the use of concrete examples; it is one that is enjoyable to read because you have entered into the spirit of the question, and have supplied hard facts and examples.

The 'S' stands for 'statement'. The word 'statement' comes from the Latin verb 'to stand'. The opening statement of your answer should make it clear where you stand on the topic in question.

'Ex' stands for 'examples'. We all come at issues from a certain angle; we cannot help ourselves. What is important is that you support your opening statement with reasons based on real-life examples.

The 'C' stands for 'conclusion'. Without a conclusion, an answer is incomplete; the examples are left hanging as if they answered the question by themselves. The function of the conclusion is to spell out the answer and confirm the opening statement.

For example, these are the components of a simple *expository* answer to a question like:

When might one country be justified in attacking another?

This is a *closed* question: it assumes that one country might well be justified in attacking another. There is little or no room for an examination of the view that such an attack can never be justified. The answer might look something like this:

Statement
Countries have attacked each other throughout history. The number of such attacks that were justified may be quite limited.

Examples
Britain might be said to have been justified in attacking Germany in the Second World War, because Britain had promised that it would assist European allies if they were attacked by Germany.

US forces might have been justified in attacking Iraq in the early 1990s when that country invaded Kuwait...

More controversially, NATO attacked Serbia in 1999 when the president of that country persecuted non-ethnic-Serbs in other parts of the former Yugoslavia...

Conclusion
Recent history gives us examples of attacks on countries that posed a real threat to their neighbours.

It is more likely that questions of a more *argumentative* sort will be asked, for example:

How far might it be said that we live in a consumer society?

This is an *open* question. In answering such a question, one might equally answer that 'we don't live in such a society' as that 'we do'.

In fact, a 'good' answer will generally acknowledge that there is a sense in which we do live in such a society, and a sense in which we don't. It is a question of balance.

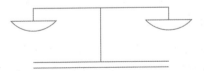

The two 'sides' of an argument might be perfectly balanced; it is more likely, though, that one side of the argument will be weightier than the other. In an argumentative essay, it is good practice to acknowledge both sides of the argument — and it is advisable to look at the lighter, less convincing side of the argument first. Thus, our:

S

Ex

C

becomes:

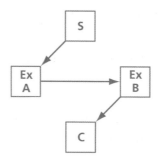

In looking at the less convincing argument first, you should show awareness that there *is* a contrary, or alternative point of view. You should then put this to one side to give prominence to the weightier point of view that leads to your conclusion.

An answer to the previous question — How far might it be said that we live in a consumer society? — could look like this:

Statement

By a 'consumer society' we mean one in which importance is attached to the buying and owning of goods. Ours is such a society to a large extent.

Ex A

Obviously, there are some people who choose to live simply. Equally, there are people who have no choice but to do this: many pensioners, single parents, the unemployed and long-term sick or disabled people.

Ex B

However, most of us, at least in the UK, buy and possess much more than we may be said to need. Many of us eat and drink more than we need in order to survive: hence (in part) the obesity problem, alcoholism and so on.

We buy and equip bigger living-spaces than we need, and we drive more vehicles than we have a rational use for. When we earn more money, we buy more gadgets with it, on the assumption that 'new means better' — indeed, we don't even wait until we have money: many of us live on credit, owing as much as we can...

Conclusion

We are not all passionate consumers, but a society that measures 'growth' in terms of the trade in non-essential goods is a consumer society.

As stated earlier, you are expected to have some knowledge and understanding of the subject content of this specification. In all the assessment units, however, you are given some support. In Unit 1, you are given a 'lead' to each question, and three cues by way of content guidance. In all the other units, texts, images and data-sets are provided, which you are asked to respond to and interpret. You are given credit for any points you make and examples you give that are not supplied in the cues or in the sources.

The knowledge that you show you have is important. But remember that a little knowledge may go a long way. What you *do* with it is just as important.

Assessment objectives

AQA sets four assessment objectives that are to be met in the teaching, learning and examining of this subject.

Assessment Objective 1
Demonstrate relevant knowledge and understanding applied to a range of issues, using skills from different disciplines (weighting *c.* 30%).

Assessment Objective 2
Marshal evidence and draw conclusions; select, interpret, evaluate and integrate information, data, concepts and opinions (weighting *c.* 40%).

Assessment Objective 3
Demonstrate understanding of different types of knowledge, appreciating their strengths and limitations (weighting *c.* 15%).

Assessment Objective 4
Communicate clearly and accurately in a concise, logical and relevant way (weighting *c.* 15%).

These assessment objectives are what all four assessment units, and all four sections of this book, are about. They call for:
- awareness of the subject content
- the ability to construct an argument
- understanding of the differences between factual statements and value judgements
- competence in the use of language

AO3 might look the most challenging. The 'different types of knowledge' is not a reference to different AS/A-level subjects; it is better understood as meaning *different ways of knowing*.

When we do A to B and the result is C; and when we repeatedly do A to B and, again and again, the result is C, we can make a *factual statement* to the effect that when A is done to B, under certain experimental conditions, the result is always C. As long as we conduct experiments in this rigorous fashion, we can be *certain* about the truth of our factual statements.

There is not a great deal that we can know with certainty — indeed, there are those who would say that we can only be said to *know* something when we are certain about it. We cannot know for certain that present-day climate change is the direct result of human activity, but we *believe* it to be the case. On balance, it does seem highly *probable*, and we feel a need to act on this belief.

It is not even probable that Elizabeth I never intended to marry any of her suitors — but it is entirely *possible*. A historian might well come to this conclusion on the available evidence. It will be his or her considered *opinion* — a matter of historical *judgement*. Fresh evidence (a hitherto undiscovered letter, for example) might render it probable, even certain, that Elizabeth's suitors were all, unknowingly, wasting their time.

This continuum from certainty, through probability, to possibility (from knowledge, through well-based opinion, to less-well-based *guesswork*) is really what AO3 is about. It is about candidates weighing the evidence in order to determine whether we can be said to *know* something, or *believe* something, or have an *opinion* about something that we may change according to whether the evidence changes.

It is one thing to present evidence and come to a conclusion; it is another to explain why you feel you have to come to this conclusion in particular. An essay is an argument, and argument is the art of persuasion. Trying to persuade a reader to adopt your point of view can be satisfying and rewarding. You may even come to enjoy doing it.

Colin Swatridge

AS

UNIT 1

CONFLICT

CONFLICT
Introduction

Each of the theme titles has been chosen because it expresses something fundamental about the human condition. What is more, the four themes are related:

- We are all different, and **conflict** arises out of **differences**.
- **Conflict** occurs within a **space**: the planet, a country, a household.
- It is often about who has **power**; who has most power often wins in the **conflict**.
- Not all **conflict** is bad; without it, perhaps, nothing would **change**.

If all four themes are fundamental, **Conflict** is arguably the most fundamental of them all:

- Knowledge is about **conflict** between new ideas and old ones.
- Justice is done when **conflict** between accuser and accused is resolved.
- Government is the product of a **conflict** of views about what should be done.
- Religion is a working out of **conflict** between concepts of good and evil.

So, we begin by looking at where conflict might arise in the five areas of study: Science and technology, Society and politics, and so on.

This is the unit in which knowledge and understanding (AO1) of the topics in the specification is most crucial. You cannot expect to answer a question like: 'Is there more to newspapers than the latest "news"'? if you have never picked up a newspaper, or you have never read non-news journalism, or you have never discussed or thought about what there is in newspapers that is not 'news'.

The unit test based on this unit does not contain source material. There are no passages, tables or illustrations supplied with the paper so all the knowledge and understanding of **Conflict** topics that you need must be in place before you enter for the unit test.

There are five questions on the paper from which you choose three. Each consists of:

- a statement
- the question
- three bullet-pointed cues (suggestions as to what you might include in your answer)

Because there are no sources supplied with Unit 1, and because you will need knowledge and understanding of the subject content in order to answer the questions, sources are supplied in the 'Content' sections in this first unit — more of them than in all the other units. There is one source for each of the 40 indicative questions in the five areas of study in this unit.

These sources do not answer the questions, but they do give you raw material for your answers. They may be all you need — but you will be given credit for any other knowledge that you apply from elsewhere.

The 'Skills' sections are also more developed in this unit than they are in Units 2, 3 and 4. You will be prepared for, and taken through the process of writing, two essays in each of the two topics, under all five areas of study. This means a total of 20 essays.

To summarise:

- You will need some knowledge and understanding of the concepts/issues in this Conflict unit.
- You should try to engage in discussion of the issues with other people so as to arrive at an opinion of your own about the issues.
- You should be aware of the format of the questions in Unit 1, and work through (perhaps timing yourself) as many of the questions in the 'Skills' sections as you can.
- You should be able to give some **specific examples** in your answers to these questions. These will always improve your answer.

AS

UNIT 1 CONFLICT
Science and technology

Human aggression

Content

Source A — **What are the causes of aggression?**

Humans, as we now know ourselves, have lived and breathed for, at most, 0.0001% of the time since the Earth came into being. We can only guess at how many species there might have been before we arrived on the scene, and the commonest guess is 30 billion. Only one in 120,000 of these species has survived in the fossil record; and of the quarter of a million species that have survived, 95% were marine creatures.

There have always been extinctions: it has been estimated that, throughout biological history, on average one species has gone extinct every 4 years, as a result of climate changes and pandemics. We do not know how many extinctions human beings have caused; but we do know that the rate of animal extinction has accelerated exponentially since humans have been around.

We know that dodos became extinct on the island of Mauritius, in the Indian Ocean, in the 1680s. They were big birds that could neither fly nor run very fast. They were shot to extinction by sailors merely because they were an easy target. They were not even very nasty.

We know that the enormous sea cow was hunted to extinction on islands in the Bering Sea, and that the species had disappeared by 1768, just 27 years after it was first sighted.

We know that, when a new lighthouse was built on Stephens Island, between the North and South Islands of New Zealand, the lighthouse-keeper's cat munched its way through the only known species of a flightless perching wren anywhere in the world.

We know that at least nine species of Hawaiian birds were shot to extinction in the 1890s by hunters in the pay of the second Baron Rothschild of the British banking family, a collector who might have thought of himself as a naturalist.

We know that there were bounties on the heads of eastern mountain lions in New York State at the end of the nineteenth century, and on a carnivorous marsupial (the thylacine), in Tasmania. The last of these creatures died in Hobart, in 1936.

Some of these species killed were deemed to be 'pests'; some were good to eat; and some — perhaps the majority — were good to look at, stuffed, in a trophy room or museum. Human aggression has taken many forms.

Adapted from Bryson, B. (2003) *A Short History of Nearly Everything*, Doubleday

Source B   How and why should we attack others and defend ourselves?

Let us face the fact fairly and squarely that Hizbullah wants to wipe Israel off the map. You only have to listen to their broadcasts to realise this. They deliberately provoked Israel's ferocious response in order to galvanise other extremist groups — yes, and governments — into supporting them in their unholy war against Israel, backed by the arch-enemy, America.

Democratic governments owe it to Israel to do all in their power to disarm Hizbullah, and show solidarity with a government that seeks only secure borders with its neighbours.

IK, Beersheba, Israel

It is perfectly clear to most of us why Israel attacked South Lebanon: she did so because Hizbullah is a terrorist organisation that attacks innocent civilians with its rockets. Hizbullah, like Hamas, had kidnapped Israeli soldiers. Israel is a democratic state with the right of all states to defend itself against unprovoked aggression. The USA does not negotiate with terrorists, and nor should Israel.

ML, Round Lake Beach, Illinois, USA

Did Hizbullah's kidnapping of two Israeli soldiers give Israel the right to bomb Lebanon, destroy bridges, put its international airport out of action, blockade ports, and make refugees of innocents? The force used by Israel was out of all proportion to the provocation. We may call it a terrorist organisation, but Hizbullah is the only real army that Lebanon has with which to defend itself.

SF, Karachi, Pakistan

As usual, it is the innocents who suffer — and I refer neither to Israel nor to Hizbullah, but to the Lebanese people. They have had to contend, over decades, with the unwelcome attentions of both Israelis and Syrians. Just when they were enjoying something like peace and prosperity, they found themselves on a battle-field again — and it is Lebanese civilians who are killed, not Hizbullah militants.

When will the world understand that there will be peace in the Middle East only when the Palestinians have a homeland of their own?

DA, Algester, Australia

Based on letters to *TIME*, 28 August 2006

Source C   **Are sports and games an effective channel for aggression?**

'Kevin Pietersen was really the man who tore into the Australians and wrenched the Ashes from their grasp.'

'The warriors of Leeds and Bradford collided with each other in a no-holds-barred battle. This was rugby as war.'

'Everton have always been at their fighting best when they have been one-nil down.'

'This was a new sort of aggressiveness that Henman showed at the net.'

'Simon Jones is a vital weapon in England's four-man pace attack.'

'Llanelli fired all their big guns in the first half at Stradey Park yesterday, but they had to fight hard to defend themselves against Glasgow in the second.'

'His colleague Giancarlo Fisichella rode shotgun early on, to hold off the McLarens.'

'His reverse swing is increasingly menacing. It is an important part of the sub-continent's bowling armoury.'

'Michael Schumacher's Ferrari was bayoneted from behind, spun round, then bayoneted head-on.'

'Cricket might have been thought a sleepy game until Warne and McGrath bared their teeth and snarled.'

'This was an epic battle that the Bulls fought to win their place at Old Trafford.'

'Arsenal's firepower was something to be seen, but they began to run out of ammunition long before the final whistle.'

Adapted from various sports reports

Source D How does technology change the nature of warfare?

Nuclear weapons were stockpiled by the western Allies and by the Soviet Union in the Cold War years. The two sides maintained what they thought of as a 'balance of terror'; the nuclear threat was thought by each side to deter the other from a first use of such weapons — retaliation would be so swift that it would bring about mutually assured destruction (MAD).

The two sides realised that the effectiveness of the nuclear deterrent would be put at risk if there was a proliferation — or runaway increase — in the number of nuclear weapons, and of states capable of developing nuclear weapons, around the world. Thus, the USA, UK and France on one side, and the Soviet Union on the other side, signed the Nuclear Non-Proliferation Treaty (or NPT) in 1970. This was intended to hold the line against 'rogue' regimes acquiring nuclear weapons of their own, and using them — or threatening to use them — in a first strike.

When China stepped forward as a nuclear state, it was made a permanent member of the UN Security Council. Israel never signed the NPT, but is widely believed to be nuclear-capable; it will neither confirm nor deny such capability. In the 1990s, India and Pakistan, then sworn enemies, both test-fired nuclear weapons. Neither country had signed the NPT — but the tests might have been little more than a flexing of muscles. Tension has since eased between these two states, and both are deemed 'friendly' towards the West.

Gadafy of Libya tried to get his hands on nuclear technology for many years, but the threat that he posed is now thought to have been neutralised. North Korea and Iran are the real threats now: both have civil nuclear-energy programmes, and both are known to have reprocessed spent fuel for weapons purposes. The big fear, of course, is that reprocessed uranium might fall into the hands of terrorists and 'rogue states' who will not be bound by any treaty. It was this fear — baseless as it turned out — that drove the USA and UK to topple Saddam Hussein's regime in Iraq.

It is estimated that there are 30,000 nuclear weapons, in the hands of ten countries, capable of destroying the planet several times over.

Members of the Security Council	1 USA
	2 Russia
	3 UK
	4 France
	5 China
Nations 'friendly' to the West	6 Israel*
	7 India
	8 Pakistan
Nations potentially 'unfriendly'	9 North Korea
	10 Iran

*Israel will not confirm or deny whether it has nuclear weapons.

Skills

The specification invites you to consider aggression at the level of both the individual and society.

It focuses on the *why* of aggression, of attack and defence, and on *how* aggression might be:
- channelled
- used effectively for particular purposes
- mitigated or counteracted

It is assumed that we are all, in some measure, aggressive. Psychologists affirm that when we are confronted by a challenge, we respond in one of two ways: *fight* or *flight*.

(i) **Think about, and write down some examples of, circumstances that might lead to either fight or flight at the level of the individual. Are these circumstances on a bigger scale the same ones that provoke countries to go to war, and others to defend themselves?**

(ii) **Groups of people in a country under attack might flee, becoming refugees but what might the 'flight' response of a country be that cannot fight?**

New Zealand all blacks performing the haka

There is a limit to the types of questions that can reasonably be asked on this topic, given that you are not expected to be in possession of specialist knowledge. The main possibilities are as follows:

1 Why do people attack each other?
2 Why do countries attack each other?
3 What can countries do to defend themselves against other countries?
4 How far can sport serve as an alternative to fighting and as a release for aggressive feelings?
5 Might sport actually encourage aggression and competitiveness?
6 To what extent are nuclear weapons a deterrent against going to war?
7 How might we reduce the threat and impact of war?

Questions in Unit 1 will give you more of a lead than questions (i) and (ii) on the previous page do. First of all, there will be a factual statement or a judgement, often in the form of a 'quotation' (authentic or not); then there will be the question itself, followed by three bullet-pointed 'cues'.

Here is an example of the type of question that might be asked, which combines the previous two questions:

> **Q1** 'Carrying an offensive weapon is against the law; so it should be against the law for countries to possess offensive weapons.'
>
> How far do you agree that this is a reasonable judgement?
>
> You might consider:
> ■ why there is a law against carrying offensive weapons
> ■ whether or not it is an effective law
> ■ how far such a law could be applied to countries

The three cues are offered as a kind of 'scaffolding' — as a guide to the way in which an answer might be structured. It is not an absolute requirement that you pick up each of the cues in turn, in such a way that an answer will be in three parts. It is likely, though, that a good answer will take note of each of the three points.

The third cue, in particular, is likely to reflect AO3, which has to do with the bases of our *opinions/judgement*; the *limits of our knowledge*; and our *beliefs* and *values*. It is important, therefore, that this third point be considered particularly carefully.

On a separate sheet, answer the following questions:

(iii) **What three reasons can you think of for the law that bans the carrying of guns, knives and other offensive weapons?**

(Note: the operative word is 'carrying'; there are separate laws against the *possession* of firearms and flick-knives *in the UK*.)

(iv) **Can the carrying of anything that might be used as an offensive weapon be prevented, in practice? Give two reasons why not.**

Note that the law does work in the main. *Most* people do not carry weapons, and road-repairers are not forced to surrender their pneumatic drills to the police. But note also that the definition of what is 'offensive' is tightly drawn at airports.

(v) **Now write down three reasons why it would be reasonable and three reasons why it would not be reasonable to make it illegal for countries to possess offensive weapons.**

You now have the raw materials with which to answer Q1. Here is a sketch of an answer:

[S] *It is reasonable up to a point; countries have a right to defend themselves, and it is not always easy to distinguish between defence and offence, as Source B makes clear.*

[Ex A] *'Carrying' weapons is one thing, when we are talking about individuals, who are subject to the law of the country; it is something else to apply such laws to whole countries. It is true that there are certain laws in place, though; Source D refers to the NPT, for instance.*

[Ex B] *The law is only partly successful in respect of individuals — as it is in respect of countries, like North Korea and Iran (Source D). Countries that are members of the UN and are part of the global economy can be monitored to some extent. The real problem arises when offensive weapons fall into the hands of groups that owe no allegiance to a state or to the UN.*

[C] *We are right to ban the possession of what have come to be called 'weapons of mass destruction', but it is unrealistic to expect countries to give up weapons that might justifiably be used in self-defence.*

A fuller answer to this question (of the sort that you might be expected to write in the 20 minutes or so at your disposal) is given in the Teacher Guide that accompanies this book.

Here is a further question that combines questions 4 and 5 from the list of seven questions on page 9:

Q2 Sport at the highest level seems to be all about winners and losers.

Discuss whether highly competitive sport brings out the worst in those who take part.

You might consider:
- football violence on and off the pitch
- sports where there is no physical contact between players
- what we might mean by 'sportsmanship'

Controversy in science and technology

Content

Why might scientific advances be a cause for concern?

Scientists have no wish to be represented as demi-gods having a secret knowledge of how the world works. They are, in no sense, in a class apart. On the other hand, they have no wish to be cast as villains, foisting innovation on an unwilling public — and being proved 'wrong'. There have been a number of cases in recent years in which scientists have been portrayed as 'ganging up' against the public interest.

BSE

The scandal surrounding bovine spongiform encephalopathy (BSE) or 'mad cow disease' arose from two sources. The first was the misguided practice among cattle-feed suppliers and farmers of mixing waste matter (including the brains) of slaughtered sheep with vegetable matter in winter feed for cows. In the desire to make use of this otherwise surplus 'protein', the possibility that infection might pass from one species to another was neglected; politicians then added to the problem by playing down any risk that there might be to humans. The

scientists working at the limits of our knowledge in this area were the 'piggies in the middle'.

MMR vaccine

The combined measles, mumps and rubella (MMR) vaccine had been administered safely and with public confidence for a generation before Dr Wakefield and his colleagues hinted at a connection between the vaccine and late-onset autism and bowel disease. No other scientist could demonstrate either that there was a connection or that there was not (it is notoriously difficult to prove a negative), and Dr Wakefield himself could not replicate his first findings. A section of the press, and even some politicians from the Conservative Party, argued that parents should be permitted to choose between MMR and single vaccinations. The government's Chief Medical Officer held his ground, arguing that the latter course would lead to deaths from measles. Scientist was pitted against scientist, and there was much unpleasantness before Dr Wakefield's research was finally discredited.

GM food

In recent years, some people became concerned that they were being encouraged to eat products that had not been properly tested. Large companies claimed that only genetically modified (GM) crops would provide enough food for the world's growing population; but it was feared that their real motive was to put small food-producers out of business and monopolise the market. Environmental groups, meanwhile, argued that the spores from GM crops would 'contaminate' crops grown organically, down-wind. The popular press caricatured the conflict as one between 'healthy' food and 'Frankenstein' food. Once again, scientists held to be in the pay of the GM companies were represented as wanting to foist novelty on a wise and unwilling public.

Stem-cell research

There is real public anxiety about whether scientists should be allowed to do everything that they now can do. Stem cells are the 'building blocks' of all cells. From these, scientists have been able to create what are called primordial germ cells: these are cells that could grow into either (female) eggs or (male) sperm. Stem-cell research has been made possible in humans by the availability of embryos discarded during the process of *in vitro* fertilisation (IVF). Thanks to this by-product of fertility treatments, science has come up with therapeutic cloning methods that could help infertile couples. (Reproductive cloning is against the law.) The same methods, though, could also help homosexual couples to have offspring genetically related to both partners; they could help a woman bear a child beyond the menopause; and even a single man (or woman) could be assisted to produce a child from an egg and sperm developed from his or her own germ cells. Such research challenges what we understand by parenthood.

These and other issues (like the future of nanotechnology) must be debated in public. Scientists make technology possible. They are only too happy to leave decision making and policy making to the elected representatives of the general public, to the extent that they are well informed and well intentioned.

Based on material by John Enderby, vice-president of the Royal Society, in the *Financial Times*, and Nic Fleming, science correspondent of the *Daily Telegraph*

Source B **Does technology cause as many problems as it solves?**

Bayer CropScience in the USA genetically modified a strain of rice that would tolerate weed killer. The company tested the rice on farms in Arkansas between 1998 and 2001 — but it decided not to apply for a licence for the rice, and the trials were discontinued.

It seems, though, that pollen from the genetically modified (GM) rice contaminated the conventional rice grown by Riceland, the world's biggest rice-growing and exporting company.

Riceland discovered what had happened in January 2006; in May of the same year, the company confirmed that it had found the GM rice in a significant number of test-samples taken from right across its growing area.

Bayer alerted the US government to what had happened at the end of July — but it was only towards the end of August that the US government informed importing nations that they had been buying rice containing the banned GM strain. The European Commission stopped all further imports of the rice immediately. In doing so, the Commission was shutting the stable door after the horse had bolted: it seems we have been eating rice contaminated by the GM crop for many months, and probably years — perhaps since 2001 when the trials were discontinued.

The Bush administration has claimed that 'there are no human health, food safety or environmental concerns associated with this rice'. This may be so, and this claim tallies with the findings of the British government's exhaustive GM Science review, which found no evidence of any ill-effects on human health.* Nevertheless, it is a matter of concern that any food that has been under a long-standing EU ban — a ban that we might have assumed the Americans were honouring — should have been allowed access to European shops and shopping baskets.

It is such a failure of controls on GM food — and in particular the entry of GM varieties into the food chain — that makes it more difficult for the British government (among others) to seek to exploit GM technology without antagonising an already suspicious public.

* Mark Henderson, 'Evidence of green effrontery', *The Times*, 28 January 2005

Adapted from Geoffrey Lean, 'Rice contaminated by GM has been on sale for months', *Independent on Sunday*, 27 August 2006

Source C | **Do we take technology too far in health and medicine?**

The announcement that 63-year-old Dr Patricia Rashbrook was about to give birth raised many eyebrows. She and her husband were delighted; and presumably, doctors at the clinic where Dr Rashbrook had benefited from state-of-the-art fertility treatment were delighted, too.

'She'll be in her late seventies when her child's a teenager,' many people said, 'when most young people's parents are in early middle age, and able to remember what it was like to be young.' It was generally believed that to give birth in one's sixties is 'unnatural'.

It is unnatural, of course, in the sense that a 63-year-old does not give birth unassisted — but then, it could be said that any medical intervention is unnatural. Fertility treatment of the kind that Dr Rashbrook received (paid for, in full, by the patient herself) has given us the power of choice. Ethical philosopher Jonathan Glover has written: 'The choice for Dr Rashbrook's child is not between having her or some other mother. The alternative is not to be born at all.' In strict fact, of course, the child had no choice either way; the choice lay entirely with Dr Rashbrook and her husband.

Assisted reproduction has given us choices that once would have been left to fate; and antenatal screening has given us the opportunity to terminate pregnancies that will result in children with disabilities. If we know that a child will be born with HIV, is it better to terminate the pregnancy because of 'what the condition does to people', as Glover puts it? Or is life with HIV — and the medicine available — better than no life at all? We would not wish some severe conditions on any child, perhaps; but there will be disagreement about conditions that are less of a threat to 'normal' life. And once we have decided on which physical disabilities we would wish to screen for, we would be confronted with the issue of non-medical disabilities, like schizophrenia. Glover reminds us that the Nazis sterilised schizophrenics, and that they sent some 70,000 psychiatric patients to the gas chambers.

We might wonder whether we send unfortunate signals to people with disabilities who live thoroughly worthwhile lives, when we seek to screen out these same disabilities in embryos. Eugenics* at its worst leads to callous

*Eugenics means improving the stock of human genes.

attitudes towards the living: parents themselves, or would-be parents.

On the other hand, as long as we do all in our power to help those with disabilities to lead the lives that they wish to lead — as long as our attitudes are positive towards individual differences — there can be nothing wrong with exploiting reproductive technologies to give the children of the future the best possible start in life. Perhaps only Dr Rashbrook and her husband know whether they can do this for their child or not.

Adapted from Jonathan Glover, 'Nazi eugenics, Virginia Woolf and the morality of designer babies', *Guardian*, 6 May 2006

Source D

Should we always do what science and technology make it possible to do?

1 The classic case of science and technology being abused is, of course, nuclear energy. Rutherford, Einstein, Teller, Bohr and co. didn't have bombs and destruction of whole populations in mind when they investigated the atom. Now some quite unstable states have nuclear weapons capability.

2 We can't let the likes of North Korea and Iran prevent the rest of us developing peaceful nuclear energy. If we want to go on using energy as we have been doing, we shall need nuclear power stations that don't emit greenhouse gases.

3 There are lots of things we *can* do that we should perhaps *not* do, that we can stop right now. It's one thing taking pictures of Mars, mapping it, naming features, like the Mars Reconnaissance Orbiter is doing; it's quite another thing to send a manned mission there.

4 The so-called Opportunity Rover has been taking the most fantastic pictures — we know so much more about Mars now. You can't stop scientists wanting to know more, and you can't stop explorers wanting to explore.

5 What did the Moon landings actually deliver? The whole programme was political. Yet politicians can stop a project when they've a mind to: look at the Bush administration and its controls on human embryonic stem-cell research.

6 And what's the result of the Bush limits to federal funding? The research is being done in Europe instead; and it's European laboratories that will reap the benefits. Stem-cell research is the big thing in medicine at the moment. It will take more than Bush to stop it.

7 No one objects to using a patient's own bone-marrow cells if they will repair damaged heart tissue, for example. It's the use of human embryo cells that is questionable. Besides, we put all this effort into trying to counteract end-of-life diseases like Parkinson's and Alzheimer's when the real killers are malnutrition and a lack of fresh water.

8 Stem-cell research might well lead to a cure for diabetes; and some heart-disease patients are in their forties and fifties. The embryos — when these are used — aren't specially created; they would be discarded if they weren't used for research. Embryonic cells have the potential to grow into any sort of tissue. It's not *either* we do stem-cell research *or* we feed the world. We must do both.

Based on articles in *TIME*, 9 and 16 October 2006

Skills

As a candidate for this and other units, you do not need to know a lot of hard science. What you do need is a handle on some of the key issues on which non-scientists are often called to decide — or, at least, to have some informed opinions. These issues might be:

- genetic modification of plants and animals
- embryonic stem-cell research
- reproductive technologies and treatments
- cosmetic surgery
- the use of animals in experiments

Certain other issues — either more or less controversial — are dealt with in later units (space research and climate change, for example, are Unit 2 topics).

Where our judgement about the rightness or wrongness of what scientists do is concerned, much will depend on whether we argue from a broadly 'religious/ principled' or 'secular/pragmatic' point of view. The difference is not (or not only) a question of whether one believes in God or not; it is whether one believes that there is some *underlying value* to be appealed to in making decisions, which make an action 'right' or 'wrong'. The 'religious/principled' thinker will, perhaps, invoke what is perceived to be God's will, the natural order of things, the sanctity of life, or the idea of the 'Good'. The 'secular/pragmatic' thinker will perhaps appeal to what is useful or does not cause harm — what seems to be 'common sense'.

Note that these are only tendencies, and they may overlap from issue to issue. It is not being suggested that we are all one of these two kinds of thinkers.

(i) **Where might the 'religious/principled' and 'secular/pragmatic' thinkers stand on the following issues?**

 1 **Choosing the gender of a child (by controlling the Y chromosome)**

 2 **Cloning a dog (as the South Korean Woo Suk Hwang claimed to have done)**

 3 **Having breast-enlargement surgery**

 4 **Assisting a childless couple in their forties to have a child**

 5 **Genetically engineering wheat so that it will tolerate periods of drought**

 6 **Extracting cells from unwanted embryos for use in tissue-regeneration research**

You could copy and complete a table like this:

	Religious/principled	Secular/pragmatic
1 Choosing the gender of a child (by controlling the y chromosome)		

The religious/principled thinker will not necessarily say 'no' to each of these possibilities, and the secular/pragmatic thinker will not necessarily say 'yes'. Both thinkers will want to be sure that scientists are:

- experimenting on living tissue only when it is absolutely necessary
- closely regulated when they do so
- acting in the public interest, rather than to advance their own reputation
- concerning themselves with significant rather than trivial problems, particularly if public money is involved

Put simply, we expect scientists to act *responsibly*. This probably means that they need to be as *independent* as possible. Of course, scientific research is expensive; how it is funded will make a difference to how much we trust it. We probably trust most the research that is done in high-ranking universities, and we probably trust least research that is paid for by commercial interests.

High-ranking universities	Government	Commercial business

Most trust ◄─────────────────────────────► Least trust

However, this rule needs to be applied flexibly. After all, government money is taxpayers' money, and this is what (largely) pays for the universities. Many commercial firms sponsor perfectly respectable research done in reputable university laboratories.

Here is an example of the type of question that might be asked on one of these issues:

> **Q3** The general public in the UK is rather hostile to the idea of eating genetically modified (GM) food. The government, on the other hand, has backed trials that show that GM food is not a threat to human health.
>
> How far is it the government's responsibility to educate the public about GM food?
>
> You might consider:
> - the benefits that GM food is thought to bring
> - the motives of the big food companies
> - the grounds for the public's hostility

There is usually some logic in the order of the cues — and it is generally the third one that is the weightiest. This question can be broken down into sub-questions:

1 Why might GM food be a good thing?

2 Why might the government be involved?

3 Why are food companies keen to push GM food?

4 Why are some environmentalists opposed to it?

5 Why is much of the public opposed to it?

(ii) Why do you think the government might want to change the public's mind about GM food?

(iii) Why do you think the public is so suspicious of GM food? (Sources A and B will give you some clues.)

Here is a sketch of an answer to Q3:

[S] *The government does have a duty to provide the conditions in which experiments might be carried out, responsibly and independently...*

[Ex A] *The food companies have profits in mind, and they might be suspected of talking up the benefits of GM food...*

[Ex B] *In view of the benefits claimed for GM food, the government does have a duty to enable independent trials to be carried out, but it must keep an open mind, and it must encourage the public to keep an open mind. The companies might be right, or the environmentalists might be right.*

The public may be hostile towards GM food because they are convinced by the environmentalists' arguments. On the other hand, the public may distrust scientists, politicians and food companies, and the media may feed this distrust.

[C] *The government has a duty to be a referee in the controversy — and this may involve explaining the rules to all the players in the game.*

Here is a further question that exploits some of the points made in Sources C and D.

Q4 Reproductive technology has given scientists and parents the opportunity to decide which of several embryos to implant in the womb.

Discuss whether parents should have the option of choosing whether their child should be a girl or a boy.

You might consider:
- whether parents would want this choice
- the effects of giving this choice to all parents
- the rights and wrongs of 'playing God'

AQA (B) Advanced General Studies

19

Tensions in society

Content

Source A — **How can we prevent young people being disaffected?**

Sir,

The Youth Justice Board published its report recently of an investigation into the workings of Anti-Social Behaviour Orders (ASBOs). It would seem that too many are being issued, often for behaviour that some would class as anti-social and others wouldn't.

Some young people are confused about why they have been issued with an order; and some actively seek such an order because it gives them prestige among their peers.

The consequence of this is that nearly half of all ASBOs that are issued are breached, and the young people concerned are labelled criminals merely on this account.

It should be made quite clear what the circumstances are in which ASBOs are issued, so that they are not handed out for trivial offences. They should be issued only as a last resort.

MM, London

Sir,

Perhaps the Youth Justice Board should have asked young people what they think of anti-social behaviour, and of ASBOs. When the British Youth Council surveyed a sample of young people aged 12 to 24, it became clear that young people themselves feel that they are misunderstood.

The government and media tend to peddle a stereotype of young people, so that the public is fully prepared to believe that British youth is 'among the worst behaved in Europe'.

A minority, to be sure, attracts disproportionate attention to itself; but when we look beyond the lurid headlines we see a very different picture.

The government ought not to be so fixated on enforcement. An inclusive society — and this is what the government says it wants — must include its young people, by engaging them in what society is and does. Their behaviour will only be pro-social if they are made to feel that they belong.

TRC, London

Sir,

If almost half the ASBOs issued are breached, then more than half are doing their job.

Here in Manchester, we are finding that they do act to moderate behaviour, and keep large numbers of young people from going further astray. We monitor those whose behaviour is a cause for concern, and before issuing an ASBO — if it comes to this — we interview the young person together with his or her parent or parents. In this way, we often head off the need for an order. The key is to involve the parents at an early stage.

There is public support for ASBOs in Manchester because they are seen to work.

Cllr EN, Manchester

Sir,

Young people are no worse today than they ever were. Those who say they are have short memories.

Most of today's young people are more tolerant, more concerned for the environment, and more hard-working than we ever were. Had there been ASBOs in my day, I and most of my peers would have qualified for one.

DBN, St Albans

Based on letters to *The Times*, 4 November 2006

Source B — How and why do we categorise people?

Most people we meet we see only fleetingly, and then we probably never see them again. We do not need to place them in categories (rich/poor; old/young; smart/stupid; courteous/abrupt), though we may do so unconsciously, or semi-consciously.

People we meet regularly we probably do categorise: for example, colleagues at work (lazy/diligent), salespeople (talkative/unsmiling), people who have authority over us (strict/easy-going), and friends of friends (well-spoken/coarse).

Those we call our friends we probably categorise quite explicitly in terms of how like ourselves we perceive them to be.

Why *do* we place people in categories?

■ Psychologists, such as Adorno, have suggested that we have a basic and immediate need to categorise people according to whether they are 'friend' or 'foe'.

■ Others, like Allport, claim that life is essentially competitive, and that if we are to succeed we need to 'size up' the competition: we stereotype people, we 'scapegoat' them, or we look up to them.

■ We categorise other people, at least in part, as a means of understanding ourselves. We know where we are 'coming from', in terms of our family and schooling, but we understand ourselves better when we compare ourselves with others.

■ We have to categorise people because we cannot *know* them as a mass, and we cannot know them all as individuals. Social scientists, market researchers and employers need ready labels for different sets of people.

There was a time when we categorised people by social class (upper class, middle class and working class), but this categorisation has ceased to be particularly useful or acceptable. We are bound to categorise people by their ethnicity, since this is (more or less) obvious to the eye — and the same goes for the way people dress.

We can tell less than we could, perhaps, from the way people talk; and even the job they do (possibly still the most useful categorisation, after gender and age) is of limited use. Most of us would prefer to befriend a likeable, sensitive, generous postman than a cold-hearted, scheming, coarse-tongued investment banker. 'Friend' or 'foe', nice or nasty, is still, perhaps, the measure that most of us apply.

Source C What factors divide society?

In 1986, the prime minister, Margaret Thatcher, privatised public bus services. Local and long-distance bus services were just one item on a long list of services that were privatised in the 1980s.

Thatcher boasted that she never went anywhere by train, and she was even more dismissive when it came to buses: 'A man who beyond the age of 26 finds himself on a bus can count himself a failure,' she said.

Twenty years later, government minister Douglas Alexander announced plans to put Thatcher's policy into reverse. He told the Labour Party Conference that what Thatcher had said was 'offensive. It was wrong. And incidentally it tells you everything you will ever need to know about the Tories.'

Local councils lost the power to regulate bus services in the 1980s. Mayor Ken Livingstone took back certain powers to regulate bus services in London. Private companies had run buses only on busy routes, in the daytime. In the 'free-for-all' competition for customers on these routes, less profitable routes were neglected.

'As a Labour transport secretary, I want to

Corel

see bus services work in every community,' Mr Alexander said. 'So, in the weeks ahead, I will bring forward proposals to change the way buses are run in this country. You know and I know that in too many of our communities we have seen a free-for-all that has left the needs of the public behind.

'So to ensure the private sector delivers the bus services our communities demand, I will act to give the local transport authorities that need them real powers to make a difference.'

Ken Livingstone lost his battle with Margaret Thatcher in the 1980s; now, well beyond the age of 26, it seems he can ride the buses again with a smile of success on his face.

Adapted from an article by Matthew Tempest, *Guardian*, 27 September 2006 (online)

Source D   **How might we encourage the growth of communities?**

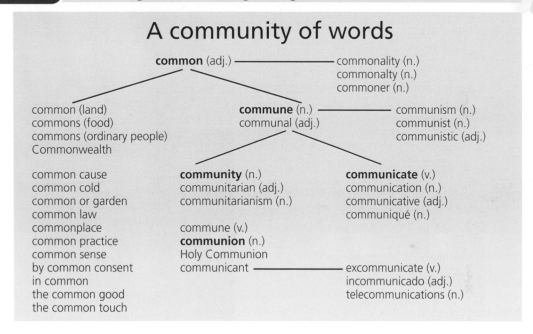

A community of words

common (adj.) —————————— commonality (n.)
                                                                    commonalty (n.)
                                                                    commoner (n.)

common (land)   **commune** (n.) ———————— communism (n.)
commons (food)   communal (adj.)   communist (n.)
commons (ordinary people)   communistic (adj.)
Commonwealth

common cause   **community** (n.)   **communicate** (v.)
common cold   communitarian (adj.)   communication (n.)
common or garden   communitarianism (n.)   communicative (adj.)
common law   communiqué (n.)
commonplace   commune (v.)
common practice   **communion** (n.)
common sense   Holy Communion
by common consent   communicant ——————— excommunicate (v.)
in common   incommunicado (adj.)
the common good   telecommunications (n.)
the common touch

Skills

In the past, we might have seen 'tensions in society' as being about:

- dysfunctional families
- the generation gap
- social class

These issues have not gone away: for example, divorce, one-parent families, and custody and access disputes. But other tensions have come to the fore.

Sources A and B both touch on the issue of stereotypes. It is easy to see all 'young people' as being of one sort. Of course, we do place all young people into this one category because it is easier (as well as more informative and more efficient) to do this than to try to understand every individual young person.

Our answer to the first question on the specification: **How can we prevent young people being disaffected?** may therefore depend upon whether we are talking about a group on a housing estate in Wythenshawe, or one living in bungalows in Poole. Still, our answer will probably involve:

- making sure their parents can provide them with housing, comfort, food and affection
- providing them with an appropriate education
- giving them plenty to do to occupy their leisure time and expend their energy
- making them feel that they have a part to play in their communities

ASBOs (see Source A) only come into play when it is too late: an anti-social teenager is already disaffected in some measure.

This question, about preventing young people from being disaffected, has a lot to do with the fourth question in the specification, about encouraging the growth of communities. A community that works is one that is concerned with some of the words found in Source D.

Teenager demonstrating anti-social behaviour

- It has things in **common**.
- It does things **communally**, i.e. together.
- It **communicates** with its members.
- It acts **by common consent**.

Here is a question that could be answered by drawing on ideas expressed in Sources A and D.

Q5	Politicians have often spoken of wanting to foster an 'inclusive society'.

Q5 Politicians have often spoken of wanting to foster an 'inclusive society'.

How might we ensure that this society includes its young people?

You might consider:
- how older people communicate with the young
- what older and younger age groups do in common
- how young people can be given a stake in the community

(i) **Write down what you think we — and politicians — mean by an 'inclusive society'. You will need to suggest a definition of this term in your opening statement when answering question 5.**

The first bullet point in question 5 (about communication) seems to be about *respect*: about older people not looking down on, or looking askance at, younger people; and treating them as equals-to-be. It is about older people bringing younger people to a state of equality, where communication is two way and on equal terms.

(ii) **The second bullet point is about work and leisure, the world beyond school. Make a note of what pursuits young and old people commonly do together.**

(iii) **The third bullet point is the one that draws threads together. Here we need some specific suggestions for ways in which young people can be made to feel valued. Write down your suggestions.**

Here is a sketch of an answer to Q5:

[S] *By an 'inclusive society' we mean one in which all members are full members: they all belong and they all have a role to play.*

[Ex A] *There used to be talk of a 'generation gap', and it was feared that older and younger people had lost touch with each other. This probably had something to do with the pace of change.*

[Ex B] *There need be no gap if parents, teachers and other adults keep talking with young people — not at them...*

Young people need older people to train them in sports; old and young people need each other when working, for example, in the theatre or on an environmental project. They complement each other at work, where experience and new ideas are both necessary...

Only if young people are given responsibility — for instance, as baby-sitters — will they prove themselves responsible...

[C] *In a really inclusive society, perhaps it would simply cease to be important how young or old people were.*

Categorising people is a way of dividing them up. The factors that divide society are the various ways in which we distinguish between one category of people and another. There are always more than two categories in any factor but let's keep things simple.

(iv) **Into what two categories might you divide people in terms of each of the following factors? Copy and complete the following table (the first factor has been filled in to give you a start). Obviously, there are no 'right' answers to this question.**

Factor	Category 1	Category 2
Birth	Planned and prepared for	Unplanned and unwanted
Family		
Schooling		
Job		
Age		
Leisure interests		
Housing		
Politics		

There may be other factors that you can think of (for example, car ownership and newspaper reading habits), and the difference between the categories is certainly not just a question of money.

Source B is about why we might categorise people — or worse, why we might stereotype them (that is, place them in ready-made categories on slight evidence).

Source C is about two factors that divide society:

Factor	Category 1	Category 2
Economics	Public services	Private companies
Politics	Left (Labour)	Right (Conservative)

Again, both have something to do with money — with wealth creation, and ownership of what Karl Marx called 'the means of production' — but not everything.

Here is a question that could be answered by drawing on some of the ideas expressed in Sources B and C:

Q6 Once upon a time there were the haves and the have-nots: the 'idle rich' and the working poor.

How far is it still money that divides society into one kind of people and another?

You might consider:
- access to a good education
- jobs available to all on merit
- what other values we use to judge people

Politics and the public

Content

What are the roles of political parties?

Interviewer: You're a member of the Labour Party?

MP: Yes, I've been a member all my adult life.

Interviewer: May I ask why Labour, and not Liberal Democrat or Conservative?

MP: Labour's always represented working people. It's always looked out for ordinary people with the same rights to a decent education, decent housing and healthcare as people with money and influence. My father worked in the motor industry in Coventry, so I was always going to be a Labour supporter.

Interviewer: And do you always toe the party line in parliament: vote the way the whips want you to vote?

MP: Labour's in government, so when the Labour front bench puts forward a bill that carries a manifesto pledge into effect, well, of course, I vote with the government. The voters in my constituency expect Labour to deliver on its manifesto promises — that's why they elected me to represent them. But if I think the government's got it wrong, and they put forward a bill that goes against what we've promised, I'll vote against them. I don't expect to be a minister now, so I don't need to curry favour.

Interviewer: If you found yourself in deep disagreement with the party, on a number of issues, say, would you join another one?

MP: I can't see myself doing that, no. If I didn't agree with my own party, it isn't likely I'd agree with either of the others. Besides, it's not the *party* I'd be disagreeing with: it'd be the way ministers — and the prime minister in particular — were taking the party.

Interviewer: What might you object to in the way that ministers…?

MP: Well, I don't much like the way the private sector's taking a bigger and bigger part in public services: health and education; health in particular. I still think the NHS is the best thing Labour's ever done, and I'd defend it to the last ditch against creeping privatisation.

Interviewer: Don't you feel rather trapped in a party that's changed — that's *New* Labour — since you first joined it? What's the point of being in a party at all? Why don't you just say what you believe in before an election, then vote accordingly in parliament, as a free agent?

MP: Well, all parties change. All three main parties have changed quite a lot since I first entered parliament. But I accept that there have to *be* parties — and with our voting system, three is about as many as we'll get. Smaller parties would never get in.

Voters must know what they're voting for. Each of the parties stands for certain principles. There's bound to be some overlap where particular policies are concerned but, broadly, voters know what they're getting when they vote for a Labour MP, or a Conservative MP, or a Liberal Democrat MP. It's a bit crude; it's a bit broad-brush — but without parties, without the discipline, if you like, of agreed platforms and policies, there'd just be a constant struggle for power…

Interviewer: Isn't it that already?

MP: No, no. Debates may get a bit rough sometimes, and Prime Minister's Question Time isn't always edifying, but it's not a free-for-all in parliament, which it would be if there weren't distinct clusters of opinion to which individuals — MPs and voters — could attach themselves. There have got to be parties, and there have got to be party leaders — but we mustn't confuse one with the other. The party's bigger than the leader. It has an identity, a function and a will of its own that'll outlast the leader.

Interviewer: So, the prime minister can count on your vote…

MP: Not all the time — I won't be lobby fodder — but, most of the time, yes. I'm not ready to write my memoirs yet.

Source B   **How do pressure groups contribute to democracy?**

Amnesty International UK has been running a campaign for asylum rights. What have we done so far?

Destitution

Amnesty International staff in the UK have interviewed asylum seekers from a variety of countries whose application for asylum has been rejected. In addition, they have interviewed the people who work with them on a daily basis. These interviews are a part of research being done into the extent of destitution in London. Our partners, Refugee Action, are conducting similar interviews in other parts of the country. We shall publish a report based on our findings, and launch a campaign at the same time.

Children in detention

The Refugee Council, Save the Children, and Bail for Immigration Detainees have organised a campaign *No Place for a Child* to call attention to the 2,000 children who are held in immigration centres in the UK every year. Amnesty International members are asked to do what they can to support this campaign.

Advocacy

The report *Seeking Asylum is not a Crime* raised a number of issues concerning legal aid and automatic bail for asylum seekers. Amnesty International has been doing advocacy work at bail hearings, and we have been having regular meetings with the Home Office to discuss all aspects of asylum policy and practice.

Events

Amnesty International has organised a number of events at the Human Rights Action Centre. These have included two plays: *The Asylum Monologues* and *The Bogus Woman*. We also showed the Michael Winterbottom film *In this World*.

And what about you? You can have your say at the next Annual General Meeting of Amnesty International. It's open to all individual and family members, local, student and youth groups. Or you can contact the Activism Team on **activism@amnesty.org.uk**, or check the website, which is regularly updated.

Adapted from information in *Amnesty Magazine*, September/October 2006

Source C — How might we foster more public interest in politics?

Why do fewer people turn out to vote?

1 The main political parties are perceived to have moved to the centre ground, and therefore to be more alike.

2 Party loyalty and membership are in decline; people do not identify with a party by virtue of their background, social class or occupation, as they used to.

3 There is a certain predictability about the outcome of elections, thanks to frequent opinion polls, and the workings of the first-past-the-post voting system.

4 The addition of European elections and elections for mayors in some cities to general elections and local government elections (and the abovementioned opinion polls) has contributed to voter fatigue.

5 Highly critical and intrusive media — which have resulted in us knowing more about politicians' private lives — foster distrust of politicians, their motives and their competence.

6 As the material conditions of most people's lives have improved, many people feel less need to register a protest vote. In addition, politicians may not receive credit for the improvement.

Adapted from information in Bennett, A. (2004) *US and Comparative Government and Politics*, Philip Allan Updates.

Source D — How can people have their say in an advanced democracy?

'Person of the year' for 2006, according to *TIME* magazine, was its own readership. Why? For 'seizing the reins of the global media, for founding and framing the new digital democracy, for working for nothing and beating the press at their own game'.

Democratising the media, at the level of entertainment, has meant that a group like the Arctic Monkeys could come to prominence on a webpage. MySpace and YouTube have given ordinary people the chance to air their views or promote their songs or video-clips. Their audience might be small, or their fame last 15 minutes; or they might ape Lily Allen, who put her song 'Smile' on the lips of people who listened to it on MySpace before the record was available commercially.

'Ordinary' people have made Wikipedia what it is, too. This online encyclopaedia published its one-millionth English-language page in 2006, thanks entirely to submissions, amendments and editorial comments made by its own users. Readers contributed examples of word-use to the editors of the *Oxford English Dictionary*, but the dictionary was engineered; Wikipedia has evolved, and is always open to revision by those who access it.

Does digital democracy go further than this? Might internet users actually exert their political influence? Might they truly beat the media commentators and parliamentary sketch-writers at their 'own game'? George Allen was expected to win a Senate seat in the US mid-term elections in 2006. He lost because a racist remark that he made was filmed and shown on YouTube within minutes, and it was played and replayed until the damage was done.

What began in the USA has come to Britain: two political bloggers, Guido Fawkes and Iain Dale made a mark in 2006 (both on the political right wing). Fawkes, intent on 'blowing up'

parliament in his own way, named Tracey Temple as deputy prime minister John Prescott's pillow-companion. It was a scoop that had eluded the paparazzi. Dale, meanwhile, blogged the Millennium-Dome-as-Super-Casino story, and Prescott's involvement with the US tycoon Philip Anschutz. It was a story that the *Daily Mail* would have liked to paste on its front page as an 'exclusive' — but Dale had got there first.

It remains to be seen whether these freelance initiatives are one-off chances, or the shape of things to come; but a mobile phone with a 2-megapixel still and video camera capability, internet links and a 1-gigabyte memory is a powerful tool in the hands of a determined democrat.

Adapted from Ed Caesar, 'Don't just watch, blog!', *Independent on Sunday*, 31 December 2006

Skills

Is politics a turn-off for many young people, for the sorts of reasons given in Source C? Or are there other reasons that are not given there? Perhaps young people never have been particularly interested in politics. It all seems rather abstract and remote — and perhaps it seems remote because politics is about power and young people feel powerless.

But politics is about conflict, too, and young people know something about that at the *micro* level. Life at home and at school must have given them a taste of politics at the level of the individual and the group; and many will have opinions about *single issues*, such as hunting, binge drinking, celebrity lifestyles, drugs and carbon emissions.

It is important to have a handle on what we mean by 'democracy'. Some of the most succinct things said about it have not been complimentary:

> No one pretends that democracy is perfect or all-wise. Indeed, it has been said that democracy is the worst form of government except all those other forms that have been tried from time to time.
> Winston Churchill, 1947

> Democracy means government by discussion, but it is only effective if you can stop people talking.
> Clement Attlee, 1957

Perhaps the kindest, most earnest praise of democracy was made by Abraham Lincoln in his famous Gettysburg Address, in 1863:

> Four score and seven years ago our fathers brought forth on this continent a new nation, conceived in liberty and dedicated to the proposition that all men are created equal. Now we are engaged in a great civil war, testing whether that nation or any other nation so conceived can long endure. We are met on a great battlefield of that war. We have come to dedicate a portion of that field as a final resting-place for those who gave their lives that that nation might live...

> We here highly resolve that these dead shall not have died in vain, that this nation under God shall have a new birth of freedom, and that government of the people, by the people, for the people shall not perish from the earth.

(i) **Using the definition of democracy as 'government of the people, by the people, for the people', is the UK a democracy? In what respects might the answer to this question be 'yes', and in what respects 'no'? Copy and complete the following table.**

The UK is a democracy in that...	It is not a democracy in that...

It is worth making the distinction between *direct* and *indirect* (or representative) democracy. Questions that then arise are:

(ii) **a Write down any examples of *direct* democracy that you can think of.**

b How representative is the UK parliament of the country's voters?

Is voting the only means by which ordinary people ('subjects' or 'citizens') can make their views known, exercise their democratic rights and engage in the political process? (Tom Stoppard, in his play *Jumpers*, has a character say: 'It's not the voting that's democracy; it's the counting.' What might this imply?)

There have always been other ways, besides voting, in which people can take an active part in politics, or — more simply — have their say. How many such ways can you think of? (Some are to be found in Sources A–D.)

(iii) **Make a note of the ways in which people can exercise their democratic rights.**

There are ways of making one's views known that involve little expenditure of time or effort, such as signing a petition. There are other ways, such as joining an active pressure group, that may involve a significant commitment of time and money.

Although people usually *vote* for a candidate who owes allegiance to a political party, only a small minority of individuals now *join* one of the parties. Answer this question:

(iv) Why might an individual join a political party?

Q7 is about political parties.

> **Q7** 'The names of the political parties no longer tell us anything useful about what they stand for. We might be better off without parties altogether.'
>
> How far do you agree with this view?
>
> You might consider:
> - what meanings we attach to party names
> - whether there are fundamental differences between the parties
> - whether a democracy can do without them

'Labour' reminds us of the party's socialist, working-class roots — but what about 'New Labour'? And what do 'Conservatives' conserve? ('Tory', the word used by headline-writers because it is short, no longer carries any of its early — Irish — meaning of 'robber'. However, we do tend to use the word to describe the more extreme right-wing Conservatives.) All but a handful of British politicians would be happy to be called 'liberal' or 'democratic'. Perhaps the party names really have become devoid of all useful meaning.

(v) As to differences between the parties, can you think of one or two policies that are unique to each party — policies by which that party can readily be identified? Copy and complete the following table:

Labour	Liberal Democrat	Conservative

You could use Source A on pages 27–28 and Source C on page 29 as source material.

Just as we wondered whether there is any example of *direct* democracy, so (in connection with the third cue) we might wonder whether there is any advanced democracy that does without political parties.

Here is a sketch of an answer to Q7:

[S] *The names of UK political parties certainly carry little meaning nowadays.*

[Ex A] *Since all the major parties have moved towards the centre ground of politics in recent years, there is little to distinguish one from the others, and they might as well be dispensed with.*

[Ex B] *The names continue to be a useful shorthand, though, for principled differences between the parties. The Labour Party will always be judged by its faithfulness to the founding principles of the National Health Service, the Conservatives by their upholding of tradition, and the Liberal Democrats by their attachment to reform — especially of the electoral system. It is difficult to imagine how a programme of policies might be presented to the electorate other than as one made by a group of representatives dedicated to putting it into effect.*

[C] *Political parties probably are necessary to the proper functioning of a representative democracy.*

Of the four general questions posed in this part of the specification, the third is perhaps the most challenging: **How might we foster more public interest in politics?**

There is an assumption here that the public is not interested enough in politics, and that more interest would be a good thing. Q8 is concerned with this issue, but before coming to that it might be worth considering whether:

- the general public has *ever* been interested in politics
- it matters if we leave politics to the politicians
- it is enough that we read the papers and watch the news on television
- there is really anything more that most people could *do* to show an interest

What would make politics more *interesting*? More direct democracy — regular referenda, for example? Can a country be governed on the basis of a constant canvassing of public opinion? Or would that just mean that the same, rather conservative (with a small 'c') majority would have the last, blocking word on everything, and nothing would change? Should there be a more frequent change of government — annually, perhaps, as the Chartists demanded back in 1848?

It was once suggested that parliament should take place in a glass amphitheatre within the shell of the Battersea Power Station, so that we could all watch it at work. This would give Londoners an advantage — unless we could all watch proceedings on our mobile phones and text in our thoughts as debates happened.

But then, as Attlee suggested, there is perhaps enough talk already.

Q8   Fewer people cast their vote, and public interest in serious political matters seems to be on the wane.

Why might this be a cause for concern?

You might consider:

- whether people ought to do more than vote
- how public interest might be stimulated
- whether democracy suffers from low public interest

The arts as a challenge

Content

> **Source A** **How do the arts challenge social norms?**

It was 1961. The grey years after the war, the 1940s and 1950s — of rationing and cleared bomb-sites — were over, and the 1960s had begun to sway, if not yet to swing.

In America, the most important painter of those grey years was Jackson Pollock, whose 'action' paintings involving

'Cloaking Movement', c.1946, Jackson Pollock.

dripping and splashing paint straight from the can onto huge canvases lying on the floor earned him the nickname Jack the Dripper. His paintings had been called 'abstract', or 'abstract expressionist'.

That action painting could be called 'art' was a shock to conservative opinion. Then Jasper Johns began painting the American flag, targets and numbers, and Robert Rauschenberg made collages of images cut out of magazines. Andy Warhol screen-printed Campbell's soup-tin labels and images of Marilyn Monroe and Elvis Presley. Roy Lichtenstein drew on hard-edge, comic-strip graphics and Claes Oldenburg 'sculpted' ice-cream cornets and hot-dogs.

In 1961 Pop Art made a splash in Britain. David Hockney, Allen Jones, R. B. Kitaj and Peter Blake were the new names bandied about, not least by Ken Russell in his BBC film *Pop Goes the Easel*. The public could see what Pop Art was 'about', whereas abstract expressionism hadn't been about anything at all. However, people said the same sorts of things about it: 'It's so simple! Is it art? I could have done that!' The point, Blake said, is that 'we did it first'.

It all seemed like a joke but it was a glamorous, accessible joke. People could understand the repeating motifs — pin-ball machines, automobiles, pin-ups, commercial brands, showbiz idioms — and the young, at least, could relate to art that was as brash and irreverent as rock music and Hollywood. It was art of its time.

But there was some confusion about whether Pop Art was making a mockery of consumerism or paying homage to it.

Adapted from *The Oxford Dictionary of Art* (2004), 3rd edn

Source B — What is the role of the arts in education?

Q. What is your favourite subject in school?

Answer 1   Art
Answer 2   Dance
Answer 3   Drama

Does this surprise you? Probably not. One or other of the arts was probably your own favourite subject lower down the school — or your favourite pastime. We draw, paint, perform for fun. Not many of us do sums, or write up experiments for fun.

Why is there such a problem with funding, then? Why is it that when budgets are cut in schools, it's art, music or drama that's cut first — or even dropped altogether? Why are the arts not given the recognition, the space on the time-table and the resources that they deserve? Why are maths and sciences always given preference?

Research over the years demonstrates that the arts are more than fun — though they'd still be justified if they were *only* for fun. They teach skills, understanding and patterns of behaviour that are essential if young people are to become successful adults. A young person collaborating on a collage, or singing, or acting in a group learns important social and emotional lessons.

Intelligence isn't all about analysis; it's about emotional engagement, too. And look how much the creative industries (design, fashion, entertainment, advertising and performing arts) are contributing to Britain's gross national product in the twenty-first century!

Is the government listening? It listened in 2003/04 when it increased the arts budget by 60% and promised additional opportunities for young people to experience the arts. But is the interest being sustained? Do we need a Jamie Oliver to go into schools and wake us up to under-nourishment in the arts that we serve up?

Adapted from Jana Ritter, 'Creative controversy: examining the role of arts in education', www.galtglobalreview.com, accessed 6 January 2007

Source C — Can the arts change our minds, or our behaviour?

Erwin Wurm is an Austrian sculptor. Some of his recent work is on display at the Baltic Centre, Gateshead.

On the terrace leading to the gallery is a bulging, white, polyester Wendy-house with a red roof. Step inside the 'Fat House', and there is another 'artwork' called *Am I a House?* This consists of a video of an animation of the house asking questions: 'Am I an artwork or a house? Am I a house more than an artwork? No house can be fat. Can an artwork be fat?'

Inside the gallery, there are two sculptures of more-than-lifesize men, dressed conventionally enough: the orange sweater of one of them, though, is stretched over a hoop, worn round his middle. This is *The Artist who Swallowed the World when it was still a Disc.* The other man, *The Artist who Swallowed the World*, presumably took a fancy to the globe as we know it, for he is simply well-roundedly obese.

There are two Coca-Cola cans on the floor, on which visitors are invited to stand; and there is a sizeable lorry whose rear end is bent back so that the wheels rest on the wall. There is also a short-legged dog, misshapen on one side, called *The Dog who Swallowed a Postbox.*

There is a fine view of the Tyne from the gallery terrace.

Your reviewer was almost as eloquent in what he didn't say about the Wurm exhibition at the Baltic as in what he did say.

What he might have added is that the show has more to do with entertainment than with art. I hesitate to give another definition of what 'art is', but I imagine we would all agree that an artist uses skill and intelligence to challenge our view of the world in some way, to reshape it, to reinterpret it, to see it — however briefly — from another (the artist's) point of view.

Could any visitor to the Wurm exhibition honestly say that their vision of the world had been enlarged or altered in any way by *The Artist who Swallowed the World*, or by *The Dog who Swallowed a Postbox*?

When the video 'artwork' *Am I a House?* has finished asking its fatuous questions, it says: 'An artwork can be good or bad, but it's still an artwork.' This is where Wurm goes wrong, and where this visitor lost patience: a 'bad' piece of work, whether it's a sculpture, a painting or a piece of music, cannot somehow justify its existence by calling itself an 'artwork'. A Rodin sculpture would be art if it stood in a super-market; *The Artist who Swallowed the World* — which might raise a laugh among children in a supermarket — does not become art because it stands in an 'art' gallery. It is still just a rather heavy-handed joke.

Adapted from a review in the *Independent Extra*, 28 August 2006

Source D   **Are the arts too elitist?**

'You can take a horse to water, but you can't make it drink.'

Some of us appreciate Shakespeare, Verdi and Rembrandt. There are enough of us, in schools and universities, who put on *King Lear*, or perform *Aïda*, or exhibit *The Nightwatch*, in the hope that we will encourage the young to like Shakespeare, Verdi and Rembrandt, too.

Not many of them do. We take them to the water, but they don't drink. Does this matter? It does in the sense that we cannot say that every-thing is equally 'good', and that it is worthwhile trying to educate the young to recognise what is 'good' and what is 'better', and why.

Of course, this is not easy because it is partly a matter of taste, and time. Is a Rembrandt better than an aboriginal painting in Australia? Would a modern western critic who said 'yes' be guilty of ethnic, cultural bias? Yes, he would, almost unavoidably. Or, to take another example

of two novelists writing at the same time, if a critic said Iris Murdoch's novels are better than those of Agatha Christie, would he be guilty of snobbery? Yes, he might, unless he could give reasons for discriminating between them that even an avid reader of detective fiction might accept. A critical preference for Murdoch over Christie need not mean disrespect for detective fiction at its best.

Picasso was inspired by the African figures in the Louvre. Bartók was inspired by Transylvanian folk-tunes. Their models were rough, 'primitive' and unsophisticated, and they made 'art' of them. We discriminate between a rough carving and a studio painting, between a simple song and a concerto, because the carving and the song do not acquire artistic merit just because they are old, or 'ethnic'. They will always be rough and simple. We can recognise this, and we can admire the art of Picasso and Bartók, without dismissing, or being snobbish about, the carving and the song.

There is no clear line between 'high' and 'popular' culture; but it is not elitist to prefer a painting, a piece of music or a play that says something thoughtful about what it is to be human, over a daub, a jingle, or a sketch that doesn't.

It is worth taking horses to water, as Lord Reith said, because 'many of them will find how good it is to drink'.

Adapted from ideas in A. C. Grayling, 'A question of discrimination', *Guardian*, 13 July 2002 (accessed online 6 January 2007)

Skills

'The arts as a challenge' is the title of this section of the specification.

What do we mean by *challenge*? In this context, the most useful dictionary definition seems to be: *a calling into question*. A novel like Orwell's *Nineteen Eighty-Four*, for instance, might 'call into question' whether truth can survive in a political dictatorship. A painting like Monet's *Impression: Sunrise* might call into question whether we *perceive* as much as we (think we) *see*.

Must art challenge if it is to be called 'art'? No: that it challenges is only one of the possible qualities of an artwork. Other possible qualities include:

- skill
- emotional intensity
- colourfulness
- subtle humour
- ingenuity

However, these other qualities do not concern us here because our theme is **Conflict**, the conflict between:

- mass and minority tastes
- popular and 'high' culture
- entertainment and art

There may also be conflict between a conventional, conservative taste in any art-form, and artworks that break the mould, ones that are in some way revolutionary or *avant-garde* (such as the 'modernists' of the early twentieth century: Pound, Eliot, Joyce, Woolf, Picasso, Schoenberg and so on).

Ballet: an example of 'high culture'

(i) **Without in any way endorsing a distinction between 'high' and 'low' (or popular) culture, which are the art forms that might be thought of as appealing to 'minority' and 'popular' tastes? Copy and complete the following table. One pair of opposites has been suggested as a starting point.**

Minority art-forms	Popular art-forms
Ballet	Pantomime

These are not opposites, of course. An opera like *Aïda* might stand at one end of a continuum and a show like *Cats* might stand at the other end — but there are plenty of song-and-dance dramas, such as the light operas of Gilbert and Sullivan, and works such as *Porgy and Bess* by Gershwin, and Robbins and Bernstein's *West Side Story*, that sit somewhere on the horizontal line, rather than either side of the vertical.

Do you think it is fair to say that 'minority' art forms are more likely to challenge social norms than 'popular' art-forms? More specifically, write down your answer to this question:

(ii) **Among 'minority' art-forms, which ones are likely to be the *most* challenging? In other words, which forms are most likely to call into question *social* norms?**

Music is perhaps the 'purest' art-form, with (apparently) least to *say*. Stravinsky's *Rite of Spring* caused a sensation in 1913, and some of Shostakovich's works displeased the Soviet authorities, but these were essentially *musical* scandals.

Paintings can be powerful: Picasso's *Guernica* (1937) is a well-known example of a painting that is a comment on the time. However, whether it challenged a social norm, and whether it can be said to have changed any minds or behaviours, is open to debate.

Perhaps the art movement that was hardest hitting socially and politically was *Dada*, or *Dadaism*. Its best-known exponents in Europe were Hans Arp, Otto Dix, George Grosz, Max Ernst and Kurt Schwitters, who flourished around 1915–22. These artists were united in their disgust at the carnage of the First World War, and their works challenged conventional notions of beauty and of what was 'art'.

Marcel Duchamp's *Fountain* (1917) was most challenging of all. This was an ordinary urinal bearing the name 'R. Mutt'. Duchamp also added a moustache and beard to the *Mona Lisa* in 1919. Again, though, it is a question of whether 'art' can do more than challenge artistic, stylistic norms — and the same question might apply to film. 'Art' films tend to call into question what film can do; and to the extent that they are social documentary and challenge social norms they cease to be art. But there is a fine line here: was Barry Hines and Mick Jackson's *Threads* of 1984, about nuclear winter, 'art'? It was certainly highly influential. The equally influential *Cathy Come Home* (Ken Loach) of 1966 was not intended to be 'art', but it might have had artistic qualities.

(iii) **Why might 'graphic' art (painting, sculpture, collage, photography, film) be effective as** *social-political* **comment? Give one or two examples.**

(iv) **Which novels, plays and poems have had most effect on our thinking? And what 'norm' opinion did each of them challenge?**

There are many possible alternative lists. The list given in the Teacher Guide is centred on the UK, and is intended to be suggestive only.

Here is a question that unites the first and third questions under this heading in the specification:

Q9 It is one of the roles of the arts to give pleasure, and it is another to provide entertainment.

To what extent is it their role to make us think?

You might consider:
■ the difference between mass and minority arts
■ the difference between verbal and graphic arts
■ whether there is a conflict between thinking and feeling

We can draw on ideas in Sources A and D in respect of mass and minority arts: Pop Art was, by definition, popular, but Pop Artists had a serious purpose; and the point is made in Source D that there is no clear line between 'high' and 'popular' culture.

There is an interesting combination of verbal and graphic elements in Wurm's *Fat House* and the secondary 'artwork' that it contains: the verbal *Am I a House?* (Source C). Source B contains a relevant observation about intelligence being, at least partly, about 'emotional engagement'.

Here is a sketch of an answer to Q9:

[S] *It is more likely to be a novel, a play or a poem — i.e. minority art forms — that will make us think, than more popular art forms like pantomime or rock music.*

[Ex A] *Much 'good' art — whether it be immediate, like a painting, or more time-intensive — is not designed to make us think. Gauguin's Tahiti nudes were meant to delight.*

[Ex B] *On the other hand, there have been many paintings that were intended to make us think, Picasso's* Guernica *among them; and there have been many novels and plays that have had serious things to say about the social-political situation of their time, such as William Golding's* Lord of the Flies *and John Osborne's* Look Back in Anger.

But there is not necessarily any tension between thinking and feeling: we think emotionally as well as intellectually. We can't listen to a Billie Holiday song, for example, without thinking on both levels.

[C] *Artworks may well give us pleasure, entertain us and make us think, all at the same time.*

Q10 combines the second and fourth questions in the specification under the heading 'The arts as a challenge'.

Q10	'Since few people seem to take an interest in art, and even they disagree about what art is, we shouldn't waste time on it in school.'
	How far do you agree with this judgement?
	You might consider:
	■ what is taught under the heading 'art' at school
	■ whether what is taught is 'useful'
	■ whether we value art for reasons other than usefulness

Here you can draw on your own experience of 'art' on the school timetable. General Studies is one subject in which you can legitimately do this as long as the experience serves as relevant evidence. Write your answer to this question:

(v) a What is done in art lessons that you consider 'useful'?

b What is done that might have value of another sort?

Sources B and D make points that are directly relevant to Q10. They contain ideas that can be explored but you will need some quite specific examples (of 'valuable' artworks) of your own.

Media bias

Content

Are newspapers about more than 'news'?

Home news

THE INDEPENDENT ON SUNDAY, 31 DECEMBER 2006

What a party! New Year's Eve with Tony, Robin and the Miami Beach set

So how exactly will Britain's first family celebrate the holiday while in Florida? **David Usborne** speculates

The four black SUVs of the Blair caravan rolled up outside Big Pink, a diner on Collins Avenue in South Beach that advertises 'real food for real people', at lunchtime on Thursday. Cherie, who had wanted to stay at the house by the pool for the day, was grumpy — it was Nicky and Kathryn who had insisted on going out. Leo, being only six, hadn't had a say in the matter.

Tony ordered a Caesar salad and a beer, wearing that forced I-love-Gordon smile of his.

Privately, he was still fuming about that fool of a British Airways captain who had overshot the runway on Tuesday (damn commercial flying), attracting the attention of the press back home to their whereabouts. A blasted nuisance, especially since he might now have to pay Robin Gibb for using that wedding cake of a house of his. Would tipping the staff do?

The last thing Tony needed now was family squabbling.

The above are the first 160 words of a 900-word article.

Above the headline was a photomontage, by Vanessa Wright, of Tony Blair, tanned and muscular in a swimming costume, Robin Gibb, one-time Bee Gees guitarist, and his wife Dwina, Cherie Blair in hair-curlers, and assorted showbiz extras. They were by a pool, against a background of sea, blue sky and tropical vegetation.

Several newspapers carried stories about the Blairs at the Gibbses' Miami mansion over Christmas 2006. Questions were asked about whether it was fitting that the prime minister and his family should be spending a (religious) holiday with B-list celebrity friends, and some wondered whether it would be the Blairs, the Gibbses or the British taxpayer who would be paying for it all.

Source B — Is it the responsibility of the press to be opposed to authority?

Some journalism needs, whatever the facts, to find a public institution to blame or criticise.

Stephen Lander, former head of MI5

Journalists do now seem to believe that The Person in Charge is Always Wrong.

Trevor Phillips, Commission for Racial Equality

Newspapers trumpet the collapse of trust in politics and politicians, as though they had not had a major role in bringing that about. They nourish a culture of contempt, engulfing the whole of public life.

Tony Wright MP, chair of the Public Administration Select Committee

The assumption is that all politicians are motivated by self-interest and ego, all public servants are either demoralised or inept, and all business people are fat cats without a conscience.

Tom Fawley, former Northern Ireland ombudsman

A lack of coverage of positive stories can create the impression that a system — in my case education — is in a perpetual state of crisis. This is simply not true.

David Bell, chief inspector of schools

Journalists are powerful people, but one of the dangers of power is not so much that it corrupts absolutely, but rather that it can make those who possess it lazy, complacent and arrogant.

Sir Michael Bichard, chair of the Legal Services Commission

The media-dominated universe presents the world in terms of opposites and polarises every issue into an extreme position.

James Jones, Bishop of Liverpool

Source: Anthony Sampson, 'The fourth estate under fire', *Guardian*, 10 January 2005 (accessed online 29 January 2007)

Source C | **Do we expect the BBC to be objective?**

It does finally seem to be sinking in at the BBC that it has a problem with impartiality. For many years, right-leaning writers on this newspaper and on the *Daily Mail* have been presenting left-leaning, liberal-minded television executives with evidence of bias in the BBC's reporting on the Middle East, the European Union and the Conservative Party, for example.

The BBC has been adept at fending off such criticism by commissioning 'research' into its coverage of these issues, and by providing 'evidence' of what it likes to think is its even-handedness. Some of us, however, are less than convinced.

Andrew Marr, a left-leaning commentator if ever there was one, admitted recently: 'The BBC is not impartial or neutral. It's a publicly funded urban organisation with an abnormally large number of young people, ethnic minorities and gay people.' He added: 'It has a liberal bias, not so much a party-political bias.'

He was dead right. The problem is not that the BBC leans to the left, in any obvious way, in its news coverage. We on the *Telegraph* and the *Mail* wouldn't be the only ones to complain if it did that. No, the problem is that there is a 'liberal bias' in all its drama, comedy and arts programming —

and the bias is more insidious there precisely because it is less explicitly political. We know we're going to hear liberal opinions expressed on *Newsnight* and *Today*, but is there a comedy-show or panel-game that isn't stuffed with *Guardian* journalists?

Linda Smith was a regular on Radio 4's *The News Quiz*. When she died early in 2006, colleagues on the panel paid tribute to her sharp left-wing wit — and they would, wouldn't they? Most of them had written for the *Guardian*.

When was the last time a *Telegraph* or *Mail* or *Express* journalist was invited on to one of these shows? The result is that when, for example, earlier this summer, a panellist called President Bush a 'war-mongering moron', there was no one there to say: 'Hang on a minute!'

And when Ken Loach was under fire for a film that was sympathetic towards the IRA, *Newsnight* interviewed two film critics. Both of them defended Ken Loach to the hilt, saying what a fine film-maker he was. One of the critics was from the *Guardian*, the other was from the *Independent on Sunday*.

The BBC should be aware, as the licence-fee comes under review, that it is only a minority of viewers who read left-leaning newspapers.

Adapted from Tom Leonard, 'The BBC's commitment to bias is no laughing matter', *Daily Telegraph*, 27 October 2006

Source D | **Do the BBC and independent broadcasting companies have quite different roles?**

The overall audience is falling for the main television channels, just as the readership is falling for printed newspapers.

BBC1 and ITV currently have an equal share of the audience at roughly 20% each.

The competition is fiercest on a Saturday evening, when BBC1's *Strictly Come Dancing* is head to head with ITV's *The X Factor*. Viewing figures vary between the shows themselves and the later declaration of results.

| Figures for 9 December 2006 were: | BBC1: | Strictly Come Dancing | 9.0m | Results | 9.8m |
| | ITV: | The X Factor | 8.2m | Results | 7.2m |

> There is nothing quite like live TV. It combines entertainment value with high emotional engagement.

Lorraine Heggessey, the former BBC1 controller, now chief executive of Talkback Thames

Peter Fincham, BBC1 controller

> Three-generation TV — that's TV you can watch with your grandparents and children. There's not enough of that about. I believe we've only scratched the surface on modern family viewing. It has a very important role on a mainstream channel like BBC1.

> Both shows being live is a big factor. It's the definitive return of the big Saturday night entertainment shows. People delay going out on a Saturday night because they want to vote and be part of the debate.

Paul Jackson, ITV director of entertainment and comedy

Adapted from Owen Gibson, 'Strictly or X Factor? BBC and ITV delight in battle of Saturday night', *Guardian*, 16 December 2006

BBC: no licence to print money

The licence fee has its downside, being a regressive, flat-rate charge that falls more heavily on poor than rich families. There is no perfect way to fund broadcasting. Once a programme is made, it makes sense that anyone who wants to can watch it, but pay-per-view would put some people off. Direct government finance would compromise independence, while moving to advertising would waste viewers' time and drain resources from other channels. In this context, and when the BBC has shown itself — through music, news and drama — to enrich Britain's cultural life, there is a decisive case for maintaining the broad shape of the status quo.

Extract from *Guardian* editorial, 23 December 2006

Skills

If newspapers ever were only 'about news', they no longer are. Source A is an example, from a 'serious', 'quality' Sunday newspaper, of the mixture of 'news' and 'views'. Though the article appeared under 'home news' in the paper, the columnist David Usborne does not 'report', he 'speculates'. The article is not news (and it is certainly not 'home' news), however we define this word.

(i) **Why is it that newspapers are looking more and more like magazines, where news and views, 'stories' and comment leak into each other?**

In order to answer this question satisfactorily, it is necessary to be able to take a long view. However, it is also useful to be aware of some of the changes that have taken place in recent years, even if it is difficult to identify them yourself.

It is worth stopping to consider whether it is legitimate for:

- photographers to stake out a politician and his or her family while they are on holiday
- a journalist to speculate about what the politician and the family might be doing and thinking in private
- a newspaper to present as news what is really subjective comment, of a quite sarcastic kind
- a picture editor to print, as part of a news story, a photomontage that ridicules public figures

In this case, perhaps the editor considered Tony Blair, in particular, to be 'fair game', and for the story to be 'legitimate' on New Year's Eve when there was no call for solemnity.

The press has traditionally seen itself as 'the Fourth Estate' (the first three being nobility, clergy and common people). It has always been a kind of unofficial opposition to those in power, and investigative journalism, at its best, can expose corruption, hypocrisy and abuse of power.

A problem may arise when a newspaper is so politically committed that it always supports one party, whether or not it is in government.

(ii) Write down why this might be a problem.

We discussed the meaning of the names of the main political parties, and outlined some of their policies, on page 32. Here, in the context of bias, we need to know what is meant by referring to Labour policies (if not always *New* Labour policies) as 'left wing', and to Conservative policies as 'right wing'.

(iii) What characterises a policy as 'left wing' or 'right wing'? Copy the following table and make your suggestions for completing the sentences.

A policy might be called 'left wing' if it emphasised...	A policy might be called 'right wing' if it emphasised...

Newspapers do not have a formal relationship with political parties in the UK, as they do in some countries. Nevertheless, some lean to the left of the political spectrum, and some lean to the right, i.e. they tend to support 'left-leaning' Labour or Liberal Democrat policies, or 'right-leaning' Conservative policies.

As we have seen, the parties themselves have tended to move towards the centre ground in recent years. Newspapers, to some extent, have also moved to the centre — and some papers do not support either of the major parties until an election comes round, when they might support one.

(iv) **What national daily papers can you think of? Which of them might be said to lean to the left, which to the right, and which might be thought of as in the centre? Copy and complete the following table:**

Left-leaning	Central	Right-leaning

In Source A, we have a left-leaning newspaper running an article that is critical of the prime minister of a left-leaning government.

In Source C, we have a journalist on a right-leaning paper, the *Daily Telegraph* (alongside other right-leaning papers, the *Daily Mail* and the *Daily Express*), accusing the BBC of sharing a 'liberal bias' with the *Guardian* and the *Independent on Sunday*. According to this journalist, the BBC has learnt how to rebut the charge that it is 'left wing', so he adopts Andrew Marr's description of it as having a 'liberal bias' instead. Most people would consider it a good thing to be 'liberal'. ('Liberal, free, generous, charitable, hospitable' are grouped together in *Roget's Thesaurus*.) However, in this context we must assume that the journalist thinks that to be 'liberal' is to be left wing, woolly-minded, high-spending, unrealistic, anti-American, undisciplined, and much else.

Q11 is about news in the media.

> **Q11** Increasingly, people read the news on the internet, watch it on television or hear it on the radio.
>
> Discuss whether we could do without printed newspapers.
>
> You might consider:
> ■ the differences in the presentation of the news
> ■ whether there would be more or less bias
> ■ whether some of the truth would be lost

Much 'internet' news is, in fact, available in printed form first; it is only because the newspapers have reporters on the ground that the news gets on to the internet in the first place.

London-based newspapers have always used news agencies, local newspapers and freelance photographers. However, increasingly, bloggers and mobile-phone users are making a contribution.

Compared to getting our news from television or radio, when we read newspapers do we get:
- more or fewer news items?
- deeper or more summary treatment?
- more analysis or subjective comment?
- more or less sports, business or foreign coverage?

Is it true that the more news media there are, the more likely it is that 'the truth will out'?

Here is a sketch of an answer to Q11:

[S] *The news comes to us along a number of channels nowadays — but daily newspapers are still among the most important.*

[Ex A] *We have less time for reading newspapers and, in consequence, circulation is dropping.*

[Ex B] *Radio delivers a number of stories, but they are rather superficially treated, while television tends to concentrate on stories that have a strong visual component. This visual component may, in fact, detract from a viewer's ability to follow an argument. Some newspapers deliver not only news stories in some depth, they also give us reflective comment and developed argument. They give us reportage and journalism.*

[C] *The more news media we have at our disposal, the more likely it is that we will be able to make up our own minds as to 'the whole truth'.*

Whenever the future of the BBC is in question, two issues raise their heads: how it should be funded, and what we mean by — and how much we value — 'public service broadcasting'.

The BBC might be funded by:
- the licence fee, as at present
- pay per view
- a government grant
- advertising, as on BBC World and independent television channels

It is worth discussing the pros and cons of each of these options (see the *Guardian* editorial in Source D).

(v) What is meant by the use of the term 'public service broadcasting' in connection with the role of the BBC?

> **Q12** 'When we have hundreds of television channels to choose from, and when only just over a quarter of licence-payers are watching the channels the licence pays for, it is time to pension off the BBC.'
>
> To what extent do you agree with this view?
>
> You might consider:
> - why fewer people watch BBC channels
> - whether the BBC offers something distinctive
> - what value the BBC may be said to add to television

This question is similar to Q11, and as the response to that question came to the defence of printed newspapers, so the response to this question in the Teacher Guide argues for the survival of the BBC.

CONFLICT
Business and industry

The market

Content

> Source A   **What are the benefits to the consumer of a competitive market?**

The market in UK postal services was opened up to full competition on 1 January 2006.

Postcomm is the independent postal services regulator. It conducted market research to test the effects of this competition, and announced its findings at the end of October 2006. It found that:

- 20% of institutional users said their mail prices had reduced significantly.
- 38% said the choice of services available had improved.
- 34% believed the quality of the Royal Mail service had improved.

Competition in the postal services market has not been with us for long, and Royal Mail still has 96% of the addressed letters market; nevertheless, more and more companies are switching to Royal Mail's competitors.

'Access agreements' allow companies to collect and pre-sort mail from customers before transporting it to a Royal Mail delivery office for final delivery. The volume of mail carried through access agreements grew between 2004 and 2006, accounting for 10.5% of Royal Mail's total volume of business in August 2006.

Postcomm chief executive Sarah Chambers said: 'The results show there is great promise for the further development of competition in the UK mail market, but it is clear that there is still much to be done, particularly to meet the challenges posed by alternative means of communication. Though Royal Mail remains by far the biggest operator in the market, competition has encouraged it to raise its game, especially on quality of service.'

Source: www.psc.gov.uk/news-and-events/news-releases/2006/postcomm-research-finds-that-competition-has-delivered-early-benefits, 31 October 2006 (accessed 12 January 2007)

Source B **By what means do producers advertise their products?**

Competitive price   Reliability   Promptness of service

By buying one of our promotional products, your customer will see the name of your business or product right through the year.

Our winter promotions include items from *coffee mugs* to *ice-scrapers*, from *ball-point pens* to *shoulder-bags*, and from *customised T-shirts* to *spectacle-cases*.

NEW!

We can imprint any one of over 6 million *Clipart* images on your giveaway pen, mug or pocket diary at no extra charge.

Giving away one of our products with your business name on it is an inexpensive way of promoting your own products. From an imprinted *golf umbrella* to a *stadium-seat cushion*, a promotional gift is a warm way to say 'thank you' to an employee or valued client, while advertising your product or service at the same time.

Our promotional products are of the highest quality — so they'll go on working for you for years to come.

✦ A *printed beach-ball* can be used year after year, exposing your business name to hundreds.

✦ A customer might see our *refrigerator magnet* with your business name on it, on a daily basis. And your telephone number and e-mail address will be there, too.

✦ Promotional products are a much more cost-effective way of advertising your brand than any newspaper, magazine, radio or TV channel.

Adapted from **www.perfectprints.com** (accessed 12 January 2007)

Source C **How susceptible are we to advertising?**

Dolce & Gabbana knife ads censured

Fashion label Dolce & Gabbana has been censured for an advert showing models with gunshot wounds and brandishing knives.

The Advertising Standards Agency said the advertisement could be seen as condoning and glorifying knife-related violence, and concluded it was irresponsible.

Teenager killed in street stabbing

An 18-year-old man died in hospital yesterday after being stabbed as he was apparently returning home from a night out. The victim was named by Scotland Yard as Dean Rashid Lahlou, of Tottenham, north London. Mr Lahlou was taken to the North Middlesex Hospital in the early hours of Tuesday morning. A 17-year-old male from the Tottenham area was arrested in connection with the incident and was still in custody last night.

Source: Home News: In Brief, *Independent*, 10 January 2007

Are sport and entertainment over-commercialised?

When the England cricket team won the Ashes in the summer of 2005, the England and Wales Cricket Board clinched some lucrative deals with companies that wished to associate themselves with success. The Australians won the Ashes back again in the winter of 2006–07 in the first 5–0 walkover since the early 1920s.

If the England and Wales Cricket Board, the Barmy Army, English followers of cricket back home, and the players themselves were all disappointed with the result, the companies that sponsored the team were not exactly full of glee.

These companies included:

■ **Vodafone**, which has sponsored the team since 1997, and which signed a deal with the England and Wales Cricket Board worth £20 million in 2005. The Vodafone logo was prominent on the defeated team's white shirts.

■ **Volkswagen**, which supplied the official cars for the England team.

■ **Hugo Boss**, which supplied grooming products (including Kevin Pietersen's hair gel) to the team.

■ **Citizen Watches**, which gave Kevin Pietersen one of its £349 ECO-DRIVE Calibre 9000 models ('Unstoppable, just like the people who wear it').

■ **Barclays Capital**, which sponsored the bat used by the captain, Andrew Flintoff.

And then there are the sponsors of the team when it plays at home: **NPower**, **NatWest**, **Marston's Ale** and **Toyota**, to say nothing of **Sky Television**, which signed a deal in late 2004, worth £200 million, for the 'exclusive' privilege of broadcasting live domestic games.

All these sponsors are big enough to know that sports sponsorship is a risky business — and they're all in it for the long haul. Contracts signed in 2005 were for 4 years, so they'll still be in place when England and Australia battle it out again, in 2009.

Based on information in Paul Kelso, 'Miserable about the Ashes result? Imagine how the sponsors feel', *Guardian*, 6 January 2007

Skills

One does not have to be an economics or business studies student to make a go of this section, but there are some basic terms that a General Studies student (and an informed citizen) should know, and be able to use with confidence. One pair of such terms is *monopoly* and *competition*.

Few people would want to defend a monopoly, and even fewer would defend a privately owned monopoly. Virgin Trains comes close to being a privately owned monopoly on the West Coast main line, but only for the duration of its franchise. Boeing comes close to being a private monopoly in the USA, and Microsoft came even closer until it ran up against anti-trust legislation.

A publicly owned monopoly is something else — and the left-wing side of the Labour Party would like there to be more state-owned industry. Network Rail is, in effect, a publicly owned monopoly, and so was Royal Mail until recently.

It might be argued that a publicly owned monopoly can:

- operate in the public interest
- distribute its profits among employees or consumers (in the form of dividends like those issued by the Co-op)
- realise *economies of scale*, i.e. the cost per customer of providing goods or services lessens as customer numbers rise (this is another term that it might be useful to know)

(i) What, according to Source A, might the benefits of *competition* **be?**

Source B is, in effect, an advertisement for advertising; it is directed at producers or at producers-as-consumers rather than at consumers. It suggests that producers place advertisements on ordinary objects in daily use.

(ii) Where else do producers place advertisements for products or services where they hope to catch the public eye?

You would probably agree that advertising, of one sort or another, is both *ubiquitous* (everywhere) and *inescapable*.

What is an advertisement for? It may have one of a number of functions:

- A company will want to bring a *new product* to consumers' attention (e.g. 'the new, versatile Kia Carens MPV...with up to 16 seat variations').

Bus-stop advertising — an advertisement for *Blair Witch 2*

- A store may want to inform customers about a *sale* or price reduction (e.g. 'Spectacular savings in our winter sale, plus nothing to pay for 12 months, at Nationwide Home Improvement Products').
- A company may want to *distinguish* itself from the competition (e.g. 'Waitrose may not be where you normally shop, but...').
- A producer may want to *remind* consumers of its existence over a long period, and raise their consciousness of the brand name (e.g. 'Glenfiddich, single malt Scotch whisky, inspiring great conversation since Christmas Day 1887').

If you choose to write about advertisements, you must refer to particular examples — preferably by name.

Here is a question that could be answered by drawing on Sources A and B.

Q13	Advertisements are everywhere. They obviously have value for producers and providers of services.

Q13 Advertisements are everywhere. They obviously have value for producers and providers of services.

To what extent do they benefit consumers?

You might consider:
- why producers advertise
- what information advertisements contain
- whether they encourage over-consumption

While the bulleted second cue suggests that advertisements may be useful to people as *individuals*, needing to know what is 'out there', the third cue is *social*. It raises the question of whether advertising is, or is not, in the public interest. It is a chicken-and-egg question:

Does advertising encourage consumerism, or does consumerism encourage advertising?

Here is a sketch of a (highly subjective) answer to Q13:

[S] *Producers need to advertise their products if consumers are to be encouraged to buy them.*

[Ex A] *Advertisements may give consumers genuine information: for example, the price of an item that they intend to buy, the specifications of an item, or where it might be bought.*

[Ex B] *For the most part, though, consumers can find out information of the sort that they need for themselves. If they really want a product — a shampoo, for example — they will probably go to one or two shops selling shampoos close to where they live and compare the claims and prices of those on offer. They may seek the advice of a shop assistant. They are unlikely to be tempted to buy more shampoo than they need. On the other hand, a seductive advertisement may tempt them to spend more than is necessary.*

[C] *Some advertising benefits consumers; some may be pernicious; most is probably harmless.*

Q14 is, in a sense, the reverse of Q13.

Q14 'At worst, advertising can be offensive; at best, it is merely intrusive.'

Comment on whether much advertising might do more harm than good.

You might consider:
- what advertising might give offence
- where advertising might be a nuisance
- what ethical standards might be applied

To answer Q14, we need to distinguish between:
- those advertisements that might be said to cause *offence*
- those that might be a *nuisance*

An example of an advertisement that might cause offence can be found in Source C.

(iii) Write down any other advertisement, or sort of advertisement, that you think might cause offence.

Of course, what causes *offence* (is blasphemous or tasteless, for example) to one person will not necessarily offend another. The same goes for what may constitute a *nuisance* — and advertisements may be a nuisance in one context and not in another. The next question, therefore, is a very open one indeed, but it is one that merits discussion.

(iv) What advertisements, or what sorts of advertisements, might be considered intrusive or irritating — in some way a nuisance — and why?

Advertisers generally try to avoid giving offence or being a nuisance since they will not sell their products if they do this.

They may not be too concerned about being rapped over the knuckles by the Advertising Standards Agency (ASA), particularly if the product they are advertising is itself 'daring', 'provocative' or 'cool' — an example of what was once called 'radical chic'. Still, for the ASA to rule against an advertisement, it must have received complaints from the public that are probably 'the tip of the iceberg'. But then again, would those people who complained about the Dolce & Gabbana advertisement (Source C) be among the target consumers of this company's products?

One last open-ended question might be considered:

Might advertisements do harm inasmuch as they lie to us (or do not tell the whole truth), and this is their explicit intention?

Business big and small

Content

Source A **How do small businesses compete with big ones?**

It's tough being a small fish in a sea full of sharks. When two small fishes swim together, they have a better chance of survival.

The two small fishes in this case are the independent publishers Profile Books and Serpent's Tail. Both companies have backed winners in recent years. Profile Books published the surprise success of 2003, Lynne Truss's *Eats, Shoots and Leaves*, which sold 3 million copies in hardback, and, more recently, Mick O'Hare's *Does Anything Eat Wasps?*, a compilation of readers' questions, and answers, from *The New Scientist*. Serpent's Tail published Lionel Shriver's *We Need to Talk About Kevin*, a novel about a school massacre in America, which won the Orange Prize.

Shriver might have been expected to score a second money-spinner for Serpent's Tail, but one of the 'sharks', HarperCollins, gobbled her up by offering her an advance of £230,000 for her next novel. Serpent's Tail could not have offered her a sweetener like this.

By merging, Profile Books gains a ready-made fiction list, and Serpent's Tail acquires a list of serious non-fiction titles. What's more, Serpent's Tail is now in a position to join the Independent Alliance. This gives it more clout when it comes to getting booksellers to stock its titles.

This is one book-trade merger from which, for once, all concerned might benefit.

Various sources, 6 January 2007

Source B **Who benefits from mergers and takeovers?**

The supermarket giant Morrisons, fourth biggest in the UK, bought the larger but ailing Safeway chain in 2004. In 2006 Morrisons posted its first ever annual loss in 106 years of trading: a loss of £313 million. There are signs now, though, that the company has begun to recover.

The Office of Fair Trading (OFT) cleared the £7 billion planned merger of Boots the Chemists and Alliance Unichem. The OFT admitted that this would reduce or eliminate competition in about 100 local areas. Celesio, Europe's biggest pharmaceuticals trader, raised concerns with the Competition Appeal Tribunal. Celesio owns the Lloyds chemists chain, which has about 1,500 outlets in the UK.

Anita Roddick founded The Body Shop in Brighton in 1976. Its distinctive pitch was that it was 'ethical': it used recycled packaging, and natural ingredients that had not been tested on animals. Then it was sold to French beauty group L'Oréal for £652 million, netting Roddick a windfall of £130 million. Although L'Oréal does not itself test its products on animals, it does not monitor whether the ingredients it uses have been so tested. The Body Shop will remain a distinct entity within the enlarged company.

Questions have been asked about the competence of the management at Vodafone, and particularly of its chief executive Arun Sarin. Its subsidiary in Japan has struggled to make an impact in a competitive market; its 3G handsets, for example, have not sold well. 'Poor name recognition' has been blamed. Now it has sold the subsidiary to internet company SoftBank for £8.9 billion, and much of this money will be returned to investors as cash payments.

The privatised British Airports Authority (BAA), owner of some of the UK's biggest airports including Heathrow, Gatwick, Stansted and Glasgow, has rejected a takeover bid from Spanish construction group Ferrovial. This bid follows the purchase of P&O by a company based in Dubai, and the attempts of Australian and German companies to buy the London Stock Exchange.

Ferrovial already owns Belfast City airport and half of Bristol airport, so the Civil Aviation Authority will be watching carefully what happens at BAA.

[Note: Ferrovial did buy BAA.]

Adapted from information in the *Guardian*, 18 March 2003 and *Today*, Radio 4, 23 March 2006

Source C

Are the managers of big companies too remote from their workforces?

All the research shows that organisations that consult both individually and collectively perform the best. Too many UK managers prefer the easy option of command and control, edict and order. But while it may be harder, a consultative approach produces more in the long run.

Brendan Barber, General Secretary of the Trades Union Congress, at the 'Unions 21' Conference, London, 4 March 2006

Democracy sounds good, but in a fast-moving business like this, you don't have the luxury of being able to spend time agonising about decisions round a table. I have to trust my designers to get on with the job they've been given to do. They won't want to discuss what they're doing or why they're doing it, all the time, any more than I would. Anything big that concerns us all — we'll get round the table to thrash that out, collectively.

Chief executive, design company

If you lined all the managers up in an identity parade, I wouldn't know which of them was the chief executive. He never comes into this department. He signs his name on notices, but I've never been consulted about any decisions the bosses take. It's all very top-down here. We just get on with the job and do what we're told. I dare say he earns a good bit more than I do, and he'll be well sorted if he's made redundant.

Admin assistant

I've been trying to encourage a bit more communication up and down the company, but the chief executive's out of the office quite a lot, and his personal assistant's very jealous of his diary.

When we do try to involve employees in decision making that affects them, they seldom have much to say. They sit in meetings and listen, but the chief executive does most of the talking, and it's he who decides at the end of the day.

Human resources director

There's the company where the boss hands out *information*: 'Here's the news', as it were. There's the boss who *consults* — views are exchanged round the table, but no decisions are reached. There's the boss who *negotiates*, one to one, across the table, and a certain amount of bargaining goes on. And then there's the boss — who isn't a boss in the old sense — who goes in for *problem solving*. Everyone says something; no idea's too silly; options are generated, and decisions are made.

Management consultant

Does big business operate in the public interest?

Margaret Thatcher was a believer in wealth creation. Her view was that when individuals get rich by establishing profitable businesses, their wealth will 'trickle down' to the poor, and all will benefit. This is capitalism with a human face. Business owners do not have to be philanthropists; they do not have to build churches and endow schools like their Victorian counterparts. They do not even have to give money to charity — they just have to spend money.

The pity is that the rich spend their money on themselves — on luxury items like art, jewellery, yachts and second or third homes, and the money they spend rarely reaches those in most need. If they don't manage to spend their money in their lifetimes, they leave it to their spouses, sons and daughters. The money does not 'trickle down'; it collects in a stagnant pool close to its source.

The founder of Microsoft, Bill Gates, and the shrewd investor Warren Buffett have offered proof that philanthropy is not dead. Gates, worth $50 billion, and Buffett, worth $44 billion, are among the world's most successful wealth-creators. They are not going to let their wealth trickle down to the needy, however: they are pouring it out, here and now, to relieve suffering caused by HIV, malaria and tuberculosis, and to promote education and food biotechnology.

Buffett is giving away 85% of the wealth that he has accumulated — and $31 billion of this will go straight to the Bill and Melinda Gates Foundation. As he said before the world's press: 'If you're accumulating wealth, it's sensible to hand it over to someone who can do it better than you can — like an investment manager. I'm handing it over to someone who can give it away better than I can.'

An Italian journalist pointed out that his readers in Italy would think Mr Buffett was 'crazy' to be giving his money away to charity instead of giving it to his own three children. They would probably survive on $2 billion apiece, Mr Buffett replied. Besides: 'I don't believe in dynastic wealth. I don't believe in inheriting a position in society based on what womb you come from.'

Neither Bill Gates nor Warren Buffett will impoverish themselves — they'll still be among the world's rich men. The question is whether they will be able to persuade some of their American contemporaries — New York mayor Michael Bloomberg (worth $5 billion), computer billionaire Michael Dell ($14 billion), and the family of David Packard, of Hewlett-Packard ($7 billion) — to follow their lead. It may be that, between them, Gates and Buffett will pioneer a redefinition of what it is to be rich.

Based on Andrew Clark, 'Sound foundation', *Guardian*, 27 June 2006

Skills

There are small businesses, big businesses, and small and medium-sized enterprises (SMEs) in the middle. An SME is officially defined as a business having between 50 and 250 employees. (This is the increasingly standard European definition, at any rate.)

When Andrew Franklin set up Profile Books, it was a small company. When Pete Ayrton launched Serpent's Tail, it, too, was a small company. The pair of them together must now be a medium-sized enterprise.

(i) **What sorts of small businesses can you think of? What goods do they produce, or (perhaps more likely) what sorts of service do they provide? Try to write down about six examples.**

(ii) **Now, what big companies can you name? List six companies from anywhere in the world, whose products or services you are sure you could identify.**

We have looked at what *monopoly* and its opposite, *competition* mean. A company might have a monopoly by:

- having been established by the government (Her Majesty's Stationery Office was a monopoly until it was privatised)
- being nationalised by the government (as the railways were before being reprivatised in 1996)
- driving rival companies out of the market, by taking them over or outperforming them

In some specialised markets, companies might achieve an *effective* monopoly, if not an actual one. Reference has been made to Microsoft and Boeing in the USA. BAE and Rolls-Royce are effective monopolies in the market for government-commissioned military aircraft in the UK, and Rupert Murdoch's Sky comes close to having an effective monopoly on satellite television.

(iii) **What is the single biggest objection to a company having a monopoly on a particular product or service?**

Sometimes, it seems that the business pages of the newspapers are all about company mergers, i.e. one company buying another. The takeover might be *friendly*, in which case the management of the company to be taken over will recommend the deal to the shareholders. Alternatively, it might be *hostile*, in which case the deal will not be recommended, and the bidding company will either have to raise its bid (perhaps beyond the company's quoted share price) or drop its bid. The American technologies stock exchange (the NASDAQ), for example, bid for the London Stock Exchange (LSE) at the end of 2006, in spite of the fact that the value of shares traded on the LSE far and away outstrips the value of shares traded on NASDAQ. It was a 'hostile' bid in that the LSE was not looking for a buyer.

In the same year (2006), two building societies were sold to the biggest mutual building society (one owned by its members) in the UK.

The small Lambeth building society was bought by the larger Portman building society was bought by the largest of all, the Nationwide

This was a friendly double-takeover of which all members (shareholders) approved. Lambeth members did rather well out of it, 'earning' a bonus at each sale.

(iv) Write down some reasons why one company might seek to take over another one.

A particularly disputed issue at the moment is whether it is good for the UK that so many British companies are being bought by foreign companies. It was one thing when the British Airports Authority (BAA) was privatised; it was something else when BAA was snapped up by a Spanish construction group, Ferrovial. But few of those who objected to this sale had objected to BAA's purchase of Hungary's only international airport, Ferihegy, in 2005.

This is a complex debate that eminent economists (such as Will Hutton on the 'left', and Madsen Pirie on the 'right') fall out about; but it is worth considering one or two of the main reasons given, both for and against.

(v) Copy and complete the following table to show the pros and cons of allowing UK companies to be sold to foreign companies.

Pros	Cons

Q15 draws on information and concepts in Sources A and B.

> **Q15** Not a day goes by without two companies merging, or one company buying another.
>
> Discuss whether these mergers and takeovers are in the public interest.
>
> You might consider:
> - why this buying and selling goes on
> - whether it has an impact on consumers
> - whether British companies ought to be for sale

Note that 'in the public interest' does *not* mean 'of interest to the public'; it refers instead to the general welfare of society.

Source A would suggest that two small companies in a competitive environment might have a lot to gain from a merger. The existence of the Office of Fair Trading (OFT), however, suggests that there are dangers from an *over-concentration* of ownership as in the case of the Boots/Alliance Unichem merger (Source B). The OFT would not be concerned about the merger of Profile Books and Serpent's Tail, but it would certainly have something to say about a merger of, for example, Sainsbury's and Somerfield, or Scottish Water and British Gas.

Here is a sketch of a response to Q15:

[S] *There have always been mergers and takeovers, but perhaps never as many as now.*

[Ex A] *It may be slightly absurd for Company A to buy Company B when the products are very different. We might worry, too, when companies grow too large to be manageable or, more importantly, accountable.*

[Ex B] *In a free market, the buying and selling of companies can scarcely be prevented. The merger of two small companies can bring benefits on all sides; and when a company is producing something worthwhile, but is not being well managed, its employees and shareholders might welcome a takeover by a better-managed and reputable company. The OFT keeps an eye on the interests of consumers, since a monopoly, or near-monopoly, is in no one's interests.*

The OFT cannot, however, prevent companies being sold because they are British, nor should it. The British flag ought not to protect a company from the consequences of either failure or success.

[C] *Mergers and takeovers are not good or bad in themselves. Only their causes and effects are good or bad. This is why we have a regulator to monitor them.*

Q16 draws on Sources C and D.

| Q16 | Company bosses are often rather remote figures, and the bigger the company, the more remote the boss.

How far can a business be run democratically?

You might consider:
- the wide range of sizes of companies
- the demands on employees
- whether democracy is appropriate in a business setting |

Our first impulse is to think that a small company (of up to around ten employees) could be run democratically, while a large one (a global corporation) could not. Perhaps it is worth considering whether a family is often run democratically — and there are many family businesses. What is more, if a country of 60 million people such as the UK can be governed democratically, why can a company like BP or Virgin not be run in a similar way?

(vi) Why might a 'business setting' make it difficult to make decisions democratically?

Bill Gates is a 'boss'; Warren Buffett is not (Source D). Microsoft was probably a democracy in its early days. How democratic can it be now, when its boss is a world-famous celebrity who has taken such a fortune out of the business that he can afford to give large slices of it away? In what sense is it his to give?

It is worth bearing in mind, when answering Q16, what is said about *democracy* in the 'Politics and the public' topic (pages 27–34).

The individual and society

Content

What rights do we have as citizens?

Sixteen basic human rights have been incorporated into UK law.

The Human Rights Act 1998 gives legal effect in the UK to certain fundamental rights and freedoms contained in the European Convention on Human Rights (ECHR). There are 16 basic rights taken from the ECHR. These rights not only affect matters of life and death, such as freedom from torture and killing, but also affect your rights in everyday life: what you can say and do, your beliefs, your right to a fair trial and many other similar basic entitlements. The rights are:

- Right to life
- Prohibition of torture
- Prohibition of slavery and forced labour
- Right to liberty and security
- Right to a fair trial
- No punishment without law
- Right to respect for private and family life
- Freedom of thought, conscience and religion

- Freedom of expression
- Freedom of assembly and association
- Right to marry
- Prohibition of discrimination
- Protection of property
- Right to education
- Right to free elections
- Abolition of the death penalty

Exercising your human rights

If you are in a difficult situation in which you believe that your human rights are being violated, it is always advisable to see if the problem can be resolved without going to court.

However, where this is not possible, under the Human Rights Act, as a victim of an alleged violation, it is for you to bring a case before the appropriate court or tribunal in the UK. The court or tribunal will then consider whether or not your human rights have been violated.

Adapted from **www.direct.gov.uk/en/RightsandResponsibilities/DG_4002951** (accessed 17 February 2007)

Source B   What duties does society have a right to expect us to perform?

Jury service

Frequently asked questions

- *Why/how have I been picked for jury service?*
  All jurors are selected at random by computer from the electoral register. Everyone on the electoral register from the ages of 18 to 70 may be selected, even if they are not eligible to serve on a jury. Some people never get called, others get called more than once.

- *Do I have to serve?*
  Yes. The Criminal Justice Act 2003 contained provision to ensure that nearly all members of society are eligible for jury service. If you have been summoned for jury service and had that summons confirmed, then you are under a legal obligation to participate in the criminal justice process as a juror.

- *Can someone else take my place?*
  No. A summons is only for the person named on the summons. It cannot be transferred to anyone else. It is an offence for someone to impersonate a juror.

- *What if I don't feel well before I reach the court?*
  Please call the jury manager as soon as possible. In some cases the trial may have to be postponed for a day. Delaying a trial is extremely costly and is not a good use of public money. For this reason it should be avoided if at all possible.

- *Can I be excused from jury service?*
  Anyone may apply for discretionary excusal. They should write the details on their summons reply. A jury officer at the Jury Central Summoning Bureau will make a decision whether that person can be excused based on the details given. If a juror is refused excusal, they have the right of appeal against this.

- *Can I have my jury service deferred?*
  Anyone can apply to have their jury service deferred. Reasons for such a request (e.g. they are going on holiday) should be clearly stated on the jury summons form. Jurors should also provide any other dates when they cannot attend within the next 12 months so that a new date can be arranged.

- *Will I get paid for being on jury service?*
  Courts can pay for loss of earnings, travelling costs, a subsistence allowance and an allowance for other financial loss incurred solely because of jury service, up to a maximum daily rate. No payment is made to third parties such as employers.

Source: **www.cjsonline.gov.uk/juror/faqs/index.html** (accessed 17 February 2007)

Source C — Do the interests of society override those of the individual?

Passports and ID cards

In 2006, all new UK passports contained a digital chip recording the facial dimensions of the passport-holder. From 2008, it is planned that new passports will incorporate iris scans and fingerprints.

The new passports, with facial dimensions, are required by international agreement to prevent fraud. Travellers to the USA will need them as from October 2006.
Government ministers

The new passports are nothing more than another part of Labour's ill-thought-through strategy for the unwanted and ineffective ID cards.
David Davis, shadow home secretary

The biometric passports with iris scans and finger-prints are likely to cost £19.2 billion over 10 years, making a new passport cost as much as £300.
London School of Economics

The scheme will cost no more than £5.8 billion over 10 years, raising the cost of a new passport to no more than £93. From 2008, passport applicants will also be given an ID card. ID cards will improve our security in the 'war on terror'.
Government ministers

ID cards will be little or no help in the 'war on terror'.
Stella Rimington, ex-MI5 chief

The government's own manifesto referred to a voluntary ID card. The government has no mandate to introduce compulsory ID, but giving an ID card with a passport is introducing compulsory ID by stealth.
Opposition MPs

No one is compelled to have a passport. Applying for a passport is a matter of choice. Of course you can't 'opt out' of having a passport if you choose to travel abroad.
Charles Clarke, home secretary, 13 March 2006

It should be voluntary for people who apply for passports to have their details entered on a national database.
House of Lords

It is thought that ministers will make ID cards compulsory once around 80% of the population has been issued with one. *Matthew Hickley, Daily Mail, 6 March 2006*

Source D Ought the privacy of public figures to be intruded upon?

We used to call them 'tabloids' (until 'serious' newspapers were reduced in size), and the *Sun* was the market leader.

Why do people read the *Sun* — still the king of the red-tops? They buy it for the sport, the race-tips and listings; but mostly they buy it for the royal gossip, the celebrity gossip and the TV-tie-in gossip.

According to the Press Complaints Commission, it is 'unacceptable to photograph individuals in private places without their consent'. What is a private place? It is one where a person has 'a reasonable expectation of privacy'. The paparazzi who waited outside the front gate of Prince William's girlfriend, Kate Middleton, on her 25th birthday had a reasonable expectation that they would be paid good money for a saucy close-up — but the paparazzi have been hate-figures since Princess Diana's death so the *Sun* called them off.

It is still the case that newspaper diary columns will pay up to £100 for a juicy story, and up to a £1,000 for a celebrity *exposé*.

The public is justified in suspecting, though, that there are times when celebrities collude with newspapers, selling stories and making themselves available for photo-shoots. Princess Diana was not above doing this herself, when it suited her.

What even the red-tops would hesitate to print

Newspapers have to pull their punches because of the libel laws and the Press Complaints Commission. Online websites are less constrained. Popbitch, in particular, has a reputation for merciless treatment of those it thinks are important. Camilla Wright set it up 7 years ago: it is now a weekly online magazine sent to hundreds of thousands of registered subscribers. Wright receives between 300 and 400 e-mails every week, from around the world, offering celebrity gossip, among other things. She also reads a number of online newspapers on a daily basis. She separates the credible from the incredible, and flies kites. When she is not certain about the truth of an allegation, or the legal position, she will print the story and let readers guess the name of the celebrity concerned. She was 18 months ahead of the *News of the World* with the story about David Beckham and Rebecca Loos. Popbitch also announced the name of Madonna's son Rocco before the baby was born, and it hinted at sexual indiscretions by two Liberal Democrat leadership contenders, long before paid newspaper reporters were on to the stories.

The site tries to be nice, rather than nasty, about the victims. This is one reason why the site manages to avoid being sued, though the Beckhams threatened to take it to court over the allegations of sexual misdemeanours on its message board. Nothing came of the threat, though (apart from notoriety for the site and 100,000 more subscribers) — perhaps because the plaintiffs would have earned nothing from the case. Popbitch has no money behind it, like the *Sun* or the *News of the World* have. It has nothing to lose.

In the days of the internet (paid for by opportunistic advertisers), the mobile-phone-as-camera and e-mail, one wonders whether there is anywhere that celebrities can go, or anything that they can do, with a 'reasonable expectation of privacy'.

Adapted from Decca Aitkenhead, 'Hot gossip', *Guardian Weekend*, 6 May 2006, and Janice Turner, 'How dare you invade my privacy! Oh, all right', *The Times*, 20 January 2007

Skills

The 16 'basic human rights' listed in Source A seem to be of two kinds: there are all-or-nothing rights, and there are rights that are matters of degree. The 'prohibition of torture', for example, is all or nothing. Torture is not to be used as a means of extracting information, in any circumstances, in any European country.

(i) What other 'all-or-nothing' rights are there in Source A? Write a list.

The all-or-nothing rights are *absolute* rights; no exceptions are allowed. All the others do permit exceptions. The 'right to life', for example, is not given to a foetus whose mother does not wish to bring it to term. The abortion law recognised that a mother's right not to bear an unwanted child overrides the 'right' of a foetus to be born (a 'right' itself, of course, that simple biology has never recognised).

Most of the rights listed in Source A are matters of degree. There is an exception, or there are exceptions, to each one of them. There is a limit to the extent to which the right can be exercised.

(ii) Think of an exception, or a limit, to each of the rights on the list that are matters of degree.

Even 'absolute' rights may not always be watertight: there is no agreement, even across the Western world, about what counts as torture, and certain 'religious' practices (e.g. 'honour killing') fall foul of the law.

It may be that you can think of other rights, not included among the 16 'basic human rights', that are worth adding. The Universal Declaration of Human Rights of 1948, for instance, enshrined the following:

- right to asylum
- right to work and to choose one's work freely
- right to earn equal pay for equal work

The International Covenant on Civil and Political Rights of 1966 added the following:

- right for ethnic minorities to enjoy their own culture
- right for linguistic minorities to use their own language

Questions might be raised on Unit 1 about any of these rights and the ways in which they are, or are not, given effect.

Source B is about one duty that UK society requires its citizens to perform: jury service. It should be noted that the jury is a British institution. It was exported from the UK to the USA and to Commonwealth countries, and had only a short-lived presence in Europe, following its introduction by Napoleon.

(iii) What other duties does society require of us? What responsibilities do we have as UK citizens? Make a list.

The list of duties may not seem to be particularly long compared with the list of rights — but there are many laws that we are required to obey. Few of these seriously limit our freedom, but the issue of identity (ID) cards is one that may bulk larger in the future. When discussing this issue, it is worth considering whose interests might be served by their introduction: the interest of the individual, or the interest of society/the state.

When ID cards were being called 'entitlement' cards (like credit cards and store cards) they might have been thought of as 'good' for the individual. In the context of the so-called 'war on terror', they take on a more surveillance-based role.

It is also worth considering whether, if ID cards were introduced, we would be required simply to be in possession of such a card, or whether we would have to carry it with us at all times.

The UK is unusual in there being no requirement for its citizens (at the time of writing) either to possess an ID card or to carry one. Some EU countries require possession only; others require that their citizens possess an ID card *and* that they carry it with them at all times. We might not object to having to possess an ID card (other than on grounds of cost). However, consider this question.

(iv) What might the objections be to a law that required us to carry an ID card at all times?

To answer Q17, you might draw on material from any of Sources A–C for evidence.

Q17 The relationship between the state and the individual in the UK has changed in recent years, and the individual is less free as a result.

How far do you share this view?

You might consider:
- rights lost or gained
- duties imposed or withdrawn
- whether attitudes to freedom might have changed

Obviously, this is a very open question. Individuals may be as free as ever, yet they may *feel* less free. They know that there are more laws and regulations, and they know that there are more people in prison (there is more of almost everything you can think of, including more people). Life in the UK *seems* to be more complicated and more demanding. However:

- We now have a Freedom of Information Act.
- We are free to work anywhere in the EU.
- Gay and lesbian couples can register civil partnerships.
- Fundamental rights and freedoms are now enshrined in UK law.
- Employees have a right to receive the national minimum wage.
- Mothers have the right to ask for flexible hours of working.

There are claims that can be made on both sides, as in any complex issue. It is as well to represent both sides in your response.

Here is a sketch of a response to Q17:

[S] *It may be that it is the perception of a change in the relationship that has changed.*

[Ex A] *New laws are constantly being introduced, and the prisons have never been more full. There is more and more surveillance, and it is expected that compulsory ID cards will be introduced.*

[Ex B] *On the other hand, the law-abiding individual is as free as ever — perhaps more so than previously. Budget airlines have freed us to travel, and the internet has freed us to communicate. If there are more laws, many of them are there for our greater security. One can even grow accustomed to high levels of surveillance.*

[C] *We might have lost some abstract freedoms, but we have gained a number of concrete freedoms in return.*

The relationship between the individual and society is especially interesting when the private individual is a public figure. Members of the royal family are a special case, inasmuch as they are public figures from the moment they are born. What made Princess Diana and, later, Kate Middleton so special was that they were transitional figures: private individuals one day, and public figures the next. And we all like a rags-to-riches story, whether it is about a young man from Stratford (Shakespeare) or a group of friends from Liverpool (the Beatles).

Who are the other public figures? Perhaps they can be divided into two kinds: the *professionals* and the *celebrities*.

Professionals	Celebrities
Politicians	Musicians (singers, instrumentalists)
Commentators (journalists, broadcasters)	Sportspeople (footballers, athletes, tennis players etc.)
Heads of institutions (businesses, charities, churches etc.)	Actors (film and television)

Is this a valid distinction? Are there other categories on either side of the vertical line? (Note that it is as well to be able to name a few examples of people in each category.)

(v) *Why* **are we 'ordinary' people so interested in the** *private* **lives of these** *public* **figures?**

Whereas once we idolised Hollywood film-stars — who were wonderfully remote from us — in the television age, the objects of our fascination are soap-stars and pop musicians, and, more recently, the inmates of the Big Brother house. Is this another sign of a progressive 'dumbing down'?

Q18 concerns public figures, and the extent to which their privacy should be intruded upon.

Q18 'Our obsession with the private lives of public figures proves the poverty of our own lives.' Discuss.

You might consider:
- whether the media are only giving the public what it wants
- the benefits to the public figures themselves of 'exposure'
- the ethics of media intrusion into private lives

Tolerance and intolerance

Content

Source A **Where do our prejudices about other people come from?**

More and more European undergraduates are studying abroad as a part of their foreign-language studies. Britons are not enthusiastic foreign-language learners, but it is normal for language students to spend a year in the target-language country.

Jim Coleman surveyed the attitudes of some 3,000 of these British students in the 1990s. He sought their views about the people in their host nation before they departed, and again soon after their return. The results were not encouraging. Most held stereotypical views before they went: thus, Germans were thought to be serious, competent, hard working, logical and a touch arrogant — they were not noted for helpfulness or good humour. The Spanish were thought to be emotional, lazy and loud — but helpful and good humoured, while the French shared some of the Spaniards' Mediterranean temperament with some of the Germans' arrogance. The French were perceived to be more hard working than the British, but to be less patient or tolerant.

What was surprising was that the British students returned from an extended period abroad holding the same opinions; their stereotypical views intact. Indeed, up to 30% of the students came back to Britain with a more negative attitude towards the people of their host nation than the one they left with.

University students of foreign languages might be expected to be among the least prejudiced of thinkers about our European neighbours. They have chosen to study a foreign language — somewhat against the grain of British society — and they have spent a number of months in the host country. They are, indeed, probably among the most travelled of young people, and the most international in their outlook. One wonders what stereotypes — what untested prejudices — their contemporaries are carrying around with them.

Based on research by Professor Jim Coleman of the Open University

Source B · How can we challenge stereotypes?

The Ulfah Collective is Britain's first Muslim female band. It performs rock, gospel and rap music, and is based in Birmingham.

On 4 November 2006 the band performed live in a women-only concert at the Birmingham Museum and Art Gallery.

What struck the audience was not only the good humour of the performance, but the very fact of seeing Muslim women wearing the hijab enjoying themselves. It is one of the objectives of the Ulfah Collective to challenge the stereotype of the Muslim woman.

Aisha Downing was in the audience: 'It was a brilliant evening and a positive view of Muslim women. Some people might think Muslim women are oppressed and it was good that people can see we can enjoy ourselves and have fun.'

Amina was there, too: 'I found it very refreshing to see Muslim women performing and letting themselves go. You wouldn't normally see that as there isn't really a stage for it.'

Naz Koser, who founded the Ulfah Collective in 2004, said: 'I really hope people have gone away with a different idea about Muslim women — we're not all oppressed!'

Adapted from Sarah Loat, 'Ulfah Collective — singing sisters': www.bbc.co.uk/birmingham/content/articles/2006/11/07/ulfah_collective_feature.shtml (accessed 15 April 2007)

Source C · Shall we ever overcome intolerance of minorities?

It's not fair to the Poles or to us

Two more countries have joined the EU, Romania and Bulgaria. Are we going to repeat the mistakes with them that we made with the Poles?

Don't misunderstand me: I have nothing against Poles. They were excellent allies in the Second World War. But what we have allowed to happen is neither fair to them nor to us.

I got on a bus at Stepping Hill Hospital and asked the driver if the bus went to Heaton Moor Road. I got no answer.

I repeated my question, more loudly, but still there was no answer. Then another passenger said: 'Yes, it is the right bus. He can't understand you. He's Polish.'

The road where I live isn't on a bus route, but a bus turned into it recently. As the driver backed it out, he knocked into a parked car. He got down from the bus, and people shouted at him. The poor fellow just stood there. He couldn't understand a word they said. He was Polish. It took the police nearly 2 hours to get to the bottom of the problem.

I don't blame the Poles. I blame the government, and the people who employ them as cheap labour.

We must regain control of our borders — and to do this we must leave the EU. Then we can choose who will come in and who won't.

In December, 26 employees in Manchester and Stockport lost their jobs, and were replaced by Poles. Why?

We must do something, or unemployment figures will race up — and there's only one party that's pledged to do it.

Adapted from a letter by a member of UKIP to the *Manchester Evening News*, 18 January 2007

Source D — What does it mean to be tolerant of others' beliefs?

Kevin Allen is a member of the British National Party (BNP). He has twice stood as a parliamentary candidate for what is regarded as a racist, even fascist party. Allen is particularly active in Halifax, in the borough of Calderdale.

Ian Eastwood is a member of the anti-racist group Calderdale Unity, which is part of the United Against Fascism coalition. Eastwood recently campaigned against the BNP in a local authority by-election, in the Illingworth and Mixenden ward. The BNP has two councillors already in this ward, one of whom was convicted of fraud in October 2006.

Given that Allen and Eastwood are active campaigners for causes in such diametric opposition to each other, in one quite confined corner of West Yorkshire, it was perhaps inevitable that they should come face to face. It is just as well that this happened in a courtroom.

Eastwood had been set upon while he was distributing anti-racist leaflets in Morley, near Bradford. He did not doubt that, though they were masked, his assailants were BNP activists. Then he received a poster with his photograph on it, taken from Redwatch, an extreme right-wing website listing the details of prominent anti-racists. The poster bore the words 'White Pride', and 'Halifax C18 to visit'. 'C18' is 'Combat 18': the 1 represents the first letter of the alphabet, A for Adolf, and the 8 is H for Hitler.

Two further posters were sent: one to Ali Ahmadi, a Labour councillor on Calderdale Council, and the other, with a skull and crossbones on it, along with the words 'Muslims will die', to Majid Ahl-E-Hadith mosque in Halifax.

Allen was arrested as he distributed BNP leaflets in Keighley. When police searched his house they found racist literature and other evidence that it was he who had sent the posters. In court, he was found guilty of sending letters with indecent, offensive and threatening messages. Sentence is to be handed down at a later date.

[Note: personal names have been changed.]

Adapted from Kevin Gopal, 'Halifax BNP activist convicted for poster hate campaign', *The Big Issue in the North*, 15–21 January 2007

Skills

Here are some important definitions:

prejudice, n. a judgement or opinion formed prematurely or without due consideration of relevant issues

tolerance, n. the disposition, ability or willingness to be fair towards and accepting of different religious, political etc. beliefs and opinions

tolerate, v. to endure especially with patience or forbearance, to put up with; to accept (a person with different religious, political etc. beliefs and opinions)

Chambers Dictionary

It cannot be good to be prejudiced; 'prejudice' is a word that can seldom have a *positive* meaning.

'Tolerance' generally has a positive meaning (particularly when it is the opposite of intolerance); it is good to be fair.

To 'tolerate' has something of a *negative* inflection: to 'put up with' is not the same thing as 'being fair to'.

(i) Put the words 'tolerant' and 'tolerate' into sentences of your own, in such a way as to express the positive sense of the former and the negative sense of the latter.

The real issue in this subsection is *difference*: we are all different from each other; the question is how do we deal with these differences? Do we:

Celebrate them	Adjust to them	Put up with them	Resist them

Here is another definition:

stereotype, n.   a fixed, conventionalised or stock image, or a person or thing that conforms to it

Chambers Dictionary

Jim Coleman (Source A) found that UK students of modern languages had stereotypical views about people whose language they were learning. Furthermore, they came back after a year in the country concerned with their stereotypes intact and — in many cases — reinforced.

(ii) Where do you think these students' stereotypes came from, and why did they remain in place after a year in the country concerned?

University students might be expected to be quite liberal in their outlook. If their stereotypes are reinforced by *knowledge*, as Source A concludes, how much more difficult it is to dislodge stereotypes that are the product of *ignorance*?

What is changing, of course, is not that more people are going to Poland, for example; it is that more Poles are coming here, to the UK. Did Britons have a stereotyped view of the Poles before Poles came to Britain in large numbers? And do we have one now? (The letter writer in Source C had a positive memory of the Poles as 'excellent allies in the Second World War'.)

(iii) Make a note of any obvious differences you can think of between the Poles and Britons of whatever ethnicity.

There *are* obvious differences between Britons and Poles — and geography and history account for many of them. But the differences between white Anglo-Saxon

Protestant (or WASP) Britons and non-white (e.g. Asian, Muslim/Sikh/Hindu) Britons are, perhaps, more obvious still.

Q19 is one for which Source B might supply relevant evidence.

> **Q19** The British are said to value 'fair play'. Why, then, do we find it difficult to get on with people from a different background?
>
> You might consider:
> - what we mean by 'fair play'
> - what it is that we might find 'difficult'
> - how we might overcome these difficulties

Of course, this is a sensitive subject: there is a danger that we might overstate differences, and in doing so we might appear to criticise people who are different from us, and even give offence.

We are most at our ease when we stick together with people who are similar to ourselves. Even the Ulfah Collective described in Source B could only perform for a woman-only audience — and it is a safe bet that most women in the audience were Muslim women. But one has to start somewhere.

Here is a sketch of a response to Q19:

[S] *If Britons value 'fair play', it may be that we are thinking of games and the rules of games. Britons did devise the rules of most games, after all.*

[Ex A] *Are we better at getting on with people different from ourselves? The fact that we live on an island would suggest that we are unlikely to be.*

[Ex B] *Nevertheless, there is no reason why we should go on finding it difficult. Britons have become familiar with many peoples thanks to the former British Empire and the Commonwealth; and there is quite a long history of people from the Commonwealth coming to the UK.*

There have never been as many migrants as now — both entering and leaving the UK. Difficulties (arising from differences of dress, language, religious observance and legal systems) will occur in the short term. There is no reason to think that we shall not overcome them.

[C] *There is resistance at first, but adjustment to differences comes with growing familiarity. Ironically, we learn to celebrate differences just as they diminish.*

Q20 focuses on what it might mean to be tolerant, or intolerant, of others' beliefs.

> **Q20** The atheist Richard Dawkins is intolerant of religious belief because of what he claims is 'the grievous harm it has inflicted on society'.
>
> How far, in your view, should we be tolerant of beliefs that we deem to be harmful?
>
> You might consider:
> - beliefs that may be 'extremist'
> - why we should tolerate or not tolerate them
> - what intolerance of such beliefs might involve

An 'extremist' is one who stands at either end of a continuum of belief, whether that belief is religious, political, social, environmental or animal-welfare related. Those who stand somewhere on the midpoint of the continuum we call 'moderates'.

Extremists	Moderates	Extremists

(iv) Write down the beliefs and behaviours that would lead us to characterise someone as an 'extremist'. What does an extremist think or do?

We would probably think of Kevin Allen (Source D) as an extremist because, as a member of the BNP, he holds racist, perhaps fascist, views. He is not only intolerant of (in this case) Muslims; he is prepared to act on his intolerance by distributing offensive leaflets and issuing threats of violence.

Would we call Ian Eastwood (also in Source D) an extremist? If racism is extremist, can the same be said of anti-racism? Would we call the UKIP letter-writer (Source C) an extremist? Would we call him a racist? We probably would not call either of these men an extremist. Eastwood, despite being an activist who distributes anti-racist leaflets, has no thought of revolution. The UKIP letter-writer appears to be prepared to leave it to the ballot box to bring about change.

An important question, in the context of Q20, is whether it is enough to counteract extremism only at election time. Consider the following beliefs:
- UK law should be replaced by Sharia law.
- Parents should be given the names of paedophiles living in their locality.
- Speed limits should be abolished on motorways.
- All shops and places of entertainment should be closed on Sundays.
- Creationism should be taught in schools alongside Darwinism.

Should we tolerate these if the person who holds the belief seems to be prepared to act upon it? And how would/should we act upon our intolerance?

AS

UNIT 2

SPACE

Space is not just 'outer space' — though this is where Unit 2 begins. It is:

- **inner space**, the atmosphere and climate change
- people moving and mixing in **intercontinental space**
- **living space**, housing, commuting, land
- communication of ideas in **cultural space**
- consumerism in the **fragile space** that is the environment

Space is about area, territory, location and mobility. As in Unit 1, you will need a certain amount of raw knowledge and understanding (AO1) of the topics listed in Unit 2. In particular, you should be able to give examples of global issues as they affect your area such as: flooding or water-shortage, the availability of green space, the quality of buildings, traffic congestion and public transport, and integration of ethnic minorities.

In other words, if you live in or around Wolverhampton and you are writing about public art, give examples of statues and installations in the Wolverhampton area. If you live in southwest London, and you are writing about transport, refer to the congestion on the Kingston Road, and the light railway from Wimbledon to Croydon. You can never be over-specific.

The examination paper based on Unit 2 contains *source material*. There are three questions on the paper, and you have to answer all of them.

The sources for Question 1 are tables of numerical data, followed by three sub-questions. You are not required to draw graphs or charts; you may be required to carry out simple calculations based on the data. The sub-questions call for interpretation of the data — for a careful reading of the information presented.

Question 2 asks you to study two visual sources. Again, there are three sub-questions relating to these two images.

Question 3 is based on a single extended passage, and it calls for an essay response in two halves. These two half questions correspond, more or less, to the 'A' and 'B' positions of the 'S/A/B/C' essay-writing strategy — to 'for' and 'against' positions, to put it simply.

Because source material is supplied on the examination paper, there is less need to supply sources here, corresponding to every question in every subsection of the specification for this unit, which we did for

Unit 1. Instead, tables of data and/or images, and one or more texts are supplied under each of the ten topics, which address as many of the questions as possible.

To summarise:

- You need to be familiar with **space**-related issues in this unit.
- You should be comfortable with the sorts of data-sets, pie charts and graphs that you see in textbooks and in good journalism; in particular, you should be able to work out simple percentages.
- You need to be able to interpret what you see in images (drawings and photographs), and to make comparisons of one image with another.
- You need to be able to present a case on both sides of an argument, and to draw on local examples to illustrate your points.

AS UNIT 2

SPACE
Science and technology

Space exploration

Content

Source A **Unmanned space probes**

Probe	Soviet Union			USA			Other			Total
	S	F	O	S	F	O	S	F	O	
Sun				6		1	7			14
Mercury				3		4				7
Venus	24	5		9	1	1			1	41
Earth					5		3		1	9
Moon	24	4		26	10		1	1	2	68
Mars	4	14		14	7	1	1	2	1	44
Jupiter				8			2			10
Saturn				4						4
Uranus/Neptune				2						2
Total	52	23		72	23	7	14	3	5	199

Notes

1 S = success; F = failure; O = ongoing.

2 'Other' includes the European Space Agency (ESA); Japan; ISRO (India); CNSA (China) and Russia.

3 There have also been 31 'flyby' probes to distant planetary moons, notably by *Voyager 1* and *2*, launched in 1979, and *Cassini*, launched in 2000.

Adapted from http://en.wikipedia.org/wiki/List_of_planetary_probes

Source B

An engraving from *De la Terre à la Lune* by Jules Verne, 1865

Source C

NASA website

The International Space Station

Source D

Welcome to the Space Tourism Society

Imagine floating in zero gravity while gazing at our beautiful planet Earth majestically rolling by your view port.

Millions of people from around the world would love to have such a wonderful life-enhancing experience.

Founded in 1996, the Space Tourism Society is the first organisation specifically focused on the space tourism industry. Our goals are:

to conduct the research,

build public desire,

and acquire the financial and political power,

to make space tourism available,

to as many people as possible,

as soon as possible.

Source: www.spacetourismsociety.org

Source E **Why explore space?**

The space shuttle was designed to ferry astronauts backwards and forwards between Earth and the International Space Station (ISS). The National Aeronautics and Space Administration (NASA) is approaching the end of the construction phase of the ISS. It has been a feat of engineering to outdo any other that has ever been undertaken.

Was it worth all the risk and expense? This was a question that the Columbia Accident Investigation Board had to ask itself following the catastrophic loss of the shuttle and its crew in 2003. The board acknowledged that it would continue to be 'expensive, difficult, and dangerous' to explore space. Nevertheless, it answered the question in the affirmative. Space research and exploration is a strategic necessity for the USA. If we don't engage, other nations will. It is vital that the USA be a 'spacefaring nation' if it is to be true to itself, to its vision of the future, and to generations of Americans to come.

Given that the costs will be significant, the objectives must be significant, too, and this means that they must reach beyond the ISS. The shuttle has been a means to an end: the ISS is not that end; it, too, is a means to the longer-term end of pushing farther out into the solar system. The US Congress gave overwhelming, cross-party approval to this Vision for Space Exploration — so it is a legal commitment.

The medium-term aim is to use the ISS as a platform on which to learn how to live for long periods in space, and how to work and carry out research there. This is where we shall develop the hardware necessary for the projected round-trips from Earth to Mars. We must learn how to live on other planetary surfaces than those on Earth, just as the Pilgrim Fathers learned to live in a new and forbidding land in 1620. Those who survived that first long winter, and sowed and harvested, prepared the way for all those who followed them. What they did, we must do.

We have been to the Moon — only 3 days away from Earth — but that was just the beginning. The ISS and the Moon are Base Camp and Camp Two on a much longer journey.

Throughout history, the great nations have been the ones at the forefront, at the frontiers of their time. Britain became great in the seventeenth century through its exploration and mastery of the seas. America's greatness in the twentieth century stemmed largely from its mastery of the air. For the next generation, the frontier will be space.

Michael Griffin, NASA Administrator

Adapted from: www.nasa.gov/mission_pages/exploration/main/griffin_why_explore.html

Skills

You are not required to re-present tabular data in a pie chart, line graph or bar graph, nor are you required to manipulate data in General Studies B assessment units. In order to interpret data fully, however, it may be necessary to assess:

- relative sizes or quantities
- such a relationship expressed in percentage terms, or fractions

- whether data need to be added, subtracted or multiplied
- trends over time

It may be sufficient to inspect the data in order to come to conclusions about it — this is all that is expected of the average newspaper-reader presented with a table as part of an article. It may be necessary, though — with or without a calculator — to work out relationships between the numbers a little more precisely. We cannot always be sure that a journalist or advertiser will do this for us, or that they will give us the whole picture.

Write down your answers to the following questions in relation to Source A:

(i) **Have the unmanned space probes, on balance, been a success or a failure?**

(ii) **On which celestial objects have the probes most concentrated, and why?**

(iii) **Why might these particular countries have been the ones involved in sending space probes?**

What we cannot deduce from Source A is an answer to the first question under this heading on the specification: **What are we learning about the universe from unmanned space probes?**

You are not expected to have exact physical-science knowledge at your disposal. It is more important to understand what scientists (and their paymasters, the politicians) hoped that we *might learn* from these probes.

(iv) **What purposes do you think unmanned space probes were designed to serve? What were the people who sent them trying to find out?**

Images, such as those in Sources B and C, will be supplied in Unit 2 questions as a prompt — an instant and concise narrative. Some interpretation of details might be called for, but it is more likely that you will be expected to form general impressions, and to use the images as points of departure, rather than as complete sources of information.

The questions that might be asked of these particular images are:
- Why have human beings (at least since Copernicus, in the sixteenth century) always dreamed of exploring space?
- Why has the space programme been so important to the USA in particular?
- Has what we have achieved in space, and what we have learnt from it in the course of manned space travel, justified all the expense?

These — and the last question, especially — will always be matters of opinion. We are all interested in space research and space travel to different degrees. The specification question: **Are we alone in the universe?** is not one that non-astronomers ask themselves on a daily basis. Nevertheless, it is worth thinking about the following question:

(v) **What might be some of the consequences of our discovering that there is intelligent life in our galaxy?**

The specification question: **Is space tourism threatening or promising?** is, likewise, one that we will answer in different ways, depending on our own interest in space. If there really are 'millions of people from around the world' who would 'love to have such a wonderful life-enhancing experience', as described in Source D, then it follows that there are plenty of people who would find space tourism promising.

(vi) **Why might most of us be inclined to take a negative view of space tourism? Write down your ideas.**

Most of us now enjoy the opportunities of tourism on this planet, although not so long ago these opportunities were restricted to a small minority of people on the grounds of:

- risks to physical well-being (of travel by ship or plane; disease; hostile 'natives')
- expense

It is worth considering whether space tourism would grow if risk and expense were both reduced to a level comparable with the risk and expense of terrestrial tourism.

The overarching question on the specification: **What value do manned space flights have?** is one that we might be inclined to ask after reading Source E. It is a question that NASA spokesman Michael Griffin seeks to answer — and it might be worth adopting some of his ideas, and incorporating them into the response to Q21. Those of us who do not work for NASA, and who are not Americans, might have reservations about the value of manned space missions, however — and these reservations would include issues of risk and expense, as described earlier.

The third question in Assessment Unit 2 is, in effect, one essay question in two halves. They correspond to the 'A' and 'B' positions in our 'S/A/B/C' structure plan. Both halves should be of equal length, though, since each is worth 15 marks. The two-part question will be based on just such a passage as Source E.

Q21a Why might we agree with Michael Griffin that, for the next generation, the 'frontier will be space'?

b Why might we *not* agree with him in this respect?

This is a good exercise in seeing both sides of a question, and in arguing on both sides, even though you will (probably) agree with one more than the other — or with one to the exclusion of the other. There is a lot to be said for not seeming to be too certain in any debate. The best answer is not always a perfectly balanced one, but there is usually something to be said for another point of view that is different from your own.

Although you are only writing half an argument, you will still need an opening statement and a conclusion. Here are some suggestions for the first half:

[S] *It is almost inevitable that the next frontier will be space.*

[Ex A] *There has always been a frontier. Humankind has always needed a fresh challenge. Space is the biggest remaining unknown.*
We are close to exhausting the resources of this planet. As Stephen Hawking has said, we may need a bolthole on another planet.

[C] *Space exploration may not be a strategic necessity, but we must understand our galaxy if we are to understand our planet.*

Here are some suggestions for the second half:

[S] *Does it make sense to speak of space as a 'frontier' when we are exploring it already?*

[Ex B] *It is sensible to be sending space probes, and to be making use of the ISS, but should we do any more?*
The next generation will have plenty to think about here on Earth: generating non-fossil-fuelled energy, conserving fresh water, feeding the billions.
Rocketry would only use up more resources and cause pollution.
Manned space missions would be a risky, expensive diversion.
Why should Mars or other planets have more to offer than Earth?

[C] *What we are learning about space, we are learning without having to waste time, money and resources on space travel.*

Climate change

Content

| Source A | Increase in carbon dioxide levels |

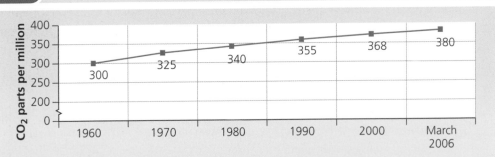

Notes:

1 The figure for 2000 is the highest carbon dioxide level for 420,000 years.

2 The EU has committed itself to a maximum of 450 ppm (*Guardian*, 15 April 2006).

3 'When 400 ppm is reached, the risk to ecosystems will grow significantly' (UN Environment Group, 2005).

Source: www.carbon-info.org

| Source B | Electricity generating costs |

	Basic cost	+ cost of stand-by generation when wind does not blow
Gas-fired combined cycle	2.2p/unit	n/a
Nuclear	2.3p/unit	n/a
Coal	2.5p/unit	n/a
Onshore wind	3.7p/unit	5.4p/unit
Offshore wind	5.5p/unit	7.2p/unit

Note: Oil-fired generating costs are not included, since these fluctuate with crude-oil prices.

Source: Royal Academy of Engineering

Source C

Source C — Pollutors and populations

Polluters	Thousand tons of CO_2	Population (1 July 2005 estimates)
USA	5,762,054	296,410,404
China	3,433,597	1,301,510,800
Russia	1,540,365	145,166,731
Japan	1,224,737	127,756,815
India	1,007,978	1,112,186,000
UK	558,225	58,789,194
Australia	332,377	20,325,926
Brazil	327,857	186,770,562
Netherlands	174,809	16,335,509
Kazakhstan	123,685	14,953,100
Iraq	78,506	25,897,848
Nigeria	48,145	140,003,542
Cuba	31,353	11,177,743
Bangladesh	29,874	123,151,246
Peru	28,193	27,148,101
Jordan	15,535	5,100,981

Sources: www.carbon-info.org; www.geohive.com/default1.aspx

Source D — Positive feedback, negative consequences

2 February 2007 may be remembered as the day the question mark was removed from whether people are to blame for climate change.

Achim Steiner, executive director,
UN Environment Programme

Hundreds of scientists contributed to the report of the Intergovernmental Panel on Climate Change (IPCC), published on 2 February 2007 — and every government in the world endorsed it.

In 2001 the same body published a report that forecast a temperature increase of 5.8°C by the end of this century, if we do nothing to cut greenhouse emissions. A more likely rise would be 4°C. Even if we did everything in our power to cut emissions, there would still be a temperature increase of 2.4°C — and anything over 2°C is regarded by the EU as 'dangerous'.

Now the IPCC has revised its most pessimistic figure to 6.4°C. Why is this? It is because scientists have learnt more about the effects of *positive feedback*. We know about three such mechanisms:

■ Polar ice sheets reflect 80% of the sunlight that falls on them. As the temperature rises and the ice melts, the soil or the sea underneath absorbs more sunlight, causing the temperature to rise still further.

■ Soils, oceans and trees absorb about half the amount of carbon dioxide emitted by human activity. As the oceans warm, they will be less and less able to absorb carbon dioxide. The phytoplankton that have absorbed it will themselves die, and this will warm the oceans still further.

■ Soils and plants will, likewise, lose their ability to absorb more carbon dioxide. As they come under stress, so microbes in the soil will break down the organic matter and release carbon dioxide into the atmosphere. Instead of being carbon sinks, plants will become carbon emitters, warming the atmosphere still further.

There may be other positive feedback mechanisms, as yet unknown, each acting to accelerate the others. They do not leave us much room for optimism.

At the same time, the IPCC would not have us think that a temperature rise at the upper end of the scale is inevitable. Susan Solomon, co-chair of the IPCC working group that prepared the report, said: 'The amount of warming will depend on choices that human beings make.'

There was much talk at UNESCO, in Paris, where the report was presented, of the need to switch to 'clean and resource-efficient technologies', and of 'global solutions to economic, social and environmental sustainability'. If these technologies and solutions were put in place, we might yet restrict the temperature increase to 2.4°C and hold off the worst of the ice-sheet melting, flooding, hurricanes, droughts, extinctions of species, and food and water shortages.

David Miliband, secretary of state for the environment in the UK, did not sound very hopeful. The debate about whether human beings are responsible for climate change is over, he said. 'What's now urgently needed is the international political commitment to take action. This has been absent so far.'

Adapted from David Adam and Ian Sample, 'Worse than we thought', *Guardian*, 3 February 2007

Skills

It is likely that all the technical information you need to answer questions about climate change will be supplied in the source(s) on the examination paper. There is no need for you to remember details about carbon emissions or the cost of electricity generation.

On the other hand, there is some basic knowledge that candidates might be expected to have — specifically in answer to the first two questions under this heading on the specification: **What is causing climate change?** and **What are the likely consequences of a global rise in temperature?**

Both questions are worth answering, to see if a cumulative answer can be reached. Write down your answers to the following:

(i) What are the underlying causes (both natural and human) of climate change?

(ii) What are some of the most likely consequences of a global rise in temperature?

Source A charts the rise in carbon dioxide levels, measured in parts per million. Questions to which this source might give rise are:

- Is it possible to judge from these figures how long it might be before we reach the EU's maximum of 450 ppm or the UN Environment Group's 400 ppm threshold?
- Is the trend consistent over the decades, or is the rate of increase unpredictable?
- What might we learn from calculating likely carbon dioxide levels for 2010, 2020, and beyond?

The number of years we have left before carbon dioxide levels become dangerous will depend, of course, on what we do as *individuals* and as *nations* to reduce carbon emissions from now on. These are the third and fourth questions under this heading on the specification: What can individuals do to minimise their environmental impact? and What global action should be taken to mitigate or reverse climate change?

Any number of good resolutions might be forthcoming in answer to the question about what individuals can do. Trite though some of them may be, they are worth collecting. Perhaps it is even worth putting individuals on the spot by asking them:

- Do you leave the television on standby?
- Do you leave the computer on all day?
- To what temperature is your house heated?
- Do you drive somewhere when you could walk?
- Do you boil more water than you need for one coffee?

Like Source A, we can really only infer anything worthwhile from Source B by simple inspection.

(iii) What observations might we make from a study of Source B?

The further question might then be asked:

(iv) What are the *future* costs likely to be of each method of generating electricity?

Of course, it may be that national or international policies designed to mitigate climate change will skew the prices we pay for energy. On the 'polluter pays' principle, carbon-emitting power stations may be penalised, and nuclear power stations may be given tax privileges for the back-up that they give when the wind does not blow.

Source C is a combination of two sets of data. From looking at the figures in the left-hand column, we learn that:

- The USA emits far more carbon dioxide than any other nation.
- In fact, the USA emits more carbon dioxide than China, India and Japan put together.
- Japan and Russia are among the top five polluting nations (though both have much smaller populations than those of the other three).

It is when we look at the two columns of figures in combination, though, that we can see who the main polluters are.

(v) What can we deduce from Source C when we calculate the emission of carbon dioxide per head of the population? Which are the most revealing comparisons between nations?

We learn from this calculation that Americans are the big polluters, both in absolute and in relative terms. We can also see that Britons are big polluters, but that we compare favourably with some other developed countries; and we learn that there are significant differences among less economically developed countries — for example, that each Jordanian is responsible for emitting 3.05 tons of carbon compared with the 1.04 tons of each Peruvian and 0.34 tons of each Nigerian.

Depending on your own opinion, it may be possible to reach the following conclusions:

- The world must challenge the USA to reduce its carbon emissions — how could it do this?
- The real threat in the future is the rapid industrial development in China and India — how could we persuade them to limit this development?
- The EU should set an example in reducing carbon emissions — how would we do it, and would others follow?
- The developed countries should pay for cleaner-energy solutions in the less developed countries.

Armed with these thoughts, let us look at Q22, based on Source D.

Q22a Why might we be optimistic that human beings will make the choices necessary to prevent runaway climate change?

b Why might we *not* be optimistic that they will make these choices?

This is perhaps the big question of our time. Whether we are optimistic or not about the future may depend upon whether we are temperamentally optimistic or not as individuals — whether we tend to think that the glass is half full or half empty. But there are some points that might be made that are more or less objectively true. These are included in the drafts of the responses to the two halves of Q22 below:

a [S] *We can be optimistic that we shall prevent runaway climate change.*

[Ex A] *We have already identified what steps can be taken, for example using renewable rather than fossil sources of energy.*

We made difficult choices in order to survive in the Second World War.

There is growing international resolve.

We know that the consequences of our not acting will affect our own children and grandchildren.

[C] *The consequences of runaway climate change are too serious for us not to act to prevent them.*

However, how hopeful can we be that we shall take the necessary steps on present evidence? You might find it easier (if less palatable) to argue for the 'B' position:

b [S] *If only we could be optimistic.*

[Ex B] *But the discoveries concerning positive feedback mechanisms do not leave much room for hope.*

The USA is dragging its heels; and the Chinese have made it clear that economic growth is more important to them than controlling carbon emissions.

There are few signs that people are driving less (or driving smaller cars), or flying less. Renewable energy sources will not be developed fast enough to replace fossil fuels.

[C] *We cannot be optimistic, but we have to make the necessary choices in any case if we are to spare the next generation real hardship.*

Migration of people

Content

| Source A | **UK migrant flows, 2005** |

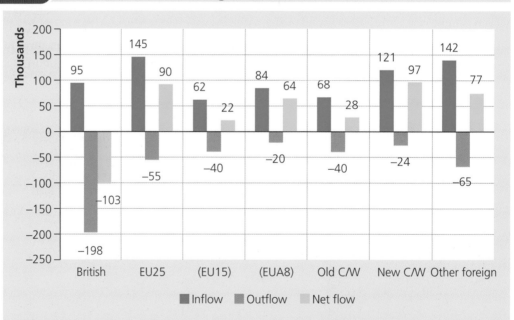

Notes:

1 C/W = Commonwealth; EU25 = the 25 members of the EU since May 2004; EU15 = the 15 members of the EU before May 2004; EUA8 = the 8 accession members of central and eastern Europe (the other 2 new members of the EU were Malta and Greek Cyprus).

2 Figures given are estimates only.

Source: **www.statistics.gov.uk/pdfdir/intmigrat1106.pdf**

Source B

UK estimates of the net number of migrants (thousands) by 5-year intervals, 1950–2000

1950–55	1955–60	1960–65	1965–70	1970–75	1975–80	1980–85	1985–90	1990–95	1995–2000
−500	−70	220	−250	−185	−50	−250	30	170	490

Source: www.migrationinformation.org/GlobalData/countrydata/data.cfm

Source C

The New Commission on Integration and Cohesion

Immigration has helped transform our economy, supporting growth and boosting productivity. London's strength as a financial centre was driven by the acknowledgement across the developed world that Britain was open to new people, to new ideas and to new products.

Immigration has helped enrich our cultural life, with the capital's diversity now commonly acknowledged to be one of its key attractions. Weekends spent at the Notting Hill Carnival or exploring Brick Lane are attracting tourists and residents alike.

And migrant workers have been vital to supporting our public services, providing critical staff to our hospitals and schools, as well as other essential services. As the prime minister has said: 'Far from always or even mainly being a drain on our health and education systems, they are often the very people delivering them'.

And I believe that we should celebrate and clearly articulate the benefits that migration and diversity have brought.

Patterns of immigration to Britain are becoming more complex. Our new residents are not the *Windrush* generation. They are more diverse, coming from countries ranging from Afghanistan to Zimbabwe, from South Africa to Somalia.

Some new migrants will put down roots. Some will move on, and find other work or return to their families.

Extracted from a speech by Ruth Kelly MP at the launch of the new Commission on Integration and Cohesion, 24 August 2004

Source D

Welcome migrants and economic growth

In 2006 the UK population topped 60 million. There was a baby boom in the mid- to late 1940s, and there was another one in the 1960s. This means that there are relatively large numbers of 60-year-olds in the country, and even larger numbers of 40-year-olds. The former are coming to the end of full-time work, while the latter are still economically active. In fact, the median age of the UK population at the moment is 39 (it is 42 in Italy and Germany, and 43 in Japan). In another 20 years, this 40-year-old generation of employees will themselves be approaching retirement, and the question arises: who will pay their pensions?

This is where the immigrants come in. Figures are very inexact, but it was estimated in 2006 that 600,000 migrants entered the UK from central and eastern European countries following

EU enlargement in May 2004. That was 600,000 entrants over 2 years, so 300,000 per year — quite a large slice of the 375,000 annual rise in the UK population. The point is, though, that 80% of these entrants were relatively skilled workers aged between 18 and 35.

To be sure, some of these young Poles, Hungarians, Czechs and Lithuanians will have competed with UK citizens for jobs; but it is estimated that, such has been their contribution to the UK economy, 250,000 new jobs have been created each year. Now, it may be asked which is the chicken and which is the egg: did the migrants bring about economic growth, or were the migrants attracted to the UK because there was economic growth here already? The only sensible answer is, perhaps, a bit of both (along with the facts that the UK kept its borders open to all EU citizens, and that English is the foreign language that these new citizens are most likely to have learnt in school).

Whatever the answer to the chicken-and-egg question, it is undeniable that migration, employment and economic growth have been mutually reinforcing in a virtuous circle. This is a far cry from the mid-1970s, when there was a brain-drain of the middle class, more deaths than births (1976), and the economy was in recession.

The trend may not last: the economy cannot go on producing jobs at its present rate indefinitely; the birth rate may rise or fall again; and the Poles, Hungarians, Czechs and Lithuanians may decide to take their UK earnings back home. For now, though, it is far better that we should have to find ways of managing growth than coping with decline.

Adapted from Hamish McRae, 'Welcome migrants, welcome growth: with fertile thinking, our "tiny" island can cope', *Independent on Sunday*, 27 August 2006

Skills

There have never been as many people migrating from one country to another as there are now. Some leave their home country temporarily; some ferry backwards and forwards; and some migrate never to return to their home country — or do so only for short periods to visit friends or family. Why is this? As the specification heading asks: **Why are so many people on the move?** And why now?

There are *push* and *pull* factors at work, which usually operate together — that is, the negative factor that causes them to leave Country A is the reverse of the positive factor that attracts them to Country B:

Country A push factors		**Country B pull factors**
unemployment	⟶	employment
lack of opportunity	⟶	many opportunities
oppressive government	⟶	open society
urban pressures	⟶	peace and quiet
unfriendly climate	⟶	warm, outdoor life
sickness and poverty	⟶	medicine and welfare

Young people will have reasons for migrating that are different from the reasons that older people might give. The young often seek jobs, opportunities, facilities and experience; older people generally seek sunshine, and the peace and comforts of retirement. In the past, old and young generally settled for what they could find in their own countries. So what has changed?

Write an answer to the following question:

(i) Why are so many people now leaving their own countries to seek a better life abroad?

Source A gives us an idea of the amount of in-migration and out-migration to and from the UK in 2005 — the first full year following the accession of eight central and eastern European states to the EU. Source B shows the net number of migrants over a 50-year period. Both sources, it should be emphasised, give us rounded-figure estimates only.

(ii) What is the most important conclusion that you come to on inspecting Source A?

(iii) Which sets of figures in Source A might most usefully be compared?

In making such comparisons, we can begin to distinguish between migrants proper, and visitors. On the other hand, is a Briton who buys a second home in Spain, and spends the winter there, a migrant to Spain or a repeat visitor?

Spain is, in fact, the second most favoured destination of British emigrants, according to the Office for National Statistics (**www.statistics.gov.uk**); the number-one destination is Australia. This goes far to answer the second question under this heading in the specification: **What are the motives of emigrants from the UK?**

(iv) What conclusions might we draw from an inspection of Source B? And can we fill in one further box, for 2000–05, from the data in Source A?

Ruth Kelly, in Source C, gives us the beginnings of an answer to the third question under this heading in the specification: **What are the benefits and drawbacks of migration?** She refers to some of the benefits for the host country. The benefits for the migrants themselves are obvious, and some of them are listed under Country B 'pull' factors on page 96.

We shall look at some of the drawbacks of migration for the host country (in this case, the UK) under the topic 'Multiculturalism' (pages 131–36). Less obvious, and less often discussed, are the drawbacks for the immigrants themselves — particularly the difficulties of settling into the UK, especially for the first generation of immigrants. The problems faced by the second and subsequent generations of immigrants may be just as numerous and substantial as those faced by the first-generation — but they will be different.

It is worth discussing what some of the problems of first-generation immigrants might be.

(v) What problems do you suppose first-generation immigrants to the UK might face? Write down your ideas.

Ruth Kelly in Source C speaks up for an inflow of young talent (and young, relatively inexpensive employees and taxpayers), as does the business editor of the *Independent on Sunday*, Hamish McRae, in Source D. However, neither of the sources would answer the fourth question under this heading in the specification: **What controls might there need to be on migrant flows?** by saying: 'there don't need to be any'. Clearly, we cannot permit anyone and everyone to settle in the UK who might find it attractive to do so. There are migrants whom we should be happy to admit, and there are would-be migrants whom we should be prepared to exclude. The criteria must be fair and be seen to be fair. Here are some suggestions:

Admit	Exclude
Those who wish to study in the UK for the duration of the course.	Those with a criminal record (unless acquired unfairly under an oppressive regime).
Those who have skills needed by the UK economy.	The unskilled and unemployable in their own countries.
Those with family in the UK, or with other close ties.	Those trafficked by criminals (and the traffickers themselves).
Those persecuted by regimes (especially those that the UK has had some part in installing or sustaining).	Those who seek to enter the UK by illegal means, unless fleeing persecution.

EU citizens, it should be noted, have the right to come to the UK whatever their skills or background. Some of them will find jobs and settle down here; others — perhaps most of them — will come for a while, try their luck, make some money (or not) and return home. Britons have these same rights in any of the 27 countries in the EU.

Now we are ready for Q23.

> **Q23a** Why should we be glad that there has been a net inflow of migrants to the UK in recent years?
>
> **b** Why might we be worried about this net inflow of migrants?

This is probably just the sort of question where a balanced answer is more appropriate than a one-sided one. McRae's argument should persuade us that there is a lot to be positive about, but common sense suggests that we may not be able to hold the door open to new migrants indefinitely.

If we were writing a single essay-answer on this subject, whether or not we were more worried than optimistic, we would have to come to a conclusion that accommodated both positions. As it is, we can keep the two positions separate.

a [S] *Migrants have brought many benefits to the UK.*

[Ex A] *They bring their youth, their enthusiasm, and their skills.*

They do the jobs that UK citizens often don't want to do.

They create many new jobs.

They pay taxes, which contribute to the pensions of older UK citizens.

They take an appreciation of the British way of life back home with them.

[C] *There is much to be glad about in the welcome that the UK has given to migrants.*

You will need to be more inventive (and less reliant on Source D) in your answer to the second half of the question.

b [S] *There is cause to worry about the net inflow of migrants.*

[Ex B] *To some extent, they compete with UK citizens for jobs.*

They put pressure on accommodation, health and education facilities.

Many are prepared to work for less than the national minimum wage, which is illegal.

Many do not learn English and fail to integrate with the host population.

[C] *There are legitimate concerns about in-migration: much may depend on how many migrants actually remain in the UK in the longer term.*

Urban and rural

Content

Source A

Semi-detached housing in Southampton

Source B

Block of flats in London

Source C

Persons killed in the UK per billion kilometres travelled, yearly average, 1995–2004

Mode of transport	Fatalities
Air (within the UK)	0.0
Bus or coach	0.3
Rail	0.4
Car	2.8
Bicycle	38.0
Walking	49.0
Motor-cycle	113.0

Source: Department for Transport

Source D · Transport 2050

The problem

Over the past 50 years, the number of vehicles on our roads has multiplied by seven. In the same period, the movement of people and freight in the UK has grown by a factor of eight.

The result is that we have the most congested roads in Europe and an annual death toll on the roads of 3,000. Transport in general accounts for about one-third of all accidental deaths but road travel alone has been estimated to be eight times as dangerous as all other aspects of our everyday lives.

Traffic congestion is reckoned to cost us £15 billion per year — and this is expected to double over the next decade. It may cost us more than this, of course, in the sense that transport is the source of many pollutants, including 38% of carbon dioxide emissions.

Traffic is likely to continue to grow by 50% by 2050, particularly on interurban and rural roads; this is the equivalent of adding to present traffic all the traffic that was on the roads in 1977.

At the same time, fares on public transport in the UK are the highest in Europe, and our provision for those without cars is among the worst.

The solution

A well-managed transport system is necessary for the economic well-being of the country: it can meet social needs, enhance the environment and contribute to long-term sustainability. Our schools and hospitals, the retail sector, industry and cultural activities all depend on our ability to move people and goods about the country efficiently.

Such a transport system would be *integrated* — that is, its parts would cooperate: timetabling, ticketing and access would all be coordinated, planned and regulated; it would make better use of up-to-date technology; and above all it would be charged at its 'true cost'.

'True-cost' charging involves those who use the system paying the true cost of their journeys. They would pay the indirect costs of providing, maintaining and improving the system; and the indirect costs of the congestion, the pollution and the accidents that the system causes. Charges would relate to the distance travelled, and would take into account whether the journeys involved used the most congested parts of the network and had the most damaging environmental impact.

The government has committed itself to reducing levels of carbon dioxide by 60% over the next 50 years. This is a laudable and necessary aim — but it will not be achieved unless we take a holistic approach to transport planning.

The Royal Academy of Engineering stands ready to play its part.

Adapted from www.raeng.org.uk/policy/reports/pdf/transport_5050.pdf (accessed 1 March 2007)

Skills

The first question under this heading in the specification is: **Is village life under threat?**

Village life could be said to be under threat from the factors mentioned in other questions under this heading: housing, the quality of urban life, and transport. It is under threat from these factors inasmuch as:

- New houses are often not built in sympathy with the older houses in the village.
- The new houses, their gardens and cars make the village look suburban rather than rural.
- Village-dwellers tend to work at a distance, and perhaps shop at a distance, too.
- Older houses may be bought as second homes by town-dwellers, who leave them empty for much of the year.
- Public transport links are poor, so residents use cars — consequently, road links might be enhanced and so further increase traffic.

Of course, a village can just as easily die from internal as from external pressures — indeed, new residents might give a small boost to the local economy. Villages typically die from within when:

- Village schools are uneconomic to run, so children have to go elsewhere to school.
- The village post office closes, and perhaps its associated general store.
- Jobs are lost as farmers struggle to make a living.
- The young migrate to the towns, and — as village houses rise in price on the second-home market — they cannot afford to return.

Perhaps it is too easy to be nostalgic for the village as it was — especially if one has never lived there. Most of us live in circumstances closer to those pictured in Sources A and B.

These are the sorts of question likely to be asked of Source A. Make your own lists in answer to them.

(i) **What are some of the *advantages* of living in houses of the sort pictured in Source A?**

(ii) **What are some of the *disadvantages* of living in such suburban houses?**

There are, as usual, no right answers to these questions: the answers you give will depend very much on your own experience of living in or near such houses. Peace and quiet, space and nearness to amenities (schools, transport links, shops, pubs) are likely to be important factors on anyone's list of advantages and disadvantages.

The same applies to housing of the sort pictured in Source B. These are the sorts of question likely to be asked of this source. Write down your answers.

(iii) What might be some of the *advantages* of living in a flat of the sort pictured in Source B?

(iv) Why might such a flat *not* be a desirable place to live?

Again, answers are likely to be subjective and to depend upon personal experience. Of course, there are some very run-down blocks of council-owned flats in and on the edges of city centres; and there are some very smart, privately owned apartments beside canals and overlooking public parks, whose prices would suggest that they are desirable places in which to live.

Now consider the following question on the specification: **Does our housing meet today's needs?** It does in the sense that most of us in the UK are housed more or less satisfactorily. We do not live on the street, or in shacks made of waste materials in shanty-towns. However, it does not meet today's needs in the sense that:

- It is expensive for young couples and those on low incomes.
- There is not enough of it of a size suitable for households of just one or two people.

Perhaps there never has been enough accommodation of the right size, at the right price and in the right place — and perhaps there never will be if the population continues to rise and people continue to move about.

The third question under the urban and rural heading on the specification asks: **How might life in towns and cities be improved?** This is a useful focus of discussion, and it might consider the following:

Feature	Improvement
Shops	More concentrated in one place? Bigger? Smaller?
Public buildings	More accessible? Better maintained?
Public spaces	More parks and gardens? More pedestrian-only streets? Seating?
Vegetation	More trees, shrubs, flowers, hanging baskets?
Transport	More cycle paths, trams, buses, parking places? Better integration of systems?

You would be well advised always to discuss *one particular town or city* — the one you know best. This will concentrate your mind on what it is possible to do. It is all too easy to generalise and to lose hold of what is *practicable*.

Transport is certainly a key issue, especially as towns and cities expand, and amenities become further away from each other. It is one thing to walk about the village of Cottingham; it is another to walk about Nottingham. Source C presents us with seven modes of transport, some of which we may use frequently and some we may never use, depending on their:

- cost
- availability
- convenience
- legal constraints
- safety

It then focuses on safety.

(v) What conclusions might we come to on a simple inspection of Source C?

Walking and cycling look like risky activities. What makes them risky is, of course, mixing them with cars, buses, taxis, vans and motor-bikes. Cycling is (relatively) safe on a dedicated cycle track; and walking is (relatively) safe in a pedestrian-only zone.

The final question is a big question — one of the big questions of our time — and it connects with other issues under this theme heading: *climate change, use of the land* and *green values*: **What solutions might there be to our transport problems?**

The Royal Academy of Engineering (RAE) has looked at the problem of traffic congestion in urban areas. It put forward solutions (see Source D) that the UK government has proposed and that many road-users have opposed (in a February 2007 petition, signed by 1.8 million people, for example, on the 10 Downing Street website). This is the subject of Q24, which is based on Source D.

Q24a What makes it likely that we shall engineer 'a well-managed transport system' in the UK?

b What makes it *un*likely that we shall succeed in doing this?

This question does not ask you to make a prediction (either optimistic or pessimistic) about the future. Instead, it calls for a judgement based on present evidence.

Here is a sketch of an answer to the first half of the question:

a [S] *A well-managed transport system is in prospect.*

[Ex A] *The government is committed to a reduction of CO_2 levels of 60% over 50 years, and Ken Livingstone is committed to this target for London.*

The congestion charge in London has already reduced traffic levels in the capital, and other cities are planning charges.

Rail services are being added to and passenger numbers are growing.

The government is pressing ahead with road-pricing trials; true-cost charging will cut unnecessary journeys and food miles.

[C] *There are good grounds for hope that we shall engineer an integrated transport system.*

Here is a sketch of an answer to the second half of the question:

b [S] *We are unlikely to be able to engineer 'a well-managed transport system' in the UK.*

[Ex B] *Rail and bus companies are in private hands, so it is difficult to coordinate them in a grand plan.*

The public transport infrastructure simply could not cope with many more passengers than at present.

Motorists are not going to be weaned from their cars without a fight; there is tremendous resistance to road pricing.

There are civil liberties implications of tracking the movements of all vehicles about the country.

[C] *The prospects for an integrated and well-managed transport system do not look good.*

Art and public space

Content

Statue by Marochetti of Richard the Lionheart outside the House of Lords, London

The Angel of the North by Antony Gormley, Gateshead

Source C

Modern buildings in the UK

Building	Location	Architect	Date
The Ark	London	Ralph Erskine	1990
Beetham Tower	Manchester	Ian Simpson	2004–06
Eden Project	St Austell, Cornwall	Nicholas Grimshaw	1996
Food Theatre Café	London	Daniel Liebeskind	2001
Glyndebourne Opera House	Near Lewes, Sussex	Michael Hopkins	1994
London City Hall	London	Norman Foster	2003
The Lowry	Salford	Michael Wilford/ Buro Happold	2000
Millennium Dome	Greenwich, London	Richard Rogers	1999
New Art Gallery	Walsall	Caruso St John	2000
Sainsbury Centre	Norwich	Norman Foster	1977
Schlumberger Centre	Cambridge	Michael Hopkins	1979–81
Scottish Parliament	Edinburgh	Enric Miralles	1999–2004
Selfridges Store	Birmingham	Future Systems	2003
Stansted Airport	Near Bishops Stortford, Essex	Norman Foster	1991
Swiss Re Building	London	Norman Foster	2000–04
Welsh Assembly	Cardiff	Richard Rogers	2001–06

Source D

Art and the travelling landscape

Since 1997, when it was set up, *Sustrans* has been responsible for developing more than 16,000 kilometres of cycle track, connecting all parts of the UK.

Some parts of the track are less pretty than others, so Sustrans has teamed up with a number of local artists to add interest to the view. Route 15, for example, linking the Clyde coast with Glasgow, was enlivened by 12 sculptures of fruit. Scott McGowan worked with local schoolchildren to create the sculptures and to paint them in their appropriate fruity colours. Unfortunately, the paint has largely worn off over the years — but the thoughts are still there.

Colliers Way runs from Monkton Combe on the Kennet and Avon Canal, along a disused railway line, for some 37 kilometres. Sculptor Jerry Ortman has stacked seven boulders one on top of another, each representing one of the geological strata of the area. Simply called 'The Stone Column', the sculpture pays tribute to pioneer geologist William Smith who was the engineer for the Dorset and Somerset Canal.

The Chalk and Channel Way links Dover and Folkestone, along the South Downs in Kent. The 'Samphire Tower' is one of the biggest of all the Art and the Travelling Landscape sculptures: it is a 10-metre tower, built by Jony Easterby and Pippa Taylor, incorporating a telescope and a small gallery of paintings.

Jim Partridge and Liz Walmsley built a capacious seat out of interlocking railway sleepers. It is both a seat and a cycle stand, providing welcome relief on an urban section of the Three Rivers cycle route, near Chester-le-Street, County Durham.

'The Wriggle' is a 3-metre length of wall on both sides of a semi-circular section of path, rising to a peak like a hump-backed bridge. This was built by artist Robert Drake, near Rowrah in West Cumbria.

There are more than a hundred of these public sculptures along the National Cycle Network, and new ones are being added all the time as Sustrans and local authorities commission local artists to lend interest to otherwise featureless landscapes, or to raise awareness of local specialities. Sally Matthews's life-size sculptures of 'Lincolnshire Red' cows and her Irish Elk, on the south Midlands cycle route, would fool you into thinking they were alive, at first glance.

There are murals, mosaics, ornamental railings, patterned pavements, and crop and stone circles. We all live within a mile of one of these cycle routes; but non-cyclists, and other stop-at-homes can view most of the sculptures on the Artwork Database pages, under Sustrans Projects, on the **www.sustrans.org.uk** website. Here begins a viewing of what must be the biggest and most geographically dispersed gallery of artworks in the world.

Samphire Tower

©David Young/Sustrans

Adapted from Craig Scott, 'A Gallery that moves at your own pace' at www.artshub.co.uk/ahl/news and www.sustrans.org.uk

Skills

We need not go too deeply into what 'art' is; we certainly need not agree about it. Once, to say of something that it was art was to make a value judgement about it. Now, it is merely to make a statement. Art is what artists, critics, gallery-owners, investors and collectors say it is. Art is what we — collectively — say it is. It is what is produced to be exhibited, reviewed and bought as what the art industry calls 'artworks'.

Whether these artworks are *good*, *beautiful* or *worthwhile* is another question, to which there can be no right answers. When everything is, or can be, art (as many artists and critics have contended), and when everyone is, or can be, an artist, the term 'art' loses all its former value-laden meaning.

Sculpture is one of the 'fine arts'. Many have said, in answer to the question raised in the previous topic: **How might life in towns and cities be improved?** that there should be some public sculpture. They would have answered 'yes' to the first question under this heading in the specification: **Should works of art feature in public places?** Of course, the art need not be sculpture; it might be a mosaic, an ornamental garden or a fountain. When art is broadly defined, it is difficult to answer 'no' to this first question.

The second question under this heading in the specification: **Does art have a function outside the gallery?** prompts the further question: does art have a function *at all?* The sculptor and the patron of the statue in Source A would have regarded it as an artwork.

(i) **What might those responsible for erecting the statue in Source A have considered its function, or functions, to be? Write down your ideas.**

Sculpture is to be found in galleries, of course; but the size of much of it, the fact that it is often a public statement, and the fact that it can often withstand most weather means that it is generally placed outside. Antony Gormley's *Angel of the North* could scarcely be placed indoors; nor could Thomas Heatherwick's *B of the Bang* near the Manchester City football ground; nor the Diana Memorial Fountain, in Hyde Park, London, designed by US architect Kathryn Gustafson.

(ii) **List the ways in which modern public sculptures, and 'art installations' (such as that in Source B), differ from the statues of the past.**

A modern piece of sculpture is, perhaps, more likely to be free standing than to be attached to a building, as Jacob Epstein's *St Michael's Victory Over Lucifer* is attached to Coventry Cathedral.

Buildings themselves, in a sense, have always been works of sculpture. All the most notable buildings have had parts that have jutted out and parts that have been recessed. These juttings and recesses have lent interest to a building — interest that straight glass towers have seldom attracted.

Just as it is important, when writing about public art, to be able to name and refer to particular works, so it is important when writing about architecture to be able to name and refer to a few particular buildings, such as those listed in Source C. The particular buildings listed here have been chosen for their geographical spread as much as for any other reason — but they are all sculptures.

We will all have our own views about the question: What makes a building good to look at? Here, let us ask the following:

(iii) What is it that makes a modern building good to look at?

The buildings in Source C are all public buildings of some importance, or prominence, and the institutions for which they were built had enough money to commission world-class architects. Many modern buildings are built rather more cheaply and tend to be less distinguished. They may *not* be good to look at because:

- They are clones of so many other bland buildings.
- There is a randomness about the positioning of windows, for example.
- Inappropriate motifs (e.g. a pediment or fake columns) are bolted on.
- Garish colours are used.
- Planes, angles, proportions — the geometry of the building — might be out of scale or just, somehow, wrong.

The first priority of any building is that it should be suitable for whatever goes on inside. However, we now tend to preserve good buildings — like a half-timbered pub, or a Regency chapel — whether or not we put them to their original use. We do our best to find a new use for them rather than knock them down. New uses will often call for new buildings, though. The question: Does modern architecture meet our needs? almost answers itself. As our needs change, so buildings must change. They must be different from before; must, in a word, be *modern*. If buildings were not modern, they would not meet these new needs.

The question is: what are the new needs, and how do new buildings meet them?

(iv) List the ways in which modern buildings might be more suitable for today's needs than old buildings.

Buildings *work* by meeting the needs that are placed on them. Architecture is not an add-on. A building might be a work of architecture, not because bits of decoration are added on to it, but because it works from the inside out. The needs are met — and they are met stylishly, with a certain grace, elegance, confidence, bravura and originality. This is why architecture is an art, and why — in a sense — it sums up all art: it is the walls that paintings might adorn, the backdrop for sculpture, and the space within which music can be heard at its best. Architecture is the art both of enclosure and of disclosure.

On the other hand, Source D demonstrates that art does not have to be enclosed at all — it has both a place and a function outside the gallery. Even the old distinction between Nature (the work of God) and Art (the work of humankind) has been blurred. Of course, what we think of as nature — the countryside — is an *artefact*, if not an artwork.

This brings us to Q25.

Q25a Why might we welcome the sort of artworks in the landscape that are referred to in Source D?

b Why might we *not* welcome them?

We might want to consider whether the artworks in question:

- are good to look at in themselves
- have a function (e.g. can be used as a seat)
- are in harmony with their environment
- are made of durable materials
- can be maintained in the long term

Here is a sketch of an answer to the first half of the question:

a [S] *Such artworks add a great deal to the landscape.*

[Ex A] *They are often beautiful in themselves.*

They allow local artists to express themselves.

They may have a functional purpose, as seats, or as exhibition spaces.

They often work with the natural environment, enhancing it, celebrating it, complementing it, and informing passers-by.

They may give encouragement to cycling, and bring in tourist revenue.

[C] *There are many reasons for welcoming these artworks to the landscape.*

Here is a sketch of a response to the second half of the question:

b [S] *We may not always welcome these artworks.*

[Ex B] *They may quickly deteriorate and be as much an eyesore as a visual asset.*

They may be quite expensive both to install and to maintain.

Some of them may intrude on an otherwise relatively wild and unspoilt landscape.

Some may be kitsch, tasteless, garish, and have little 'art' about them.

[C] *There may be good reasons for doubting whether these artworks will always add to the landscape.*

Global media

Content

Source A   Estimated audience figures (millions) for BBC World Service radio

Language	2004	2006
English	39.0	44
Persian	20.4	22
Hindi	16.1	21
Urdu	10.4	12
Arabic	12.4	16

Notes:

1 The BBC World Service broadcasts to 66 million listeners in Africa and the Middle East, of whom 18.7 million listen to English broadcasts.
2 The BBC World Service also broadcasts in 32 other languages.
3 There are fewer European-language broadcasts since the majority of European listeners tune into English broadcasts.

Source: http://en.wikipedia.org/wiki/BBC_World_ Service

Source B   BBC World

BBC World is the BBC's commercially funded, international 24-hour news and information channel.

■ It broadcasts in English in more than 200 countries.
■ Its estimated weekly audience is 65 million.

■ It is available in over:
  – 28 million homes
  – 1.3 million hotel rooms
  – 48 cruise ships
  – 32 airlines
  – 29 mobile-phone platforms

Source: www.bbcworld.com

Source C — BBC faces expulsion from Cuba

The Cuban government reviews annually the credentials of foreign journalists posted to that country. In February 2007, reporting rights were withdrawn from Stephen Gibbs, the BBC's correspondent in Cuba. The BBC was given no reason for this action by the Cuban authorities.

Accreditation was withdrawn from Gary Marx, the *Chicago Tribune*'s correspondent, who has been reporting from Cuba since 2002. He was told his stories were 'too negative'.

Another victim of the crackdown was César González Calero, the Havana-based correspondent of the Mexican newspaper *El Universal* since 2003. He was told by the authorities that his reporting was 'not the most convenient for the Cuban government'.

Adapted from Dan Bell and agencies, 'BBC facing expulsion from Cuba', *Guardian*, 24 February 2007

Source D — Business activities of six large media companies

	Film companies	TV channels	Book publishing	Newspapers and magazines	Internet portals
AOL Time Warner (USA)	12 (inc. Warner Bros)	29 (inc. CNN)	24 (inc. Time-Life)	35 (inc. *TIME*)	10 (inc. AOL, AOL International, CompuServe)
The Walt Disney Company (USA)	8 (inc. Walt Disney, Miramax)	10 (inc. ABC TV)	Disney Books	4 newspapers 5 magazines (in USA)	18 online ventures
Bertelsmann (Germany)	—	22 (inc. RTL)	Random House (20 UK imprints)	9 newspapers 80 magazines	Lycos, Barnes & Noble.com
Viacom (USA)	Paramount, United Cinemas International	200 (inc. CBS, MTV)	2,000 book titles p.a.	—	—
News Corporation (USA)	14 (inc. 20th Century Fox)	22 (inc. Fox TV), 74 news networks (inc. Sky)	8 imprints (inc. HarperCollins)	8 national newspapers (inc. *Times, Sun, The Australian*), 200+ local papers	—

	Film companies	TV channels	Book publishing	Newspapers and magazines	Internet portals
Vivendi (France)	Universal Studios	Canal+ (France), Universal TV	60 imprints	—	Many, under vivendinet umbrella

Adapted from *New Internationalist* (online)

Source E   **A country with a split personality**

Belgium is a country divided into three parts: Flemish-speaking Flanders in the north, French-speaking Wallonia in the south, and bilingual Brussels in the middle. The country only came into existence in 1830, and ever since that time, there has been a certain tension between the two language groups. Flanders is better off than Wallonia, and some Flemings would like to break with the south. Whether Belgium is a viable country at all is an issue that never really goes away.

On Wednesday 13 December 2006, the French-speaking television station RTBF broadcast a docu-drama announcing the sudden collapse of the kingdom and the abdication of King Albert II. The announcement was made by a well-known newsreader, François De Brigode, and film-footage was used that gave the programme — which had been 18 months in the making — the appearance of breaking news.

Nine out of ten Belgians are said to have believed what they saw and heard, and certainly until the words (in French) were flashed across the screen, 'This is fiction', half an hour into the programme. When they realised that they had been duped, many viewers were angry: 'It was irresponsible!'; 'How can we know when newsreaders are telling the truth?' Others applauded the programme-makers: 'It took courage'; 'it's made us face up to reality'. Certainly everybody was talking about the programme for days afterwards.

The story filled eight pages (out of 24) of the French-language evening paper *Le Soir*, on Friday 15 December. Much of the front page was given over to a cartoon: a woman is watching television news, and there is a picture on the screen of a poor black child in Darfur, Sudan, who has a bloated belly, and is surrounded by flies. The woman's husband comes in from work, takes off his coat, and — looking at the screen — asks: 'What's their fiction this evening?' 'Nice one!' says his wife. 'I believed it for the first 5 minutes.'

It was an important story for Belgians: the country's very existence was on the line. It was an important story for Europe, too, since not only was Belgium one of the original six members of what is now the European Union, but also many of the EU's key offices are located in Brussels. The break-up of the country that precipitated the UK's entering two world wars should have caused a stir in the British media, too, but it did nothing of the kind. Britons were far too fixated on the serial killings of prostitutes in Ipswich to notice that a near-neighbour was contemplating (mock) suicide.

Belgium did not break up, but how many of us would have known where to look for Belgium on the map if it had?

Adapted from stories in *Le Soir*, 15 December 2006

Skills

At the time this book was written, news from abroad mainly concerned:

- civil conflict in Iraq
- the conflict with the Taliban in Afghanistan
- Hamas–Fatah rivalry for power in Gaza
- the beginnings of the long presidential election campaign in the USA
- George Bush's tour of South America
- the kidnappings of five UK diplomats in Ethiopia

As a general rule:

- News from *Europe* usually focuses on an EU directive.
- News from *Africa* is most often about a disaster or atrocity.
- News from *Asia* is either about a disaster or about the economic growth of India and China.
- News from *South America* concerns drugs, paramilitaries or the destruction of the Amazon.
- News from *Australasia* often relates to sport of one kind or another.

War, *disaster*, *scandal* and the occasional *human interest story* are the staples of international news.

Consider the first question under this heading on the specification: **Are we open to foreign news and cultures?** Only up to a point, it would seem.

(i) **Why do you suppose there is only a limited amount of foreign news in our newspapers and on our screens? (And why do the media concentrate on so few 'staple' stories?)**

The 'quality' papers contain more foreign news stories than the 'popular' papers — and these stories tend to be more 'serious' in nature. Occasionally, a programme about a foreign culture appears on television, too — even if it only serves as a backdrop to the travels of Michael Palin.

(ii) **What evidence is there in the sources that the West (North America, Europe and Australasia) dominates the media? Write down your ideas.**

Does it matter that the West dominates the media? The BBC is generally reckoned to be a 'good thing' — it is politically neutral, and its journalism is acknowledged to be evidence based and impartial — so surely it is beneficial for it to broadcast in English in more than 200 countries, to 65 million people weekly? It may seem so to a Briton; but would we say the same thing of CNN, Fox TV or Sky News? People from other countries might not see the world, or want to see the world, through the eyes of BBC, CNN or Sky News journalists.

How would non-Muslims in the UK feel if our foreign news came from Al-Jazeera? How would non-Indians feel if most of our films came from 'Bollywood' (i.e. Mumbai, previously Bombay)?

What are the effects of the West's domination of the media?

Several effects can be inferred:
- The English language is rapidly becoming the global *lingua franca*.
- The West imposes its views on the rest of the world ('cultural imperialism').
- Non-western countries have to buy their news and entertainment from western agencies, in a transfer of wealth.
- Non-western voices are seldom heard.
- Poorer countries have scarcely any access to media resources.

Hugo Chávez, the left-wing leader of Venezuela (not one of the very poorest countries) has set up a state-owned film studio, in order to counteract what he perceives to be the right-wing propaganda issuing from right-wing, American-owned media companies (Gyula Hegyi, *Guardian*, 22 December 2006). We would probably agree with Gyula Hegyi that this is a good thing, and in similar circumstances, we would want to do the same. It is surely better than trying to block, or censor, those western media outlets. But then Chávez caused consternation by not renewing the licence of RCTV, a popular television channel that had campaigned against him (Rory Carroll, *Guardian*, 9 June 2007).
- The BBC is banned from reporting in Zimbabwe, so has to do so clandestinely or from neighbouring South Africa.
- According to Source C, the BBC, the *Chicago Tribune*, and *El Universal* are to be banned from reporting in Cuba — or, at least, particular correspondents are to be banned.
- Western media (including internet) companies are subject to controls placed on them by the Chinese government.
- The Islamic regime in Iran bans a number of western book titles, including Tracy Chevalier's *Girl with a Pearl Earring* and Dan Brown's *The Da Vinci Code* because they serve 'a poisoned dish to the young generation' (Afar Nafisi, *Guardian Review*, 25 November 2006).

So, the answer to the question in the specification: **Are the global media subject to** any form of control? is, plainly, yes. But this is hardly surprising: the media are subject to controls in the UK, too.

(iii) What controls are media companies (foreign or domestic) subject to if they publish or broadcast in the UK?

There are limits to what you might be asked to do with your calculators when answering questions about Sources A, B and D — but a simple percentage-growth question might be asked of Source A. You ought to be able to carry out the calculation called for in this question.

(iv) By how much, in percentage terms, have audiences grown between 2004 and 2006 in the five major languages listed in Source A?

Hindi wins by a narrow margin over Arabic (though the latter is likely to grow faster because the BBC is withdrawing from an increasingly English-speaking Europe, and is raising its profile in Arabic-speaking countries).

(v) What conclusions might we come to about the global media from a close reading of Source D (apart from those already mentioned)?

Source E concerns a story that consumed Belgium for some days, but that had no impact in the UK media. It is a particularly interesting story because it has something to say about:

- the ambiguous nature of the docu-drama (is there a merging of fact and fiction, news and views, in modern media?)
- the way in which a news story can be big in one country yet be ignored by the media in neighbouring countries
- the ease with which apparently sophisticated viewers can be duped into believing what they are told by an 'authority'

There are some interesting paradoxes here, not the least of which is the observation made by psychologist Jacques Van Rillaer that 'people tend to believe what they read or hear, uncritically'; yet the message of the front-page cartoon is that viewers are just as inclined to *dis*believe what they see, once the seed of doubt has been sown.

Here is a question that might be asked about Source E (although a candidate might draw on any information in this section to answer it):

Q26a 'The UK media tell us enough about what is going on elsewhere in the world.' How far do you agree with this statement?

b How far do you *dis*agree with it?

This is another of those questions to which it is probably as well to give a balanced answer, unless you want to give the impression that you do not care what is going on beyond the English Channel. If, of course, you really do not care, it is even more important that you try to see things from another point of view.

Note that, although the words 'how far...?' are used in both halves of the question, you can assume that you are not expected to write the same answer twice. Here is a sketch of an answer:

a [S] *We do get enough foreign news in the UK media.*

[Ex A] *Much of the news on television seems to be about Iraq, Afghanistan, Gaza, Lebanon and other conflict zones.*

There is never any shortage of news from Washington.

Newspapers keep correspondents in Brussels, Paris, Berlin and Moscow.

Our politicians are always jetting about the world, and their journeys are reported on.

In a global village, we quickly hear about a ferry-boat disaster in Indonesia, or the plight of refugees in Darfur.

[C] *The media give generous coverage to events overseas.*

b [S] *We hear little about what goes on in certain parts of the world.*

[Ex B] *There is certainly blanket coverage of a serious atrocity or an earthquake when such events happen; but the journalists don't stay at the scene long.*

Foreign news tends to be rather patchy in the popular press.

There are certain countries and parts of the world that we rarely hear about: the Baltic states, the Pacific states of South America, much of Central Asia and Indochina — even certain EU states. Does nothing happen in Slovakia?

We are too wrapped up in the trivia of domestic news to notice more significant events elsewhere.

[C] *Reporters hunt in packs, staying in urban hotels, and file only the most sensational stories from foreign lands.*

SPACE
Business and industry

Use of the land

Content

Source A

Land by agricultural and other uses, 1998–2005 (thousand hectares)

	1998	2003	2004	2005
Crops and bare fallow	5,005	4,507	4,622	4,583
Grassland	6,665	6,884	6,866	6,904
Rough grazing	5,848	5,565	5,563	5,590
Other agricultural	285	276	356	289
Forest and woodland	2,758	2,807	2,816	2,825
Set-aside land	313	681	560	559
Urban and other	3,219	3,373	3,531	3,501

Source: www.defra.gov.uk/environmentstatistics/land

Source B

New homes built on previously developed land in England, 1989–2005

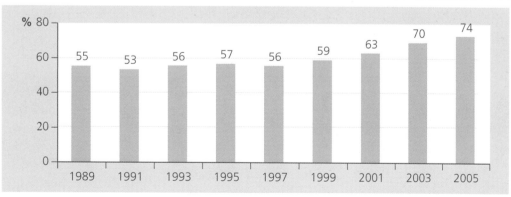

Source: Department for Communities and Local Government

Land ownership in the UK

Landowner	Acres
Forestry Commission	2,400,000
Ministry of Defence	750,000
National Trust	550,000
Crown Estate	400,000
Duke of Buccleuch	270,000
Prince of Wales (Duchy of Cornwall etc.)	141,000
Duke of Westminster (including 300 acres in central London)	140,000
Church of England	135,000
Queen (Duchy of Lancaster) (Balmoral etc.)	50,000 75,000

The right to roam

The right to wander at will in the countryside is one that seems 'natural' — our birthright — but it is one, in fact, that has had to be fought for over more than 100 years. The Rights of Way Act 2000 began the process of opening up large areas of downland, heathland, moorland and designated common land.

Access to this land was granted by an Act of 19 October 2004 to ramblers, bird-watchers and climbers — but not to campers, cyclists, horse-riders or any vehicle other than a mobility scooter — so that they no longer had to stay on public footpaths. Landowners could dedicate further areas of land to cyclists and horse-riders if they wished, and be released from legal liability for any personal injury suffered by users of the land.

The new 'right to roam' includes some of the wildest and most dramatic landscapes in England and Wales. It did not grant automatic access to forest and woodland; nevertheless, the Forestry Commission — the biggest landowner in the country — did begin to designate all its freehold land as access land. The 2004 Act opened up 865,000 hectares of downland, moorland and heath to the public. This constitutes 6.5% of all the land of England and Wales. By January 2006, the Forestry Commission had added 36,122 hectares to this sum.

The 'right to roam' also did not extend to coastlines and beaches. Landowners might grant 'permissive' access to privately owned coastal land at their discretion, and there are some ancient rights of way. However, the Ramblers' Association is campaigning for a legal right of access, in the belief that to be able to walk among dunes, on beaches and on cliff-tops is a part of our heritage.

The right to walk along estuaries and beside rivers and canals is another access right to be fought for. The British Canoe Union has combined with the Ramblers' Association in this fight. Clarity and consistency are needed in the first place: there are public rights of way, permissive paths and informal agreements going back years; and a certain amount of 'open countryside' was designated under the Countryside and Rights of Way Act of 2000 — but there is no accepted procedure for ensuring continuing access when building development or coastal erosion impedes access.

The new Ordnance Survey Explorer maps have been updated to show access land, and the countryside code has also been revised (Scotland has its own outdoor access code). This asks land-users to:

- be safe, plan ahead and follow any signs
- leave gates and property as you find them
- protect plants and animals, and take your litter home (this includes cigarette ends, which should never be stubbed out on the ground)
- keep dogs under close control
- consider other people

Rights come with responsibilities.

Sources: www.countryside.gov.uk/LAR/Access/open_access; www.ramblers.org.uk/freedom/improvingaccess

Skills

We may assume that the word 'industrial', in the question: **How is land in the UK put to industrial use?** is being used in its broad sense to mean 'resources put to economic use'. It is not a contradiction in terms to speak of the 'farming industry', the 'forestry (or timber) industry', or indeed the 'fish-farming industry'.

(i) **If we sum all seven figures in the 2005 column in Source A, will this give us a total of all the land in the UK that is available for use in that year? Explain your answer.**

We may assume that the figure in Source A (3,501,000 hectares) for 'urban and other' land includes all the land that is built on. This will certainly include land put to industrial use in the narrower sense of the term: land developed for quarries, factories, oil refineries, mines and mills.

(ii) **a What proportion of all the land put to economic use in England and Wales was accounted for by 'urban and other' development in 2005?**

b By what percentage did the 'urban and other' category grow between 1998 and 2005?

It is likely that much of the growth of 'urban and other' development between 1998 and 2005 will be the result of house building. House prices are still rising, and they will probably continue to rise because *demand* for houses is continuing to exceed the *supply*.

The demand for houses — and particularly for small houses or flats — is growing all the time because:

- people are living longer
- more people choose to live alone
- more couples are getting divorced and require separate dwellings
- there is a net inflow of migrants
- growing numbers of university students require accommodation

One problem is the lack of available land; another is the time and expense involved in securing planning permission to build houses on that land.

How is land allocated to housing? Another way of putting this is by asking this question:

(iii) On what sort of land is it *not* possible (at least in theory) to build new houses? Write down as many types as you can think of.

To this land unavailable for housing we can add coastland that is subject to erosion (part of the east coast of England, in particular), and uplands and remote land with poor transport links and no local employment.

So, what land does this leave us with that *is* available for house building? There are three major categories of such land:

- former farmland that has been reclassified for house building
- land that was previously used for industrial purposes on which there are, perhaps, derelict buildings, mine workings etc.
- urban land that has been privately owned but which is offered for sale by its owner (part of an extensive garden, for instance)

(iv) a What conclusion do you come to on inspection of Source B?

b Why is it so important that as many homes as possible are built on previously developed land?

We can conclude that land is increasingly being allocated to housing that has previously been in industrial use — indeed, the buildings themselves (mills, warehouses and station buildings) may be converted to residential use.

In the future we may be forced to:

- reclaim land from the sea
- live in houseboats on canals and other stretches of (rising) water
- build on all the thousands of tarmacadamed acres currently used for car parking

How do we protect land against development?

You might already have discovered some of the ways in which we protect land against development, in answer to question (iii): we classify it as a National Park (Peak District, Lake District, Snowdonia, Dartmoor, Exmoor etc.), or as an Area of Outstanding Natural Beauty (the West Wiltshire Downs, the Cotswold Hills, the Sussex Downs etc.), or as a Site of Special Scientific Interest (SSSI).

Forestry Commission land is protected, of course; the *Ministry of Defence* is fiercely protective of the land that it uses for military exercises (for example, on Salisbury Plain, in Wiltshire — not far from the World Heritage Site: Stonehenge); and the *National Trust* is a landowner that preserves 550,000 acres (Source C) of countryside and coastland against building and other development.

Privately owned land in general cannot be developed, although the Duke of Westminster's estate in central London and the Prince of Wales's property in Kennington yield a handsome return from residential and office rents.

(Note: Source C is expressed in acres, so these values would have to be converted into hectares in order to be compared with the values in Source A. 1 acre = 0.4 hectares.)

Who owns the land and who has access to it?

When answering the fourth question under this heading in the specification it is important to remember that who owns the land is one thing; who has access to it is another. Source D makes reference to a number of different sorts of land in Britain:
- downland, heathland and moorland
- forest and woodland
- coastlines, beaches and dunes
- estuaries, rivers and canals

Reference is also made to a number of different sorts of land-user:
- ramblers and bird-watchers
- climbers
- campers
- cyclists and horse-riders

Ramblers and bird-watchers have the least restricted 'right to roam'; climbers will only be interested in certain kinds of rocky landscape; while campers, cyclists and horse-riders have, understandably, limited rights of access. Most of us would want motor-bikes and off-road vehicles to be banned altogether from land that is attractive to walkers by very virtue of its inaccessibility to vehicles.

Here is the question, and a sketch of an answer to the two halves of it, that is most likely to be asked in connection with Source D.

> **Q27a** Why might we welcome a public right of access to all the land in the country that is not built on?
>
> **b** Why might we *not* welcome such access?

a   [S] *In principle, such access would certainly be welcome.*

[Ex A] *It is a 'natural' right: one that we are reclaiming after centuries of undemocratic land ownership.*

Often, the right being claimed is to use ancient rights of way denied by men in power at the time.

A more urban population needs access to the countryside, for fresh air and recreation. Town-dwellers must understand the countryside if they are to vote for measures to help to conserve it.

   [C] *There are many reasons for increasing access to the countryside by people who would respect it.*

b   [S] *The right to roam cannot, in practice, be given too open-handedly.*

[Ex B] *Much of the land is in private hands, in just the same way as our own back gardens are off-limits to strangers.*

Many of those who would claim the right might abuse it by lighting fires in woodland and on dry heathland, or by riding motor-bikes and quad-bikes on it.

Many cliff-top paths might be dangerous, and riverside paths might be subject to flooding — these could be dangerous and raise insurance issues.

   [C] *There are many reasons for restricting access to 'heritage' land.*

If you were writing a rounded 'S/A/B/C' essay on this subject, you might well want to reverse the above order of the 'A' and 'B' positions, so that the open-access position came second and led straight into your conclusion.

Buying and selling

Content

AQA (B) Advanced General Studies   125

Source A

Revenue shares of grocery retailers (%), 2001 and 2005

	2001	2005
Tesco	24.6	30.6
ASDA	14.4	16.5
Sainsbury's	17.7	15.9
Morrisons	5.3	11.2
Safeway	10.7	0.0
Somerfield	3.8	4.1
Waitrose	3.0	3.7
Discounters	3.4	5.2
Co-ops	5.5	4.6
Independents	5.1	3.0
Other	6.5	5.2

Note: Morrisons bought Safeway in 2004.

Source: www.competition-commission.org.uk; Taylor Nelson Sofres 52-week grocery data, June 2006

Source B

Village shop in Suffolk

Source C

ASDA superstore in Hartlepool

Source D

At a clone town near you

'Always low prices'

'Every little helps'

'Helping you spend less every day'

'More reasons to shop at Morrisons'

'Try something new today'

'More for you for less'

You are probably familiar with these slogans as you will have seen them on the plastic bags bearing the logos of the big four retailers: Tesco, ASDA, Sainsbury's and Morrisons.

The first of the slogans above was ASDA's — and it was the company's boast for 30 years. Then, in 2006, its American parent company Wal-Mart decided that there is more to today's retailing than being 'cheap and cheerful': customers look for quality, too — so it adopted the last slogan in the above list.

Will its rebranding mean that customers will return to ASDA's aisles? Or is there a deeper consumer disquiet about the impact of the big superstores on our lives? The charge sheet is a long one:

■ Nearly 30,000 independent retailers have gone out of business in the past 10 years as a result of superstore penetration (that's 50 small shops every week).

■ Most towns are clones of each other, with the same names above the shop-fronts.

■ Tesco already sells one-third of the nation's groceries, and it has between 40 and 45% of the market in 19 UK postal districts.

■ Supermarkets bully their suppliers into selling standard products at low prices that put small farmers out of business.

■ They source their products at a distance, adding to food-miles and disadvantaging local suppliers.

■ They reduce customer choice, and add to traffic congestion and unsustainable waste that comes from over-packaging.

The Office of Fair Trading (OFT) has expressed concern about the effects of supermarket penetration on competition in the high street. Bicester, in Oxfordshire, for example, has no fewer than six Tesco stores, and there are ten Tesco outlets on just one road (Fulham Road in London).

Two matters in particular are under investigation by the OFT and the Competition Commission: the amount of land that the supermarkets have bought for future store development; and the increasing numbers of Sainsbury's Local and Tesco Express high-street outlets.

It is estimated that the big four supermarkets have a land-bank between them of 300 sites. Tesco is far ahead of its rivals in terms of the number of sites that it owns. Justin King, Sainsbury's chief executive, has estimated that if Tesco were to build stores on all its sites, its share of the grocery market would leap to 40% and even 50% in places.

The OFT formerly made a distinction between out-of-town superstores and high-street convenience shops: it regarded them as two separate markets. As Tesco's onslaught on corner-shops continues, however, the OFT is considering whether the retailer might be abusing its market position.

Tesco, of course, argues that its success demonstrates that it is giving the public what it wants, and that it should not be penalised for this. But it may take more than a slogan ('Every little helps') to convince the Competition Commission that 'Tescopoly' is in the public interest.

Adapted from articles by Teena Lyons, *Mail on Sunday*, 5 March 2006; Pete May, *Earthmatters*, Friends of the Earth, spring 2006, and Julia Finch, *Guardian*, 20 January 2007

Skills

There are many ways of describing the times we live in, all of them much used (often unthinkingly) by journalists:

- the jet age
- the electronic age
- the information age
- multicultural society
- consumer society

The question: **Do we live in a consumer society?** seems to answer itself. It is obvious that we buy a lot of things — that we *consume*. Do we consume more now than our parents did, or than their parents did? Again, the answer seems to be 'yes'.

(i) Why do we, in the present generation, buy more now than our parents' generation did, and than the generation before them?

Perhaps all societies have been consumer societies; what is different now is that, whereas previous generations spent much of their incomes on what they *needed*, we are more inclined to buy what we *want*. What we buy may satisfy us for a shorter time, and it may be that more of it goes to *waste*.

We welcome a *choice* of products. Consumer choice is spoken of almost as if it were our right — it is certainly thought of as *desirable*. Yet the more choice we have, the more it seems that the products we buy are the same, or similar. This brings us to the second question under this heading in the specification: **Why are consumer products increasingly standardised?** One reason is obvious, as can be seen in Source A.

(ii) What are the main lessons that we learn from Source A concerning the market share of retail stores between 2001 and 2005?

The biggest retailers, and Tesco in particular, have increased their market share over the 5-year period. This alone will have had a standardising effect on products — each retailer will want to restrict the number of its suppliers to keep costs down (i.e. those arising from shelf-space and storage, administration and wages for staff processing orders etc.)

In addition, consumer products may be increasingly standardised because:

- Consumers are influenced by standardised advertising more.
- Products are subject to (health and safety, nutrition and other) regulations, which have a standardising effect.

- As the market for products grows, so those products are more mass-produced by bigger — and fewer — companies.

Products tend to cost more in small shops like the one pictured in Source B than in superstores such as the one shown in Source C.

(iii) Why do small shops tend to charge more for their products?

The key phrase, and concept, is *economies of scale* — that is, the bigger the size of the operation, the lower the unit costs of stock, storage, transport, staff etc. The more tins of baked beans you sell, the less you need to charge for each tin. Big stores are able to exploit economies of scale, while small shops are not.

There are, of course, some advantages of the small shop over the big one:

The small shop is more likely to:	The big store is more likely to:
be situated close to where you live	be a car-drive away
stock specialised goods	stock a standard range of goods
offer an after-sales service	prefer to replace defective goods
offer a personal, more knowledgeable service	be impersonal and employ staff who are simply there to sell goods

The UK used to be a major manufacturer of *goods*; now we tend to be more a purveyor of *services*. Gone are the days when the UK was the 'workshop of the world' — when we made Morris, Austin, Humber and Hillman cars, de Havilland aeroplanes, Pye televisions, Wills and Player's cigarettes, Crossley carpets and BSA motorbikes.

We do still produce goods, of course.

(iv) List as many goods as you can think of that are produced in the UK (whether or not they are UK owned).

Is the UK still a major producer of goods? Not if we compare the UK of today with the UK of 50 years ago; but the UK still produces a distinctive range of goods — and foreign manufacturers set up operations in the UK. (Honda, Nestlé, Siemens, Nissan and Pfizer all have plants in the UK.)

However, the service sector is now much greater in the UK than the manufacturing sector. Hairdressing, teaching, advertising, mortgage lending, nursing, marriage guidance counselling and taxi driving are all services, but they are services of a domestic kind. They are *invisible* in the sense that they produce no visible, tangible product. They are not services that we export — services by which we pay our way in the world.

Teaching, for example, is a cost borne by taxpayers; it is only profitable, in a strictly business sense, when foreigners buy UK teaching services. When UK teachers sell their services abroad, or when foreign students come to study in the UK, we can then say that teaching is an **invisible export**. We can put this at the top of quite a long list of services that earn foreign exchange:

- English-language teaching and book publishing (e.g. Oxford University Press)
- school and university-level courses and examinations (e.g. Cambridge examinations; Nottingham University's campus in Ningbo, China)
- fine-art auctions (e.g. Sotheby's, Christie's, Philips)
- insurance and reinsurance (e.g. Lloyd's of London)
- financial services (e.g. private and merchant banking — Coutts, Barclays, Hambro; trading on the London Stock Exchange)
- tourism (i.e. foreigners visiting the UK)
- creative industries (e.g. UK bands and orchestras, theatre groups and choirs performing abroad)
- telecommunications, broadcasting and online services (e.g. Vodafone, BBC World, newspaper websites)

The UK still buys and sells. It may not now sell cars and textiles to the rest of the world, but instead, it sells music, investment opportunities, gallery space, data, the English language, Shakespeare and other aspects of its culture to countries with less well-established institutions.

Q28 is the type of question that might arise from Source D. Below is a sketch of an answer to the two halves of the question.

Q28a	Why should we welcome the fact that Tesco is increasingly as successful abroad as it is in the UK?
b	Why might we not be pleased about Tesco's success abroad?

a [S] *We should be pleased that Tesco, a British business, is successful abroad.*
[Ex A] *Tesco will be more able to exploit economies of scale.*
It will earn foreign exchange for its UK shareholders.
It will give foreign consumers the same choice and competitive prices that UK consumers enjoy.

UK tourists, when abroad, can shop in familiar surroundings and know that they are getting value for money.

[C] *There are many reasons for being pleased that Tesco is as successful abroad as it is in the UK.*

b   [S] *We may not be altogether pleased to hear about Tesco's success abroad.*

[Ex B] *It is not healthy that one store should achieve market dominance either at home or abroad.*

There is evidence that Tesco comes close to putting its suppliers out of business by demanding low prices; we should not be exporting dubious business practices.

We should not welcome Tesco's putting yet more small retailers out of business, anywhere.

We should worry about all the other problems caused by big retailers being exported to countries with a weaker regulatory system than in the UK.

[C] *Tesco's success abroad may not be entirely in the public interest.*

Multiculturalism

Content

| Source A | Population of the UK by ethnicity (2001 census) |

Ethnic group	%
White	92.1
Indian	1.8
Pakistani	1.3
Bangladeshi	0.5
Black Caribbean	1.0
Black African	0.8
Chinese	0.4
Mixed	1.2
Other ethnic minorities	0.4

Source: www.statistics.gov.uk/cci/nugget.asp?id=273

| Source B | Religion in England, Scotland and Wales (2001 census) |

	Thousands	%
Christian	42,079	71.6
Buddhist	152	0.3
Hindu	559	1.0
Jewish	267	0.5
Muslim	1,591	2.7
Sikh	336	0.6
Other religions	179	0.3
All religions	45,163	76.8
No religion	9,104	15.5
Not stated	4,289	7.3
All no religion/ not stated	13,393	23.2
Total	58,789	100

Source: www.statistics.gov.uk/cci/nugget

Source C — Multiculturalism and integration

Put simply, multiculturalism seemed to imply that we should accept, even rejoice in, the differences between cultures and the ways in which they express themselves. This appeared to include the wearing of the veil, the *hijab*, which covers a woman's hair and neck, and even the *niqab*, which covers everything except for the eyes.

Then Trevor Phillips, chair of the Commission for Racial Equality (CRE), who is himself from a black Caribbean background, said it was not multiculturalism that we should be aiming for, but integration.

Jack Straw, Leader of the Commons, writing in his local newspaper in Blackburn, expressed his unease about meeting Muslim women in his constituency who — though they had sought a 'face to face' meeting — nevertheless wore the *niqab*. He thought that, by so doing, they seemed to be wanting to emphasise their separateness.

In December 2006, Channel 4 had a young convert to Islam, in full *niqab*, deliver a Christmas message in which she criticised Jack Straw under, literally, a veil of anonymity. If this was some kind of stunt, as many felt, then it had gone too far.

Prime Minister Tony Blair endorsed the views of Trevor Phillips and Jack Straw, in a speech to an invited audience at 10 Downing Street, in the same month. He said:

'For the first time in a generation, there is an unease, an anxiety, even at points a resentment that our very openness, our willingness to welcome difference, our pride in being home to many cultures, is being used against us; abused, indeed, in order to harm us.

'The 7/7 bombers were integrated at one level

in terms of lifestyle and work. Others in many communities live lives very much separate and set in their own community and own culture, but are no threat to anyone. Religions have a perfect right to their own identity, to practise their faith and to conform to their culture.

'But, when it comes to our essential values — belief in democracy, the rule of law, tolerance, equal treatment for all, respect for this country and its shared heritage — no distinctive culture or religion supersedes our duty to be part of an integrated United Kingdom.'

Specifically, on the issue of the veil, Mr Blair said: 'It really is a matter of plain common sense that when it is an essential part of someone's work to communicate directly with people, being able to see their face is important.'

It does seem that a change has taken place in official thinking: 'common sense' suggests that we can tolerate difference only so far, and no further. There comes a point at which we must lay emphasis on what it is that we share. Britain as a 'multicultural society' must give way to Britain as an 'integrated society'. The *niqab* might have been the symbol of, or the catalyst for, the change in emphasis and policy.

Adapted from articles by Nigel Morris, *Independent*, 6 October 2006; Will Woodward, *Guardian*, 9 December 2006; and Joan Smith, *Independent on Sunday*, 31 December 2006

Source D   Integrated communities

Integrated communities

Note: this is a second extract from a speech by Ruth Kelly MP. An earlier extract can be found in Source C on page 95.

We have moved from a period of uniform consensus on the value of multiculturalism to one where we can encourage debate by questioning whether it is encouraging separateness.

The Commission [on Integration and Cohesion] will look at how we can encourage local authorities and community organisations to play a greater role in ensuring new migrants better integrate into our communities and fill labour-market shortages. For example:

- increasing the availability of English teaching
- mapping where local jobs exist
- ensuring that migrants are able to develop a sense of belonging, with shared values and local understanding, as we underline their responsibility to integrate and contribute to the local community

There are already communities rising up to tackle these issues and equipping themselves for the changes they face:

- There are school twinning programmes and sporting events across the country that focus on children mixing at an early age.
- Local communities are developing Charters of Values or Local Citizens' Days that aim to develop a sense of belonging in multicultural towns and cities.
- There are community-led projects springing up in communities facing cohesion challenges that focus on mediation and conflict resolution — learning from the best inter-national practice.
- There are more specialised projects such as the work in Bradford aimed at developing a citizenship curriculum for Madrassas [Islamic religious schools].

What we need to do is to consolidate these pockets of good practice and spread the lessons learnt much further. Then we can begin to develop a more consistent national picture.

Extracted from a speech by Ruth Kelly MP at the launch of the new Commission on Integration and Cohesion, 24 August 2006

Skills

Source A presents us with a breakdown of the population of the UK by ethnicity, in 2001. The data might have been presented in the form of a pie chart — but most of the slices would have been very narrow and difficult to distinguish.

(i) **What are the main points that can be learnt from a simple inspection of Source A about the extent to which the UK is a 'multicultural society'?**

The proportions might have changed somewhat since 2001, of course; but the question: **What do we mean by multiculturalism?** cannot be answered by saying 'lots of different ethnicities living side by side'. This is because, ethnically, the UK is still predominantly 'white'. Non-whites are only in the majority in certain districts of certain towns and cities.

Many different *cultures*, of course, are represented among the 91.9% of whites. There are Poles, Czechs and Hungarians; but also Americans, French and Italians who have settled in the UK. There are Jewish communities who have been in the UK for decades — and the Orthodox among them would not describe themselves as having *integrated* into British society.

Multiculturalism as a policy was defined as lying on this continuum:

Tolerating differences   Celebrating differences

⟵————————————————————————————⟶

How and why should we celebrate our differences?

It seemed that we should celebrate differences because to express one's cultural identity is a basic human right. No one in liberal, democratic Britain would seek to prevent anyone from believing and worshipping as they chose, for example. Source B presents us with data on the state of belief, or unbelief, in England, Scotland and Wales, at the time of the last full census. (The question about religious belief was included for the first time, though it had been asked before in Northern Ireland.)

(ii) What conclusions might we come to about religious belief in England, Scotland and Wales, from inspection of Source B?

Of course, religion is not culture but it is an important part of a culture — even a *proxy* for culture — inasmuch as it has connections with art, food, customs and (to some extent) behaviour. So, one way in which we might celebrate our differences is by accepting, witnessing and participating in the religious art, meals and rituals of another 'faith community'. Short of this — and leaving religion to one side — we can enjoy many aspects of other communities:

- the music (e.g. Bob Marley, Ravi Shankar, Klezmer music, Russian Orthodox chant)
- the cuisine (e.g. Chinese, Indian or Italian)
- the literature (e.g. the novels of Rohinton Mistry and Orhan Pamuk, the poems of Shi Tao)

(The list is endless.)

Language is something else: this is central to culture. We would not want migrants to stop using their languages among themselves, but presumably we *would* want them to learn English as well, so that they can function fully in civil society.

Is 'integration' desirable?

We have another continuum here:

Multiculturalism   Integration   Assimilation

←──→

Assimilation is the complete absorption of migrants into the host society, so that they become no different from members of that society.

(iii) Is assimilation of migrants into British society possible or desirable? Explain your answer.

Assimilation will not happen in the short term, and if it happens in the long term, it will be unforced. Many groups, even in Europe, have often resisted assimilation after centuries of oppression, for example: the Basques, the Jews, the Estonians, the Roma-gypsies, the Hungarians, Muslims in the Balkans, and Catholics in England (between 1558 and 1829).

Integration, however, *would* seem to be desirable. There are some differences that we ought not to tolerate — that we cannot tolerate if we are to function as a society.

(iv) What did Tony Blair say were the matters we must all agree about if we are to achieve an 'integrated United Kingdom'?

Paradoxically, we ought not to tolerate intolerance: we cannot allow one community (fundamentalist Islam or British nationalism, for example) not to allow other communities to be different. We do not expect different cultures to be so integrated (or so assimilated) that there will be no significant differences between them.

Ruth Kelly MP, in Source D, has something to say about the question under this heading in the specification: **How could integration be brought about?** She speaks of the need for:

- access to classes in English
- better information about job opportunities
- schools of different faiths and no faith to work and play together
- local events that focus on what it means to be a citizen, locally
- exercises in conflict resolution

These are rather abstract ideas, on the face of it. It is important to be aware of what concrete problems there might be ('cohesion challenges', as Ruth Kelly calls them) in a particular locality, and what steps are being taken, or might be taken, to solve them.

If we are to write on this topic, *examples* will be need.

Q29 is based on Source C, but other sources might be drawn on when answering it. Here is a sketch of an answer to the two halves of the question.

Q29a Why might it be a problem if certain communities in the UK choose to live separately, and differently, from the host community?

b Why might this *not* be a problem?

a [S] *Difficulties can arise if certain communities hold themselves apart from the host community.*

[Ex A] *Language and cultural differences may mean that minorities will not gain employment and be able to access the benefits of UK citizenship.*

We cannot allow cultural/linguistic ghettos to form, or 'no-go' areas for policing.

There may be mutual suspicion arising from a lack of understanding and cultural mixing.

This may lead to alienation and to the sort of radicalism exemplified in the 7/7 bombings.

[C] *If there is not social integration, there is a danger of its opposite occurring: disintegration.*

b [S] *Cultural minorities have a perfect right to hold themselves apart from the host community.*

[Ex B] *This is, after all, how most Britons behave when they migrate to culturally different countries.*

The vast majority of migrants settle in the UK, and contribute to British life and the economy, without behaving in 'white' British ways.

There is, besides, no homogeneous 'white' British way of life to which migrants might be expected to conform.

[C] *Integration will be a gradual process; it is not one that we need artificially to accelerate.*

Green values

Content

Source A

Selected European countries' waste record (% of rubbish recycled or composted)

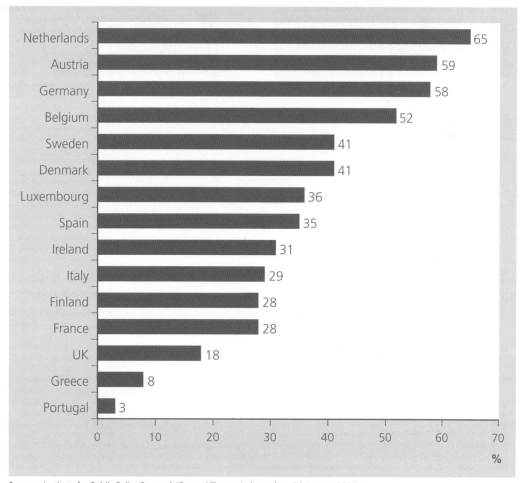

Country	%
Netherlands	65
Austria	59
Germany	58
Belgium	52
Sweden	41
Denmark	41
Luxembourg	36
Spain	35
Ireland	31
Italy	29
Finland	28
France	28
UK	18
Greece	8
Portugal	3

Sources: Institute for Public Policy Research/Green Alliance; *Independent*, 28 August 2006

Source B

A landfill site in Lanarkshire

Source C

Waste paper at a recycling plant in North London

Source D

Water pressure

In parts of the south of England, underground water resources are at their lowest for almost a century. This is hardly surprising: every year since 1997, temperatures have been above average and as temperatures rise, so more ground water evaporates.

Across the country, each individual uses — on average — 150 litres of water per day; in parts of the south, the average is closer to 170 litres. What does each of us do with so much water?

Water use per person per day (litres)	
Baths and showers	65
Toilet flushing	35
Cooking, cleaning etc.	25
Washing machines	20
Garden watering	15
Dishwashers	10
Total	**170**

The figure for garden watering may seem to be exaggerated: most of us water the garden — if we do so at all — on relatively few days in the year; but when you consider that a hosepipe or sprinkler uses 540 litres of water per hour the daily figure of 15 litres makes more sense. This is why sprinklers and unattended hosepipes are banned already in some areas, and why a ban is likely to be placed on all hosepipe use.

Most of us pay a fixed sum every year for the water that we use, no matter how much or how little the total amount may be. Water meters are fitted in all new houses and, in particularly water-stressed areas, companies will be empowered to fit meters in all properties.

The 150 litres of water used by each of us daily, referred to above, may be an underestimate. The Centre for Alternative Technology puts the figure at 278 litres per person per day, on average. Whatever the true figure is, it is rising. We are using more water, and more of us are doing it. Leakages still account for 40% or so of 'consumption' — and this is not just the fault of the water companies and poor maintenance: a tap dripping at 30 drops per minute adds up to wastage of about 25 litres per month.

Do you take a bath and use 90 litres of water, or a shower (30 litres)? Do you need to shower every day? How long do you stand under the shower? Do you flush the toilet even when you throw a used paper handkerchief into it? Have you installed a new, small or dual-flush cistern?

Do you leave the tap running when you clean your teeth, shave or rinse dishes?

If you are 16, 17 or 18 now, you probably won't be alive in 2080; but your children will be. Whether they have enough water, even for their basic needs, depends on how careful we are with it now — and if we are not careful by choice, we may find that water companies will have to be careful on our behalf, by shutting off supplies at critical times.

Information from: *Observer*, 3 July 2005; *Pipelines*, Sutton and East Surrey Water, spring 2006; Centre for Alternative Technology (accessed online, 13 March 2007)

Skills

Friends of the Earth, Greenpeace, the Department for the Environment and the Green Party all came into existence many years before there was talk about global warming or climate change. As the world population rose (as we began to win battles against disease and infant and maternal mortality), and as technology enabled us to develop more of the land for agriculture and raw materials for industry in the 1950s and 1960s, so ecologists began to warn us of the long-term effects of our exploitation of natural resources.

The key dates were:

- **1969** — the photograph of the Earth taken by the Apollo astronauts, which seemed to show just how fragile the planet is and how important it is that we are careful with it
- **1972** — the publication of *The Limits to Growth* by Donella H. Meadows and others, commissioned by the Club of Rome, in which graph after graph detailed the speed at which we were using up the finite resources of the world.

We began to use the word 'environment' rather a lot.

What is it to be 'environment-friendly'?

To be a 'friend of the Earth', to be 'environmentally friendly', was (and is) to be concerned about:

- the pressures of *population growth*
- the *over-exploitation of natural resources* (oil, coal, other minerals, wood, water)
- the *waste* of these resources

- *pollution* caused by the burning or spillage of materials
- *deforestation, desertification* and the over-rapid development of 'green-field' land

(i)   What does a 'friend' of the environment do?

We are urged to 'think globally, act locally'. It is, of course, easier to do the first of these things than to do the second. Thinking costs us nothing. It is easy to deplore acid rain, the destruction of the Amazon rainforest, and polluted rivers; it is less easy to turn down the heating, insulate the loft, queue for a bus and invest in a compost bin.

(ii)   What conclusions might we draw from Source A?

The graph has something to say about the second question in the specification: **What does it mean to be 'green' politically?**

Governments in northwest Europe (the UK and Finland are the exceptions) are generally greener than governments in central and southern Europe (Austria is the honourable exception). Why should this be the case?

It should be added that the UK government has acted in accordance with EU regulations to:

- require manufacturers and importers of electrical and electronic equipment to collect, treat and recycle such equipment; it cannot just be dumped
- make landfill waste disposal more expensive and restrictive, so that recycling is more attractive

All EU countries will need to be up there with the Netherlands and Austria soon.

(iii)   What waste disposal measures have been taken in your own local area? Make a list.

Sources B and C provide pictorial evidence of the problem of waste disposal, and one solution to it (recycling). The type of questions that might be asked of these sources will relate to:

- why the waste disposal problem has grown
- what the answers to it might be
- how we as individuals might waste less

Being 'green' politically has a meaning at the level of government, but it also has a meaning at the level of the individual — whether we:

- live 'green' lives ourselves
- vote for a party with 'green' policies

- belong to or otherwise support a 'green' pressure group
- campaign on 'green' issues

Perhaps to be 'green' politically means that one must be something of an *activist*. It may mean that an individual will take up a position on such issues as *genetically modified (GM) food,* and on building a new generation of *nuclear reactors.* Greenpeace and Friends of the Earth are both anti-GM and anti-nuclear energy — yet there are 'green' arguments on both sides, in both debates.

Should we use nuclear energy?	
Yes	**No**
Nuclear power stations do not burn a fossil fuel.	A great deal of energy goes into building a reactor.
They do not emit greenhouse gases.	Decommissioned plant is very costly and hazardous to dispose of.
The technology is more efficient and safer now than ever.	There is still no answer to how waste might be stored in the long term.
Reprocessing means long-lasting fuel supplies.	

There are few natural resource issues to which there is one cut-and-dried 'green' answer.

Are the great religions green?

(iv) Why might one expect the Christian church, for example, to take a lead on green issues?

Whether the Christian church, or any other of the great religions, has taken a lead on green issues is an open question. The USA is a 'Christian' country, but it took a politician (Al Gore) to tell his countrymen about climate change in *An Inconvenient Truth.*

Hindus revere the Ganges as a goddess, but will this save the river from drying up as the Himalayan glaciers retreat? And will Hinduism ensure that India's present rapid industrialisation is a 'green' revolution?

If 'green values' are to do with: using resources sparingly; minimising waste; recycling materials where possible, **how might we teach green values?**

Or, perhaps, *where* might we teach green values: at home or at school? The answer must be both, and in both places the best way of teaching is *by example*. A parent who searches for a litter bin to put sweet wrappers into is teaching a child not to drop litter.

(v) What do you remember about how (or whether) green values were taught at your primary school? How effective was the teaching?

Q30 relates to the use of water, the subject of Source D. Here is a sketch of an answer to the two halves of the question.

Q30a	'It is time to tax water in the same way that we tax oil.' Why might this be a reasonable proposal?
b	Why might it be *un*reasonable to tax water like oil?

a [S] *We should indeed tax water as we tax oil.*

[Ex A] *We need to send the message to consumers that water is not an inexhaustible resource. It costs money to collect, treat and distribute water, and mend leaks; so it should be charged at its true cost.*

Consumers must be made more aware of the pattern — and cost to the Earth — of their water use.

It is likely that water shortages will be more acute in the future; conserving water may be a matter of life and death.

[C] *Water should be taxed to reflect its true value.*

b [S] *It would be unreasonable to tax water like oil.*

[Ex B] *Water is a fundamental need in a way that oil is not.*

Large families will have more need of water than single individuals who perhaps earn an equivalent income.

Taxing water would amount to taxing health and cleanliness.

Such a tax might encourage people to collect and use rainwater and river water in unsafe, and perhaps anti-social, ways.

[C] *Taxing water like oil would be fraught with difficulties.*

A2

UNIT 3

POWER

POWER
Introduction

When we think of **power**, it may be that power stations or power politics come to mind, but — like the other three unit titles in this specification — power comes in all shapes and sizes.

Consider the following ways in which we use the word:

- His **power** base is in the City.
- She has been em**power**ed by the assertiveness class.
- He put forward a **power**ful argument.
- She has perfected the art of **power** dressing.
- In so doing, he exceeded his legal **power**.
- It is a novel with the **power** to move the hardest hearts.

Power is not all about muscles, guns and turbines.

At AS, each of the five areas of study is divided into two topics; at A2 each area of study is divided into *three* topics. Thus, 'Society and politics', for example, is divided into:

- Distribution of power
- Equal opportunities
- Law enforcement

This does *not* mean that, at A2, there is half as much material again to learn as there is at AS. It *does* mean that you will need to think about the idea of **power** in many dimensions — that you will need to be flexible in your thinking about the many ways in which **power** is exercised.

A2 is intended to be more challenging than AS: questions are likely to be more open, and to answer them adequately, you will need to draw on more of your knowledge (from the General Studies course, and from elsewhere), on your imagination and on your own experience, than you might have done at AS.

Texts are provided on both A2 unit tests (Assessment Units 3 and 4). They are not 'sources' in the way in which the data-sets, images and passages are in AS Unit 2: there, most of the information you need is presented to you; here, at A2, the texts are no more than points of departure. You should not base your whole answer on them. Instead, read them and then lay them to one side; consider what other knowledge you may have that will serve as relevant evidence, and make a note of it before beginning to write an essay answer.

Unit 3 is a further development of the question 3 text-based question in the Unit 2 specification. There, you adopted first position 'A' in an argument, and then position 'B'. Here, for question 1 in Unit 3, you do much the same thing. The paper is laid out as on the next page.

Section A

In **Section A** candidates are required to argue first from one point of view (in 1a), and then from a different (perhaps opposing) point of view (in 1b).

Use the texts and your own knowledge to answer **both** parts of Question 1.

1 a Read **Texts A** and **B** and argue the case for doing…   (20 marks)

   b Read **Texts C** and **D** and argue the case for *not* doing…   (20 marks)

Section B

Use the texts and your own knowledge to answer **either** Question 2 **or** Question 3.

You may draw on some of the ideas expressed in **Section A** in your answer.

Either

2 'It is a fact that…'

   How far do you agree with this view?   (40 marks)

Or

3 'Common sense would suggest that…'

   How reasonable do you consider this judgement to be?   (40 marks)

The whole unit is about putting together an 'S/A/B/C' argument. The four texts will give you much — but not all — of the evidence that you will need. They may be in the form of:

- bullet-pointed factual statements from a website
- a piece of news or reportage
- an article from the 'comment' section of a newspaper
- an extract from a book

To mount a really persuasive argument in Section B of the paper in particular, you will need to be able to draw on evidence, examples and experience of your own. Remember, it is the *Ex* for examples that makes a response *sExy* and half-way *Ex*citing to read. Examples/evidence are what will **power** your argument.

What follows are five examples of a unit test. Each example has a 'Content' section that includes four texts; the first two of these four texts relate to each of the five areas of study in turn. Each example also has a 'Skills' section, which addresses what you need to do to complete sections A and B.

Content

Science and technology

The energy debate

> **Text A**   **A waste of energy**

- The UK emits about 150 million tonnes of carbon each year; it has pledged to cut this by 60% by the year 2050.
- One in five office workers admit to leaving their computers on overnight at least three times per week; this wastes more than £100 million of electricity per year.
- On average, a television is left on standby for up to 17.5 hours per day. While on standby, it uses about 8% of the energy it would consume while fully switched on.
- If we turned unnecessary lights off, 375,000 tons of carbon dioxide would not be emitted, and £55 million would be cut from our electricity bills.
- When we leave dishwashers on at the end of their cycle, they consume 70% of the power they use when they are running.
- When washing machines are left on standby, they use just under 20% of the power used when in operation.
- Televisions, DVD players and other appliances left on standby in UK homes are responsible for 1 million tonnes of carbon emissions.

Adapted from Martin Hickman 'Office workers who leave computers on all night "add to global warming"', *Independent*, 6 October 2006

Science and technology

The ethical responsibilities of scientists

> **Text B**   **Science and the public interest**

The vast majority of papers and articles published in scientific journals are of little interest to the public: they are about obscure matters, or they have no implications of a practical kind.

Occasionally, though, there is a paper that sparks a more general interest, especially when a newspaper or television channel picks it up and runs with it. Then the scientific community is asked: 'Why were you keeping this a secret? Why didn't you tell us about this before?' The answer, of course, is often that the researcher or researchers concerned are still cagey about their findings; they aren't totally confident about the data or they want other researchers — not journalists or politicians just yet — to join in the debate.

The UK Freedom of Information Act 2000 makes a useful distinction between research findings that might be 'in the public interest' and those that might be 'interesting to the public'. The challenge to researchers is how to be as open as possible, yet not to be premature in the release of findings and risk misunderstanding of these findings, and even misuse of them.

Science that is publicly funded — where researchers are working in universities or in government laboratories — is one thing; but the challenge is particularly fraught when researchers working for private pharmaceutical companies, or weapons manufacturers for example, are bound by confidentiality clauses in their contracts.

Who owns the findings that researchers come up with? Whose intellectual property are they, and for how long? Researchers have a duty to assess the public importance of the work that they do then — if they do judge their findings to be important — they have a duty to consider, not *whether*, but *when* and *how* they should communicate their findings. They must be sure that their research:

- is accurate, following proper peer review
- has been conducted in an ethical way
- makes clear the zone of uncertainty
- is honest about risks
- takes into account previous results, public perceptions and the 'accepted wisdom' on the subject

Adapted from The Royal Society, *Science and the Public Interest*, at www.royalsoc.ac.uk/downloaddoc.asp?id=2879

Beliefs and values

Nationalism and internationalism

Text C — The United States of Europe

'This is an age of great combinations. The United States was welded even in the lifetime of the older ones among us by the arbitrament of war. People talk in Europe today of a United States of Europe.'

This was Conservative prime minister Stanley Baldwin, speaking to his party in 1929. Already, in 1929, people were talking about a United States of Europe — and this at a time when fascists were in power in Italy, and the First World War Allies were still occupying the Rhineland.

'The first step in the re-creation of the European family must be a partnership between France and Germany...The structure of the United States of Europe, if well and truly built, will be such as to make the material strength of a single state less important.'

This was the Conservative prime minister

Winston Churchill speaking in Zurich in 1946, at a time when the Second World War Allies occupied Germany and Austria, and much of Europe had been laid waste.

It took a long time to re-create 'the European family' — a family that, at the best of times, had been dysfunctional. First there was the Coal and Steel Community, then the Common Market, then the European Economic Community (EEC), then the European Community (EC), and then there was — and is — the European Union (EU). It has a parliament, a flag, an anthem and a civil service. What it lacks — if it is to be anything like a *country* — is a constitution and a president.

A committee under ex-president of France Valéry Giscard d'Estaing remedied this deficiency, in order that the EU should be ready for enlargement, from 15 to 25 members in 2004. Just as Baldwin and Churchill had been Conservatives, so it was a Conservative, Ted Heath, who masterminded the UK's membership of the EEC in 1973 — yet it was the Conservative Party that raised the loudest objections to a European constitution. They spoke darkly of 'federalism', a European 'superstate', and the end of British 'sovereignty'. It

seemed clear that, if Britons voted in a referendum on the constitution, they would vote 'no'.

But, so far, Britons have not been called upon to vote because, in 2005, the French and the Dutch both voted 'no' in referendums of their own. It appeared to most people — even committed 'Europeans' — that the constitution, that the dream of a United States of Europe, was dead.

If the Belgian prime minister is to be believed, it is not. He spoke to the Radio-4-listening public on the *Today* programme in late March 2006, and he referred more than once to 'the United States of Europe' as if it was an about-to-be-accomplished fact. If Europe was to compete in the global marketplace with America, China, India and Japan, it would need not just to *be* a union, but to *act* as one.

It seems we live in an 'age of great combinations' again, but now they are economic as well as political. Britain was one of the Allies in both world wars. Why do we find it more difficult to think of ourselves as one of the United States of Europe, than as one of the states united with America?

Adapted from Middlemass, K. and Barnes, J. *Baldwin* (1969); Heath, E. (1998) *The Course of My Life*

Society and politics

Law enforcement

Text D   **Murder is murder, life means life**

Most people would agree that for a person to kill another person is the most serious of crimes. The crime is now divided into three from the point of view of level of seriousness, and punishment:

1	**Murder**	(a) with an intention to kill
		(b) with an intention to do serious harm
2	**Manslaughter (voluntary)**	(a) with an intention to kill but with provocation
		(b) with an intention to kill but with diminished responsibility
		(c) with an intention to do serious harm but with provocation
		(d) with an intention to do serious harm but with diminished responsibility
3	**Manslaughter (involuntary)**	(a) with knowledge of risk of death or serious harm
		(b) with gross negligence as to the risk of death
		(c) in the course of the commission of a crime

Under the present law, murder carries a mandatory life sentence. That is the theory: in practice, judges exercise discretion in the context of 1(b) offences, so that life may not, in fact, mean life. The following is an example of a 1(b) murder:

John and Yvette have been in dispute over a parking space. Yvette stands in the space to prevent John parking in it. He drives at her quite deliberately, and runs over her foot, knowing that this will break it. Yvette is treated for a fracture but complications set in that lead to her death.

Because John intended to do serious harm, he is guilty of murder and therefore liable to life imprisonment.

The Law Commission, at the end of 2005, proposed that murder with an intention to kill should be reclassified as first-degree murder; murder with an intention to do serious harm and voluntary manslaughter should be reclassified as second-degree murder; and involuntary manslaughter would then simply be called manslaughter. (There would also be some redefinition of 'provocation' and 'diminished responsibility'.)

Thus, John would be charged with second-degree murder, but perhaps, in the event, be found guilty of manslaughter.

Adapted from Joshua Rozenberg and George Jones, 'The jury is out over two-tier murder charge', *Daily Telegraph*, 21 December 2005

Skills

Text A will generally be in the form of a bullet-point list of statements giving facts and figures. Here, the text plainly relates to the fourth question under 'The energy debate': **What scope is there for energy conservation?**

Text B relates to the third question (and to some extent the fourth as well) under 'The ethical responsibilities of scientists': **Ought scientists always to work in the public interest?**

Text A gives rise to a number of possible issues:

- Should manufacturers be required to produce appliances that waste less energy when they are on standby?
- Should appliances not have a standby facility at all?
- Should people be required to turn off appliances when they are not in use?
- How could such a requirement be enforced?

We do pay for all the energy that we waste, of course — but perhaps if we had to pay more, we would waste less. Maybe if everybody *knew* how much they were wasting, they would act.

Text B is about *knowledge,* too: the public's right to know about the content of scientific research papers. The two texts might be brought together in a question like the following:

Wasted energy? — a London office block lit up at night

 Q1a Read Texts A and B and argue that a well-informed public ought to be trusted to make important decisions.

You are only asked to give one side of the argument here. Most of the points you make will come from the two texts, but you will be given credit for any other relevant points that you make. *You may disagree heartily with the case you are being asked to make, but this is not the place to express that disagreement.* You may have a chance to express your own opinion on the issue in the longer answer, to question 2 or 3. You will be given credit, too, for reaching the appropriate conclusion — with reservations or not.

Text C unites the first two questions under 'Nationalism and internationalism': **How far can we transcend nationalism?** and **Does sovereignty matter?** The text gives a little history of the concept of a United States of Europe, and makes reference to the role of a referendum in finding out what the public thinks about an EU constitution.

A *referendum* is a vote on a single issue with a question of a yes/no kind. There has only ever been one UK-wide referendum: that was in 1975, when Harold Wilson asked the British people whether or not they wished to remain in the EEC (as it then was). The vote was a quite conclusive 'yes'.

The issue in 2005 was a little more complicated, and there was some doubt about whether the public knew enough about what was being proposed to vote one way or the other. There are not many questions in politics that have a simple 'yes' or 'no' answer. Much hangs on how the question is worded.

Text D concerns another complex issue: how we define 'murder', and what the penalties for different kinds of murder — or actions that cause another person's death — might be. It addresses the third question under 'Law enforcement': **Does the present legal system ensure justice?**

The public is unlikely ever to be asked to vote on whether or not murder should be redefined (just as the public was not asked whether or not capital punishment should be abolished).

Texts C and D might be combined in the following question, which counters question 1a:

Q1b Read Texts C and D and argue that, in complex matters, decision making should be left to experts.

You will not have written (two-sided) essays in response to the two halves of question 1 in Section A of the paper; indeed, your responses will have been *list*-like. They will have been arguments in the sense that each was a series of claims leading to a conclusion — but it will not have been a *debate*. In these two responses, though, you do have the *ingredients* of a debate.

It is in the response to question 2 or 3 that you will conduct a debate proper: where you will make an opening statement (S), consider position 'A', then consider position 'B', (which has more evidence to support it), before reaching a conclusion (C) that is in line with the original statement.

Remember, the instruction at the top of Section B of the paper is as follows:

Section B

Use the texts, and your own knowledge, to answer **either** Question 2 **or** Question 3.

You may draw on some of the ideas expressed in **Section A** in your answer.

Both questions take the form of statements or propositions taken from, or suggested by, one or more of the texts. Neither statement may be directly related to those argued for in the two parts of question 1 in Section A. *Question 2/3 in Section B is not a mere re-run, or combination of the two cases, of Section A.* It would be rather tedious if it were.

You can reuse some of the ideas that you used in question 1 in your response to question 2/3, but the statements in question 2/3 take us on to new ground — perhaps to other topics within the unit. What we can be sure about is that the statements will have something to do with aspects of **power**.

Here is a possible question 2:

> **Q2** 'It is no good the general public having "freedom of information" if they are not empowered to act upon it.'
>
> How far do you agree with this statement?

This statement does give you the opportunity of rehearsing some of the points made in Q1, but it also gives scope for taking the argument in new directions. If its focus is on any one place in the unit, it is most obviously 'Distribution of power'.

Draft an 'S/A/B/C' response to Q2.

Here is a possible question 3:

> **Q3** 'We ought not to entrust important decisions to scientists and other so-called experts.'
>
> How reasonable is this claim in your view?

This statement reverses the position taken in Q1b. It arises most naturally out of 'The ethical responsibilities of scientists', but the reference to other experts means that we can bring in the judges who featured in Text D, as well as the Law Commission and similar bodies.

Draft an 'S/A/B/C' response to Q3.

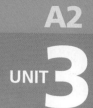

Content

Society and politics

Law enforcement

Text A   **Security, crime and justice**

- According to a recently published government review, *Building on Progress: Security, Crime, and Justice*, crime has fallen by 35% since 1997.
- 6 million fewer offences are committed each year, it claims, than 10 years ago.
- From March 2002 until September 2006, the number of offenders brought to justice increased by 37%, according to the same review.
- A total of 53 law and order bills have been introduced to parliament since 1997.
- Nearly 3,000 new criminal offences have

been created over the 10 years of Tony Blair's government.
- The prison population has risen to a record 80,300 in that time.
- Nevertheless, there is a 'perception gap': two-thirds of the public believe that crime has been rising, when, in fact, crime levels have been falling since 1997.
- To ensure that this fall continues, the report says, 'citizens are asked to accept the gathering of greater levels of information and intelligence'.

Adapted from Henry Porter, 'For Blair, it's child's play to make us all criminals', *Observer*, 1 April 2007

Society and politics

Distribution of power

Text B   **Fools' Paradise**

At the beginning of April 2006, Lord Ashcroft turned 60. Ashcroft was treasurer of the Conservative Party in the 1990s, and is still one of the party's biggest lenders — it was revealed that he had lent the party no less than £3.6 million to help fund its 2005 campaign.

In 1996, at his fiftieth birthday party, he

promised to shift out of the 'fast lane' and to live more modestly in the 'middle lane'. Ten years on, he said: 'I lied. I'm still in the fast lane and intend to stay there.'

Lord Ashcroft is a banker, and much of his wealth has come from banking interests in Belize. It is for this reason that the ballroom of the Grosvenor House Hotel in Park Lane, where his sixtieth birthday party was held, had a tropical theme, and guests were invited to 'Fools' Paradise'.

These guests, some 700 of them, included the whole front bench of the parliamentary Conservative Party. They were entertained by the Band of the Scots Guards, and Jasper Carrott, as master of ceremonies, introduced singers Lulu, Sir Tom Jones and Sir Cliff Richard, as well as Denise Van Outen and television impressionist Jon Culshaw. Dancers were let down from the ceiling on ropes, darts were thrown at images of less-than-popular politicians, tarot cards were read, and a drag artist impersonated the Queen.

When it is considered that some of the artists will have charged fees in six figures, and that guests drank Krug champagne at £700 per bottle, and vintage Pouilly-Fuissé, it is not surprising that the whole affair cost in the region of £1.5 million.

Lord Ashcroft's wife Susi, who planned the whole thing, charged some of it to the account of the Bank of Belize. If this was indeed a 'fools' paradise', one is tempted to ask: who were the fools?

Adapted from Alexa Baracaia and Pippa Crerar, 'The £1m Tory party', *Daily Mail*, 4 April 2006

Arts and media

Media pressure and impact

Text C · Gallows humour

Davis Lucas, 45, sells pet-food from a shop in the village of Mildenhall, Suffolk. In 2005, Mr Lucas saw a photograph of a hangman's noose on the front page of a tabloid newspaper. Being an enthusiast of capital punishment, he had the idea of building a full-size gallows of his own. With the permission of the landowner, Brian Rutterford, Mr Lucas erected the gallows outside the shop.

In May 2006, an undercover reporter from the *People* newspaper turned up at the shop, posing as an official from Zimbabwe. Apparently, Mr Lucas offered the reporter a 'multi-hanging execution system' on a lorry. 'You can get rid of five people at a time,' he is reported to have said. Mr Lucas mentioned to Mr Rutterford that a 'coloured chap' had come to see him from the Zimbabwe government, and was interested in buying a set of gallows. When the *People* rang Mr Rutterford to check the story, he confirmed that he had given his partner, Mr Lucas, permission to erect the gallows on his land. In confirming this, he inadvertently gave the story legs.

The story had no sooner appeared in the *People* than it was taken up by 'more than 30 top newspapers' (according to *The Times*) including the *Daily Mail*, *Guardian* and *Sydney Morning Herald*. Jeremy Vine raised the issue on BBC Radio 2, and commentators discussed Mr Lucas's 'shocking opportunism' in having sold 'mobile execution units' for up to £12,000 a time to Robert Mugabe of Zimbabwe and Muammar Gadaffi of Libya, among other despots. The BBC and Sky News sent camera teams to David

Lucas's pet-food shop in Mildenhall; even Amnesty International weighed in, accusing him of making 'a mockery of the UK's efforts to oppose the death penalty around the world'.

What had begun as a joke had spun out of control. Mr Rutterford understood that his partner, David Lucas, had enjoyed talking to the media about capital punishment, but — to his certain knowledge — he had not sold a single set of gallows to anyone. He had built one set only — the set outside his shop — and all that would ever hang from it was a shop-sign.

Adapted from Rajeev Syal and Ian Young, 'Deadly serious — or gallows humour?', *The Times*, 1 June 2006

Business and industry

Large corporations

Text D   **Foreign takeovers**

JOURNALIST: Surely globalisation is having some very negative effects. Look at the way foreign companies are buying British firms — well-established firms, some of them, household names.

ECONOMIST: Globalisation is, simply, the workings of the free market on a world scale. Potentially, it benefits everybody.

JOURNALIST: How does it benefit Britain when we sell BOC — the *British* Oxygen Company — to the Germans? Or when an Australian bank bids for the London Stock Exchange? Or when a Spanish investment company buys three London airports?

ECONOMIST: They don't take those airports back to Spain with them, do they? They invest Spanish money in them. That's money coming to Britain that was previously in Spain.

JOURNALIST: It's beginning to look like an invasion: Americans buy Manchester United, a Russian buys Chelsea…

ECONOMIST: Yes, and look how well those clubs are doing, and how many millions of people round the world pay to watch British premier-league football.

JOURNALIST: And now Americans are wanting to buy Sainsbury's, which has always been British.

ECONOMIST: You're making it sound like winners and losers — like a chess game. It isn't like that. Safeway was American, but when Morrisons bought it, no one said: that's a victory for the Brits — because it wasn't. We all win when there's investment going into a company. Preventing British companies being bought by foreigners means we'd be refusing foreign investment, cocooning British CEOs [chief executive officers], and letting them run their companies like private empires — a dynamic takeover market is a guarantee of efficiency.

> JOURNALIST: So, if we gain when Nissan builds a successful car factory in Sunderland, we lose when Burberry shifts production to China.
>
> ECONOMIST: The employees in South Wales do, I'll admit — but better that a British company should make profits in China than go bankrupt in Wales. It's only when you make profits that you can afford to make investments; it's only when you invest that you put money to work — that you grow the economy.
>
> JOURNALIST: Yes, but is it the *British* economy that's growing? If Americans buy Sainsbury's, it's the American economy that's growing.
>
> ECONOMIST: Not so. It doesn't matter where the person comes from who signs the cheque; it's where the person comes from who cashes it that matters.

Adapted from James Surowiecki, 'Foreign lesions', *Guardian*, 18 March 2006

Skills

The first two texts here are from the 'Society and politics' area of study. Of the four questions under 'Law enforcement' in the specification, perhaps it is the fourth: **How might we deter, punish, and rehabilitate criminals?** that is the focus of Text A. If crime levels are falling, and more offenders are being brought to justice, maybe we can claim to be deterring would-be criminals. With a record number of offenders in prison, we can certainly be said to be doing more punishing. However, reoffending rates would suggest that we are doing little to rehabilitate offenders.

Two questions that seem to arise from this text are:

- Do we, by creating new criminal offences, create new criminals?
- Why, if crime levels are falling, does the public believe that they are rising?

Inside Wandsworth prison

These are questions that might be worth discussing, although since they arise from just one text, they are not the type of questions that will feature on the third examination paper (GENB3).

Text B might be thought to be either a 'Distribution of power' issue, for example: **What makes for high status?** or an 'Equal opportunities' issue, for example: **How might inequalities be mitigated?**

The *Daily Mail* favours the Conservative Party, yet the authors of the article were quite critical — at least implicitly — of the extravagance shown at Lord Ashcroft's party, perhaps because it shows a Conservative Party that is anything but conservative. The final question: 'who were the fools?' is left hanging in the air. It is one to which there are several possible answers.

Here is a question that might be based on Texts A and B:

 Q1a Read Texts A and B and make the case that justice has different meanings for the rich and the poor.

You may take the view that *civil* and *criminal* justice is meted out in equal measure to rich and poor in the UK, but here you are asked to reflect on the broader, *social* meaning of the term 'justice'.

Text C might be thought of as a comment on the third question under: 'Arts and media commentators': **What is the role of individuals in shaping the news?** Three individuals might be said to have had a role in Text C: David Lucas himself, Brian Rutterford (his partner) and the undercover reporter from the *People*.

Alternatively, or additionally, the text seems to have something to say about the second question under 'Media pressure and impact': **Is journalistic objectivity possible or desirable?**

Did David Lucas 'set up' the reporter from the *People*, or did the reporter 'set up' David Lucas? They both appear to have been keen to create a story when all that there was, by way of evidence, was an elaborate shop-sign. Again, one might ask, who was the fool?

The original of Text D was a long article on a complex subject. The issue has been simplified (it is to be hoped not *over*-simplified) here and re-presented in dialogue form. (One complicating issue that did not feature in the article was whether 'we all win when there is investment going into a company' when the investment is made by a private equity firm. But this is, perhaps, not a matter that need concern us as students or teachers of General Studies.)

Text D, most obviously, has to do with the third question under 'Large corporations' in the specification: **What are the benefits and drawbacks of globalisation?**

Here is a question that might be based on Texts C and D:

 Q1b Read Texts C and D and make the case that justice will be served when there is a free flow of money and ideas.

This is not exactly the contrary of Q1a — the 'A' and 'B' sides of an argument may not always diametrically oppose each other; they may be different angles on the issue. Q1b certainly presents a different point of view from that expressed in Q1a — indeed, it may well be the point of view that Lord Ashcroft from Text B would adopt.

Remember, *all questions should be answered in continuous prose.* This does not mean that the responses to questions 1a and 1b in Section A are expected to be fully fledged essays. However, it does mean that if you jot down items that you think ought to be included in the responses, and you number these items so as to put them in a logical order, you should then write out the items in complete sentences, removing the numbers.

It *is* expected that the responses to questions 1a and 1b will be based largely on the two pairs of texts, respectively.

It is in response to question 2 or 3 in Section B that it is hoped that you will provide material not found in the texts.

Here is a possible question 2:

 Q2 To what extent do you agree that: 'In a free society, it is right that individuals and companies should be free to accumulate wealth'?

To answer this question, you might draw in particular on Texts B and D. It is important that you bear in mind that the question is about both *individuals* and *companies* — so both should feature in your answer.

The likelihood, but by no means the requirement, is that your response will be: [A] yes, it is right, because... [B] But...

Draft an 'S/A/B/C' response to Q2.

Here is a possible question 3:

> **Q3** 'If there is a gap between reality and the public perception of reality, it is the press that is to blame.'
>
> How far is this judgement a reasonable one?

The question arises from the reference to a 'perception gap' in Text A. Texts B and C — particularly the latter — are also relevant. But you ought to be able to cite a case of press misrepresentation from beyond the texts, as well as to name other agents of misperception.

Draft an 'S/A/B/C' response to Q3.

Example 3

Content

Arts and media

Arts and media commentators

Text A — **Reality television**

- After 7 or 8 years of *Big Brother*, television critics assert that the series has run its course; it is running out of ideas, and its popularity is flagging.
- In spite of what the critics say, between 5 and 6 million viewers are still tuning in to *Big Brother* at peak time — that is, at least one quarter of the available audience.
- In the 2006 edition it cost 50p to use a landline to vote a housemate off the show. When producers changed the rules to allow evicted housemates to return, 2,700 viewers complained to the television regulator.
- The net worth of bets taken on the 2005–06 *Big Brother* series was estimated at £6 million.
- 15% of the votes cast in August 2006 might have been through company phones, in company time. This would have cost business something like £510,000.
- Media regulator Ofcom received 33,000 complaints following 'racist' remarks by Jade Goody directed at Bollywood star Shilpa Shetty on *Celebrity Big Brother* in January 2007.
- Carphone Warehouse, which had sponsored *Celebrity Big Brother* since 2003, withdrew its £3 million sponsorship. Channel 4 relies on revenue from business to finance the series.

Adapted from articles by Mark Lawson, *Guardian*, 19 August 2006, and by Elizabeth Judge and others, *The Times*, 19 January 2007

Arts and media

Art as empowerment

Text B — **Art comes to Castleford**

Castleford is a town near Wakefield in West Yorkshire that was once dominated by coal mining and the manufacture of glass and pottery. These industries are now history. How was Castleford to reinvent itself? It did so by involving its 40,000 inhabitants in decisions concerning big, local art and design projects. It *empowered* them.

The sculptor Henry Moore was born in Castleford. It was only natural, therefore, that the redesigned town square should be named after him. The French artist, Pierre Vivant, who has been commissioned to install an artwork in the square, is just one of a number of international artists who have come to work in Castleford.

The town was chosen from among 100 to be the recipient of major arts funding as well as the subject of a series of programmes on Channel 4. It was considered vital that local people should not merely assent to hosting the works of renowned artists but that they should contribute artworks of their own. It was no small matter for people whose livelihood had disappeared to pick themselves up again and look ahead with confidence.

Artists Wolfgang Winter and Berthold Hörbelt created a vast sculpture out of shipping containers and bottle crates, called *Cratehouse for Castleford*. Their aim was to 'open people's eyes to the fact that art is an important vehicle to increase the quality of life'. It did not meet with

Cratehouse for Castleford

universal approval, but at least the approval of the people of Castleford was sought; and it is a landmark, in an important sense, *owned* by the townspeople, as a result.

The town centre, the *Cratehouse*, a new bridge over the Aire, an art gallery, a heritage centre, and new retail and leisure complexes promise to raise awareness of art's power to revive and refresh, long after the Channel 4 camera crews have moved on.

Adapted from: www.idea.gov.uk/idk/core/page.do?pageId=5901137 (accessed February 2007)

Science and technology

The ethical responsibilities of scientists

Text C   Whose pain?

Dr Richard Ryder, former chairman of the RSPCA Council, has argued that 'pain is the one and only true evil'. Whether our behaviour towards others is moral or not depends ultimately on whether or not it causes, or alleviates, pain.

The question here is whether 'others' includes

animals or not. Ryder is adamant that it does: 'All animal species can suffer pain and distress,' he says. 'Animals scream and writhe like us: their nervous systems are similar and contain the same bio-chemicals that we know are associated with the experience of pain in ourselves.' For this reason, he says, there is no *moral* justification for treating animals any differently from the way in which we treat members of our own species.

We know that we cause animals pain when we experiment on them in science laboratories. Thus, 'an animal in a toxicity test, poisoned with a house-hold product, may linger in agony for hours or days before dying'. We know this, yet we conduct 2.7 million experiments on live animals in the UK every year.

We cause these animals pain — we exploit them — because 'the simple truth is that we are more powerful than they are,' Ryder claims.

A rather less than simple truth is that we have inherited the view that human animals are more significant than non-human animals. We accept the lesser evil of causing pain to animals in scientific experiments, in order to prevent the greater evil of pain in humans. This view, on the analogy of racism and sexism, Ryder calls 'speciesism'.

Experiments on live animals — or vivisection — have been much in the news lately. This is partly because of the ongoing campaign of the Animal Liberation Front (ALF) against the work of Huntingdon Life Sciences, in the UK and the USA; and partly because of the building of a new research centre in Oxford. The ALF threatened a 'campaign of devastation' against virtually everyone associated with the centre or with the university.

All major advances in medicine have come about because of experiments with live animals. Indeed, so important is it that any new drug or treatment be tested on live tissue before it is applied to humans, that such a drug or treatment must be tested on two live mammals, by law, before it is tested on human volunteers.

All such tests have been subject to a strict code of ethics since 1831, and the 1986 Animals Act imposed tougher standards for UK laboratories than those applied anywhere else in the world. Thus, only the minimum number of animals must be used. These must not include great apes, and experiments may only involve more developed mammals — cats, dogs and primates, for example — in exceptional circumstances (in less than 0.5% of cases). Of all tests on animals, 84% are done on mice and small rodents bred for the purpose. A MORI poll found that 75% of the population support vivisection in medical research.

Laurie Pycroft, 16, launched the aptly-named Pro-test campaign in response to the threats of the ALF and another anti-vivisection group 'Speak'. Pro-test gives its backing to the Oxford research centre on the grounds that 'Animal testing saves lives'.

Information from the *Guardian*, 6 August 2005 and 7 March 2006

Beliefs and values

Attitudes towards authority

Text D — Argument from scripture

There are still believers in God who base their belief on what they call the 'evidence' in the Bible. The book has been handed down to them as the 'Word of God', and therefore as The Truth, and they have accepted it as such without asking the obvious questions, like: Who wrote it? Why? and When? They would ask these questions of any other book before they committed themselves to accepting it as 'true', so why don't they ask them of the Bible?

Biblical scholars since the early 1800s, particularly in Germany, have pointed out that the books of the Bible — indeed, different chapters, even different verses of the books of the Bible — were written by many authors, over many generations, who had heard the stories from the mouths of many story-tellers before them. The stories were told, and finally written down, and copied, recopied, edited, and altered, by one set of men to demonstrate that the Jews were God's chosen people, and by another set of men to demonstrate that Jesus was God's son, who was sent to offer hope of forgiveness for sins and a new life to non-Jews as well. They were men with a mission, not historians with an eye for detail.

It is not surprising, therefore, that Matthew, for example, traces the descent of Joseph, the father of Jesus, from King David through 28 generations, while Luke presents us with a genealogy consisting of 41 generations — and there is only a handful of (common Jewish) names occurring in the two lists. These are two men, not living far apart in time, who both wanted to prove something about the respectability of Jesus's parentage, presenting us with 'evidence' that is close to being worthless.

So much for any literal reading and understanding of the Bible. So much for its being a 'true' record of events — the unimpeachable word of God. And Matthew and Luke are only two of the four gospel-writers whose books survived the editorial process: Bartholomew's didn't, and nor did the gospels of Philip, Nicodemus, Thomas and Peter. Even the Church feared to multiply the 'authorities' to whom it would appeal.

Adapted from Dawkins, R. (2006) *The God Delusion*, Bantam Press

Skills

In this example, the first two texts come from the 'Arts and media' area of study. Text A is a collection of items from two articles, focusing on the shows *Big Brother* and *Celebrity Big Brother*. The text responds in some measure to the first question under 'Arts and media commentators': **What contribution do critics make to the arts?** (although, admittedly, it may be stretching the definition of 'arts' in this case).

It also, in some measure, responds to the third question under 'Media pressure and impact': **Are print and broadcast media sufficiently open to complaint?** Certainly, there was a good deal of complaint about the showing of *Celebrity Big Brother* on Channel 4 on 18 January 2007, when Jade Goody made a slighting reference to pappadoms in connection with Bollywood star Shilpa Shetty. Government ministers voiced their disquiet, and Gordon Brown, in India at the time with prime minister Manmohan Singh, had to field questions about the show at a press conference.

Channel 4 is also involved in Text B. The text goes some way to addressing the question: **How important is art to our identity?** In this case, it is the identity of ex-mining town Castleford, in West Yorkshire, that is in question.

Here is a question that unites Texts A and B:

 Q1a Read Texts A and B and make a case for saying that we look increasingly to the arts and rely on our feelings to make sense of our lives.

The two key words here are *arts* and *feelings*: the 'soft' or 'emotional', side of ourselves. It is a bold claim, but one that should not be too difficult to support.

Text C presents two sides of a debate in answer to the first question under 'The ethical responsibilities of scientists': **What place do animals have in scientific research?** A case is made for and against animal testing. The original texts go back to 2005 and 2006, but the issue has not changed since then. There are still no easy answers.

It might be instructive to draw up a table like the one below to see what your current knowledge and beliefs are on the subject. Following a re-reading of the text, the table might then be added to, or amended.

Animal testing	
For	**Against**

Text D is loosely based on a reading of pages 92–97 ('The argument from scripture') in Chapter 3 of Richard Dawkins's book *The God Delusion* (2006). The passage goes some way towards answering the second question under 'Beliefs and values: attitudes towards authority': **To what extent do we still appeal to authority in argument?**

It is Dawkins's view that religious believers (certainly those following the religions of 'The Book': Judaism, Christianity and Islam) appeal to the authority of scripture. In other words, they will try to clinch an argument about what is right or wrong by saying 'According to the Law of Moses...', or 'Matthew's Gospel says...', or 'It is written in the Qur'an that...'

We appeal to authority in argument when we seek support for a position from:

- an ancient text
- a post-holder set 'above' us (for example, the Pope)
- a recognised expert

Richard Dawkins himself, a zoologist, is appealed to as a 'recognised expert' in the field of evolutionary biology by other writers in this field.

Here is a question that unites Texts C and D:

 Q1b Read Texts C and D and make a case for saying that we look increasingly to the hard evidence of science to make sense of our lives.

This question runs almost diametrically counter to Q1a: the 'soft' arts and the 'hard' evidence of science are set in opposition to each other.

Of course, neither of the cases made in Q1a and Q1b is persuasive on its own. We make 'sense' of our lives in both creative-emotional *and* rational-scientific ways.

We live emotionally:	We live rationally:
when we take a sick dog to the vet's and pay more money to save him than we give to Save the Children.	when we take the train into town because the fare is less than a car-parking fee.
when we 'drown our sorrows' following the break-up of a long-standing relationship.	when we stop smoking because our doctor has warned us about shallow breathing.
when we fear to sleep in a house that we have been told is 'haunted'.	when we keep expenditure down in order to save for the future.

You might come up with other examples.

You might be able to combine the two cases made in Q1a and Q1b in an answer to Q2. Bear in mind, though, that a good answer will do more than rehearse the points already extracted from the four texts. It will (probably) strengthen the 'B' position with examples from elsewhere.

> **Q2** 'Art is an important vehicle to increase the quality of life.'
>
> This is the view of artists Winter and Hörbelt. How far do you agree with it?

You might agree that art does increase the quality of life, but:

- wonder about the quality of much 'art'
- think of other, more effective, vehicles for increasing the quality of life
- concede that there are other ways of increasing the quality of life, but argue that art is more 'important'

Draft an 'S/A/B/C' response to Q2.

The issue of 'authority', which was not really picked up in Q1 and Q2, might well be the focus of Q3. Although Text D is most explicitly about argument from authority, other texts do have leads about whom we might trust — on whose findings and judgement we might, or might not, choose to rely.

> **Q3** 'In a sceptical age, there is no one whose authority — in any field — is beyond question.'
>
> To what extent do you share this view?

It is open to you to:

- deny that this is a sceptical age, and claim that religious authorities still have the last word
- accept that no one has all the answers
- claim that in certain fields, and provisionally, there are authorities whose judgement can be trusted implicitly

A judicious combination of the second and third options is probably the safest route. It is difficult to think of anyone who might be said to have *all* the answers.

Draft an 'S/A/B/C' response to Q3.

Content

Business and industry

Free trade, fair trade

Text A — The British chocolate market

- The annual British chocolate market is worth more than £4 billion.
- Easter alone accounts for something like £440 million of this total.
- The Co-op was the first big retailer to sell fair trade food, starting with Cafédirect in 1992.
- Now all the major supermarkets stock fair trade products.
- Divine Chocolate is the biggest producer of fair trade chocolate in the UK. Comic Relief and The Body Shop were behind its founding in 1997.
- Ghanaian cocoa farmers own one-third of Divine Chocolate.
- Easter sales of Divine Chocolate rose by 17% in 2006.

- In 2001 turnover of Green & Black's organic fair trade chocolate was £4 million; by 2006 this had risen to £40 million.
- Cadbury's, the UK's biggest chocolate maker, was impressed by Green & Black's 50% annual growth rate.
- Cadbury's bought the company for £20 million, but will continue to run it as a separate business.
- The non-organic, non-fair-trade Cadbury's Creme Egg is still the best-seller in the Easter chocolate market.

Adapted from Fiona Walsh, 'This year's Easter message: go organic', *Guardian*, 15 April 2006

Business and industry

The impact of advertising

Text B — Image building

Of all the efforts by advertisers to build a brand, none has been more controversial than the United Colors of Benetton campaign in the 1990s. One of the first images to cause a stir was that of a priest (dressed in black) kissing a nun (dressed in white), in 1991. In the same year, a white child with silver ringlets was pictured with a black child whose hair had been drawn up into 'horns'. The caption 'Angel and Devil' seemed to reinforce racist stereotypes — but at least the images still had something to say about colour.

In 1992, the image of a named AIDS victim, David Kirby, on his deathbed, caused real offence. His grieving relatives, pictured at his bedside, had given their permission, but this did not quieten objections to what was considered a piece of exploitation by the clothing company.

Other disturbing images followed: Bangladeshis wading through flood-waters; migrants on an overcrowded ship; poor black people in a steel container. Three advertisements, in particular, were the subject of a court case in Germany. The illustrated magazine *Stern* published three Benetton advertisements depicting a duck covered with oil floating on an oil-slick; children doing manual labour in an economically undeveloped country; and naked human buttocks branded with the words 'HIV POSITIVE'. The Central Institute for Combating Unfair Competition took the magazine publisher to court, in Berlin, on the grounds that Benetton was seeking to exploit 'the misery of the world', merely for the purpose of identifying public pity with the name of the company.

The Federal Court of Justice finally ruled, in 2000, in favour of *Stern*. The photographer Oliviero Toscani, responsible for the 'HIV POSITIVE' image, claimed that: 'With this poster, I wanted to show that Benetton is still willing to intervene, as we stand up against the exclusion of AIDS patients with the same force as against racism.' Whatever the court might have thought of the advertisements, it upheld the right of publishers to publish them on grounds of the 'free exchange of ideas'.

It must remain a matter of critical, not legal, judgement whether Benetton's campaign in any way violated the human dignity of children, of the poor, and of AIDS patients.

Based on information at **www.bundesverfassungsgericht.de** and **www.benettongroup.com**

Society and politics

Equal opportunities

Text C   Teaching equality

JOURNALIST: The Equal Opportunities Commission has been replaced by the Commission for Equality and Human Rights. The chief executive of this new equality watchdog is Nicola Brewer.

Now, we understand that it's your belief that children should be taught from a quite young age that they shouldn't discriminate against ethnic minorities, women, the disabled, and gays and lesbians. But can all discrimination be avoided?

BREWER: If kids come up against discrimination at school, it can have a multiple negative effect later on. What kids learn about how to get on with people who are different from them is hugely important.

JOURNALIST:	There has been a lot of anti-discrimination legislation in recent years, though, hasn't there? This must have had its effects.
BREWER:	Most people today believe that racism and sexism are unacceptable…
JOURNALIST:	But you worry that discrimination against older people, disabled people, homosexuals isn't dealt with…
BREWER:	Some forms of discrimination are like drink-driving; you know you definitely shouldn't do it. But other forms are like speeding, where people tend to do it if they think they can get away with it; even if people know it's wrong, they don't regard it as illegal.
JOURNALIST:	The view that equality should be taught to young children in school has caused concern in some quarters. Andy Hibberd is co-founder of the Parent Organisation.
HIBBERD:	I've got two young children under the age of 10 and I honestly don't believe that they understand what racism, homophobia or homosexuality is. I don't think that they need to be taught something they don't yet understand.
JOURNALIST:	On the other hand, it should be said that Brewer's comments have been welcomed by anti-discrimination charities like PeaceMaker, which campaigns against racism in the playground.

Adapted from Jamie Doward and Helen McKenna, 'Give young pupils lessons in equality', *Observer*, 1 April 2007

Science and technology

Medicine and health

Text D — Prevention is better than cure

School dinners used to be thought of as the means by which we could ensure that children from poorer homes had at least one substantial meal in the day. Some schools even run breakfast clubs so that all children have some sustaining food in their stomachs at the beginning of the school day. Concerns have been expressed about the sweet or salty snacks that children bring with them, or buy on their way, to school; and many schools have terminated contracts with the suppliers of food and drinks vending-machines.

At last — and thanks in part to pressure applied by 'Naked Chef' Jamie Oliver and dinner-lady Nora Sands — we are paying some attention to what children eat at school. Oliver concerned himself with school dinners. Nutritionist Yvonne Bishop-Weston has some advice concerning what parents should be putting in children's lunchboxes: 'Kids should be eating more anti-oxidant-rich fruit and vegetables.'

Wholegrain carbohydrate food — for example, rice, bread and wholemeal pasta —

is necessary for fibre; and B vitamins can be obtained from wholemeal bread, yeast extract and fortified cereals. Wholegrain food of this sort will give children some immunity from illness and help to build their bones.

Proteins are vital for tissue repair and for the nervous system. Among the best sources of protein are beans and pulses, nuts, seeds and good-quality white (chicken or turkey) meat. Fish is another good source, and oily fish are rich in omega 3 and 6 fatty acids which are good for the skin, the heart and the brain.

'Meanwhile,' says Bishop-Weston, 'kids should avoid sugary and salty foods, deep-fried food, excess saturated fats from red meat and dairy products, processed and hydrogenated fats, additives and preservatives.'

A well-balanced packed lunch is the best means of ensuring that children have the nutrients they need to see them through the school day, and to establish in them the habit of healthy eating.

Adapted from http://health.uk.msn.com/family/parenting/article

Skills

The first two texts come from the fourth area of study: 'Business and industry'. (It should be noted again that, while it is the case in this book that Texts A and B are from the same area of study, this will not necessarily be the pattern adopted in assessment units.)

Text A is about free trade and fair trade, and it is most obviously relevant to the third question under this heading: **Is international trade fair to small producers?** It would appear to suggest that:

- International trade has not been fair to small producers in the past.
- The market for fair trade products is growing.
- Fair trade companies might find themselves attracting the attention of big (hitherto *un*fair trade) producers.

Text A features one well-known and one less well-known brand of chocolate; Text B features one very famous brand (United Colors of Benetton) that came close to being infamous in the 1990s for its advertising campaigns.

Text B most obviously addresses itself to the first indicative question under 'The impact of advertising': **How are images and motifs used in advertising?**

It also relates to the second and third questions under this heading, as well as to the first question under 'Large corporations': **How is corporate identity established?**

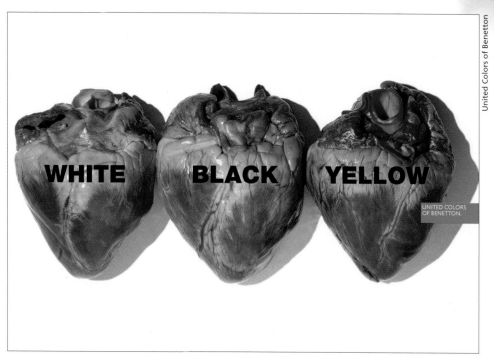

Benetton 'Hearts' campaign, March 1996

Before addressing Q1, which unites these two texts, it might be worth thinking about some of the issues raised by Text B. The images concerned, as well as others, can be viewed on the Benetton website, **www.benettongroup.com**.

- What might have been the objections to the priest and nun image?
- The caption 'Angel and Devil' appears on the website (it might not have featured on the advertisement itself). Is it apt?
- Why do you think the David Kirby image caused offence?
- Do you accept the objectors' view that Benetton was exploiting the disadvantaged merely to build its brand; or do you accept Benetton's explanation that it genuinely wished to campaign against injustice?

Where this last question is concerned, much might depend on what we know about what Benetton did with its profits in the 1990s.

 Q1a Read Texts A and B and support the claim that big companies have too much power.

This question is not very different from the corresponding question in the specimen assessment unit on the AQA website.

It is open to you to refer to companies other than those (Cadbury's and Benetton) referred to in Texts A and B, and, therefore, to other aspects of corporate power.

Texts C and D both relate to children in school — hence the thrust of Q1b, which is not the simple opposite of Q1a.

Text C goes some way to addressing the question, under 'Equal opportunities': **Is true equality of opportunity achievable?** It raises some interesting suggestions that might be discussed before Q1b is answered:

- Is legislation against sexism and racism actually working?
- Can 'anti-discrimination' be taught in school?
- Should young children be taught that we are all equal?

It is worth teasing out the difference between *equality* (meaning: we are all the same) and *equality of opportunity* (in this case, perhaps, meaning: equality of respect).

Text D, under 'Medicine and health', relates (in both cases, loosely) to the questions: **Is all illness preventable?** and **Is our health in our minds, or in our genes?**

Healthy food is, of course, a good long-term insurance against ill-health, and what are called 'eating disorders' are very much 'in the mind' — though research suggests that there may be *some* genetic predisposition to obesity.

Similar questions arise in relation to Text D as above:
- Can healthy eating habits be taught in school?
- Should schools concern themselves with the contents of children's lunch-boxes?

Behind Q1b there lurks the familiar complaint that we live in a 'nanny state'.

 Q1b Read Texts C and D and support the claim that certain groups and individuals have too much power to interfere in schools.

Note that this question also relates to a question under 'Distribution of power': **What checks are there on the power of particular institutions, groups and individuals?**

You could argue that in a democracy, schools are accountable to society, not merely to government, and that education policy should therefore be open to scrutiny and comment by informed outsiders. You could equally argue the opposite.

Whether the focus is on influencing young minds, or on the minds of all of us, all four texts have something to do with the extent to which we are susceptible to influence — and, in particular, to the influence of advertisers and advertising.

The fourth question under 'The impact of advertising' is an interesting one: **How far is public information influenced by advertising?** This may seem like a preposterous or 'scare-mongering' suggestion at first, but consider:

- the dependence of much print and broadcast media on advertising and commercial sponsorship (remember Carphone Warehouse sponsoring *Celebrity Big Brother*, as described in Example 3, Text A on p. 160)
- the advertising-style 'spin' to which much information issued from government and political parties is subject
- the marketisation of public institutions and services — for example, contracted-out sectors of the NHS and sponsorship of city academies
- the privatisation of 'security services' and prisons, and the commercialisation of aspects of school and college external examinations

Here is a question on this theme:

Q2 'We have allowed advertisers to exert too much influence on the way we think.'

How reasonable is this claim in your view?

The claim is not very different from the claim that 'we live in a consumer society'. Texts A and B and, to a lesser extent, D should supply ideas to answer this question.

In position 'A', you could concede that 'advertising is everywhere', and not least on the clothing that we wear. In position 'B' you could point out that one can watch and listen to BBC programmes, read books instead of magazines, and live in the country, and therefore be confronted by few advertisements. Alternatively, you could turn these arguments around, and accept the claim as it stands.

Draft an 'S/A/B/C' response to Q2.

Q3 'Pressure groups and concerned individuals are a necessary counterweight to the power of politicians and big business.'

How would you support this claim?

Few people would actually want to say: 'In a democracy, all the power must be in the hands of politicians and big companies' — hence the bias in the question. You are expected to support the claim, and several 'pressure groups and concerned individuals' are referred to in Texts A–D. You would also be expected to refer to a few others.

What might you say in a brief paragraph 'A'? Although there must be space in a democracy for voices other than those of politicians and chief executives, it is nevertheless necessary that we leave much of the talking and deciding to our elected representatives. We probably do not need to make special provision for business people; they seem to manage to make their voice heard well enough as it is.

Draft an 'S/A/B/C' response to Q3.

Content

Beliefs and values

Rights and responsibilities

| Text A | DNA databases |

- The UK has the biggest DNA database of its citizens in the world.
- It contains 3.1 million samples, more than 5% of the total UK population.
- The police have the right (according to a law passed in 2003) to take and retain a DNA sample from anyone who is arrested.
- Nearly 125,000 of the samples are of people who were released without charge or caution.
- Non-whites account for 24% of the samples, even though the non-white population is 8%.
- DNA profiles of about 24,000 young people, aged 10–18, are on the database, though they have not been charged with any offence.

DNA databases: Europe and North America		
	Population (millions)	**Total on database**	**Proportion (%)**
UK	59.8	3,130,429	5.23
Austria	8.1	84,379	1.04
USA	298.4	2,941,206	0.99
Switzerland	7.4	69,019	0.93
Finland	5.2	32,805	0.63
Estonia	1.5	7,414	0.49
Germany	82.4	366,249	0.44
Slovenia	2.0	5,782	0.29
Hungary	10.2	28,278	0.28
Canada	32.3	75,138	0.23
Croatia	4.6	10,744	0.23
France	59.3	119,612	0.20

(continued)	DNA databases: Europe and North America		
	Population (millions)	**Total on database**	**Proportion (%)**
Norway	4.5	6,745	0.15
Netherlands	16.1	14,747	0.09
Belgium	10.4	4,583	0.04
Sweden	9.0	6,115	0.07
Denmark	5.5	4,084	0.07
Spain	40.4	2,656	0.01
Portugal	10.3	0	0.00

Adapted from Nigel Morris, 'More Britons have DNA held by police than rest of world', *Independent*, 14 April 2006; table from Home Office

Beliefs and values

Rights and responsibilities

Text B An act of disobedience or of conscience?

Malcolm Kendall-Smith had been a university tutor in moral philosophy. In 2006 he was sentenced at a court martial to 8 months in prison for disobeying an order to deploy in Iraq as an RAF doctor. Kendall-Smith claimed to be acting according to his conscience: he would not serve in Iraq, he said, because he believed the war to be illegal.

Obedience of orders is at the heart of any disciplined force. Refusal to obey orders means the force is not a disciplined force but a rabble. Those who wear the Queen's uniform cannot pick and choose which orders they will obey. Those who seek to do so must face the serious consequences.

We have considered carefully whether it would be sufficient to dismiss you from the Royal Air Force and fine you as well. We do not think we could possibly be justified in taking such a lenient course. It would send a message to all those who wear the Queen's uniform that it does not matter if they refuse to carry out the policy of Her Majesty's government.

Judge Advocate Jack Bayliss

It is right that Flt Lt Kendall-Smith was prosecuted for disobeying legal orders. British troops are operating in Iraq under a United Nations mandate and at the invitation of the Iraqi government.

Spokeswoman for the RAF Prosecuting Authority

Hostility to the war is not just confined to the public at large; many members of the armed forces share their concern and have genuine moral objections to serving in Iraq.

    This case illustrates the legal quagmire that has developed over the government's decision to go to war. The government has repeatedly had to hunt around for legal justification for this war.

Nick Harvey, Liberal Democrat spokesman on defence

Many people believe the war in Iraq was an illegal war and therefore we would consider he was quite within his rights and it was indeed commendable; he believed it was right to stand up to what he considered to be an illegal instruction to engage in an illegal war. We have full sympathy for him and he has our full support. We consider it to be a commendable and moral act.

Kate Hudson, chairwoman of the Campaign for Nuclear Disarmament

From an article by Kim Sengupta, *Independent*, 14 April 2006

Arts and media

Art as empowerment

Text C

The social impact of the arts

A lot of public money goes into the arts — even if those who work in the 'creative industries' would like the amount to be much higher. Is this money well spent? What exactly is the *beneficial* impact of the arts on society?

    One-time minister for the arts, Estelle Morris, answered these questions succinctly in 2003: 'I know that arts and culture make a contribution to health, to education, to crime reduction, to strong communities, to the economy, and to the nation's well-being but I don't always know how to evaluate or describe it. We have to find a language and a way of describing its worth. It's the only way we'll secure the greater support we need.'

    We have largely, but not entirely, moved from a view of 'the arts' as European high culture, to a view that includes 'popular culture' among the arts. John Carey in his 2005 book *What Good are the Arts?* came to the conclusion that: 'a work of art is anything that anyone has considered a work of art'.

    This may be good social democracy but it doesn't help Estelle Morris's successors decide what should be funded, and what should not. The 'social impact' of some art-forms and artefacts will be greater than others; and some will have more impact on one group in society than others. How can we tell which are the most *powerful*, which will have *long-lasting* impact, and on which people this impact will be the most *beneficial*?

    The arts do bring measurable economic benefits, of course, but we all know that this is not really what the arts are *for*, even if we can't always explain what we think they are for. The arts must bring other benefits, if we are to believe several hundred years of art history. The problem for funding bodies and for the creative industries themselves is that there is little agreement about what they are and about what *evidence* there might be for them.

Based on Belfiore, E. and Bennett, O. *Rethinking the Social Impacts of the Arts*, Centre for Cultural Policy Studies, University of Warwick (accessed online, 10 April 2006)

Science and technology

The energy debate

Text D — 'Addicted to oil'

In his State of the Union Address in January 2006, George W. Bush said of Americans that they were 'addicted to oil'. This was not news to anyone, least of all to Americans. But it was significant that the president seemed to be suggesting, perhaps for the first time, that the addiction might be unhealthy, and that it might be unsustainable.

In the past, the message had always been that the American way of life is 'not negotiable'. As Tom Baldwin of the London *Times* put it, in the USA, 'the unfettered freedom of the individual to drive across wide-open spaces is almost part of the Constitution'. The president's own background is 'big oil', and it is no exaggeration to say that the American economy is thoroughly oil-dependent.

Domestic supplies of oil in the USA were slow to recover from the damage to oil refineries on the Gulf Coast caused by Hurricane Katrina, in the autumn of 2005. They were put under further pressure by the ban placed on the petrol additive MTBE, and its replacement by ethanol. This is an alcohol-based product, and refineries were hard put to secure enough of it.

Then there were the petrol price rises of 2006 that affected consumers all over the world. These were put down to:

- the exploding demand for oil in China and India
- the interruption of oil supplies from Nigeria (and the threat of something similar in Venezuela)
- continuing problems with supplies from Iraq
- tensions with oil-rich Iran over its uranium-enrichment programme

Saudi Arabia has been a major supplier of oil to the US economy. China is now the world's second biggest consumer of oil after the USA, so when Chinese president Hu Jintao visited Saudi Arabia in April 2006, it was more than a courtesy call. He was there to cement relations with a country that shares China's resentment against the USA for its criticism of the countries' human rights records, and to ensure that, in the event of any shortfall in the supply of oil, China's needs would be taken account of by the Saudis.

When Americans began to complain that petrol prices had risen on the forecourts by one-third in 12 months, George W. Bush was moved to observe, a touch defensively, that: 'The

American people have to understand what happens elsewhere in the world affects the price of gasoline you pay here.' To Europeans, this was a statement of the obvious. To Americans, who pay less than half for their petrol what Europeans pay for theirs, it was an unwelcome reminder of their vulnerability — and one more of the repercussions of 9/11.

Adapted from articles by Tom Baldwin, Carl Mortished and Richard Beeston, *The Times*, 24 April 2006

Skills

The 'Beliefs and values' area of study is the focus of this fifth example. Text A breaks ranks with previous examples to the extent that a shorter list of facts and data is accompanied by a table of data such as might appear in AS Assessment Unit 2 (GENB2). The format of the sources presented in A2 Assessment Unit 3 (GENB3) will not be uniform: hence the dialogues in Example 4, Text C on pp. 168–69, and Text B in this example, which collects together four quotations by protagonists in a recent legal case.

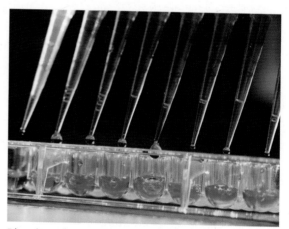

Blood can be tested to determine a DNA profile

Text A, about the retention of DNA samples by the UK police, relates to the question: **How are [human rights] infringed and safeguarded?** The text has rather more to do with an alleged infringement than with safeguards. Is the UK ahead of the world in respect of DNA profiling, or are we setting an unfortunate example for authoritarian regimes elsewhere to follow? Of course, the text also has something to say in answer to more than one of the questions under 'Law enforcement'.

Text B is concerned with the more general question: **What do we mean by human rights?** This text gives rise to a number of sub-questions that might serve as the basis for discussion:

- Did Kendall-Smith give up any rights when he joined the Royal Air Force?
- Was it right that he should be prosecuted for disobeying orders?
- In what sense can what British troops have been engaged in, in Iraq, be called a 'war'?

The last question may seem an odd one, but coalition forces invaded Iraq with a view to confronting the regime; war was never declared *against Iraq*. To the extent that there has been 'war' in Iraq, it might be referred to as a civil war that was an unforeseen outcome of the removal of the Sunni regime.

Here is a question that unites Texts A and B:

> **Q1a** Read Texts A and B and argue the case that we do not do enough to defend our rights.

Of course, this question could have been constructed from the opposite point of view. A case could certainly be made on the basis of these texts that we are over-insistent on our rights that:

- If we want to be protected against crime, we must give the police the tools to do their job (and many unsolved crimes have been cleared up thanks to DNA evidence).
- If we enlist in the armed services, we waive certain of our rights to go where we want and do what we want; we take on a duty to serve and to obey orders.

There may be an opportunity to make these points, or similar ones elsewhere in the unit.

Text C is concerned with the questions: **Does art have a civilising function?** and **Can art change our minds or our behaviour?** The text grapples with the question of whether there is any hard evidence for the arts having any real impact — for their being worth all the public money that is devoted to them. (Ministers do not, apparently, doubt this worth, but their case for funding is strengthened when there is such evidence.)

Text D takes us back to where this unit began: 'The energy debate'. It has to do with both the first and the last questions: **Do fossil fuels have a future?** and **What scope is there for energy conservation?** While it is true that the article is about America's being 'addicted to oil', there are lessons here for all of us in 'the West'.

Q1b is not the exact opposite of Q1a, but it is concerned with 'responsibilities' rather than 'rights':

> **Q1b** Read Texts C and D, and argue the case that we do not always take the responsibilities that we ought to take.

It would certainly be hard to argue that we never fail to take the responsibilities that we ought to take. Do we always:

- attend class?
- earn whatever money we may be paid?
- help in the home as much as we might?
- justify the public money spent on our education?
- treat people with respect, even if we don't like them?
- drive with care?
- exercise our right to vote (if we have it)?

There are several issues that arise from the four texts under consideration, and there are more than two ways of framing questions 2 and 3. The focus of such questions could easily be:

- the balancing of our rights and responsibilities
- how the sciences and the arts benefit the country as a whole
- our rights in the UK as compared with other countries
- questionable law-enforcement measures
- difficulties that have arisen from the invasion of Iraq

Questions 2 and 3 will not often draw on all four texts — and certainly not equally — but one of them, at least, will normally follow on from the issues raised in question 1. So the focus on responsibility in Q1 carries over into Q2.

 Q2 'We can only be expected to take responsibility for ourselves and for our children — not for others.'

To what extent do you share this view?

Is this view a charter for selfishness? The answer will depend upon what we mean by 'taking responsibility' for others. We could be said to be taking responsibility for others when we:

- raise questions about police retention of DNA samples of those citizens released without charge (Text A)
- join the armed forces or the Campaign for Nuclear Disarmament (Text B)
- contribute to 'arts and culture', and therefore have a beneficial impact on society; or when we bid for funding, or do without it, as artists (Text C)
- consume less oil and live more sustainably (Text D)

Draft an 'S/A/B/C' response to Q2.

Q3 takes its rise from 'Rights and responsibilities', but also takes us back to 'Society and politics: distribution of power'.

 Q3 'A government has no rights, only responsibilities.'

How far do you agree with this statement?

In some ways, this question is the opposite of Q2 — or, at least, of the response to Q2. Perhaps the following could be argued:

If citizens have a responsibility to:	Then the government has a right to:
elect a party to form the government	govern according to its manifesto promises
give children a good moral and material start in life	expect parents to do this
pay taxes	decide how the revenue will be spent
defend the country, if necessary by being conscripted	require that those who enlist will obey orders
conserve the planet's resources	legislate to ensure their conservation

A government *may* therefore be said to have rights, even if the points listed above could be reworded so as to be responsibilities. Position 'A' might acknowledge the rights listed above; but position 'B' will probably list the formidable responsibilities that any government assumes when it takes office.

The texts will suggest some of these:

- to justify having a DNA database of its citizens (Text A)
- to ensure widespread public support for ethical military engagement (Text B)
- to support artistic endeavour (Text C)
- to supply energy needs in a sustainable way (Text D)

You will be able to come up with others.

Draft an 'S/A/B/C' response to Q3.

A2

UNIT **4**

CHANGE

CHANGE
Introduction

Both A2 units, 3 and 4, are *synoptic*. This means that they bring together all that you have done so far. Unit 3 is synoptic in that it is all about constructing an argument; Unit 4 is synoptic in that it is about **change**:

- **change** in the nature of conflict
- **change** in geographical space
- **change** in the distribution of power
- **change** — above all — over time

It is an over-arching theme, since there is very little in this world that is not subject to change.

The questions in Unit 4 are as demanding as those in Unit 3, because they are open questions to which there are no right answers. You should be familiar with as much of the content of Unit 4 as possible, but more important than learning content is to be able to:

- think of what is changing in each of the five areas of study: science and technology, society and politics, arts and media, business and industry, and beliefs and values
- identify specific changes that you could give as examples to support the case that you make in your answers to questions

There are three questions on the examination paper, of which you must answer two. Question 1 in Section A is compulsory. This is based on a text that consists of a prose passage of about 450–500 words, and a table of data of some kind related to the passage. Much of the information that you need to answer question 1 is in Text A — but not all of it. You will need to draw on knowledge and examples of your own to answer the question adequately.

In Section B, question 2 is *loosely* based on Texts B and C; and question 3 is loosely based on Texts D and E. You have time (2 hours altogether) to read all four texts, B–E because they are all quite short; but you must answer **either** question 2 **or** question 3.

Again, the texts are mere starting points: read them, and then lay them aside. Draw on your own knowledge, and call up your own examples, to answer the question; try not to be dependent on the texts given.

A challenging paper it may be, but because there are no right answers, and because the questions are 'big' questions, it is also the most stimulating paper. Indeed, perhaps it is the most stimulating paper you are likely to take in any subject at A-level.

As in Unit 3 of this book, what follows are five complete examples of assessment units, each with a range of texts and questions. The five examples of Text A are taken from each of the five areas of study, in rotation; and each of the 15 topics under these areas of study will be represented by at least one of the total of 25 texts.

A2

UNIT 4

CHANGE
Example 1

Content

Science and technology

The idea of progress in science and technology

Text A — **Britain's noisy cities**

The ring-tones of mobile phones, background music in clothing stores, street musicians, the siren of an emergency vehicle, the beeping of a reversing lorry, the hum of a tram, the shouts of children from a school playground: these are all friendly, urban noises that most of us take for granted, and almost wouldn't be without. Indeed, if we have not been listening to the car radio or been wired up to an iPod, many of us — as soon as we arrive home and shut the front door behind us — turn on the radio or television for background music, chatter, recorded laughter and studio-audience applause.

There is a volume control on our domestic communications equipment, of course, but we cannot control the volume of traffic noise — and this is growing. Professor Deepak Prasher of the Ear Institute at University College London worked with Widex, a hearing-aid manufacturer in Denmark, to find out just how serious the problem is. Widex measured noise levels in decibels at points where pedestrians are in close proximity to traffic in 41 towns and cities the length and breadth of England, in October and November 2006 (see table).

The noisiest city in England is not London, perhaps surprisingly: it is Newcastle upon Tyne, a city that with 263,000 inhabitants is only the twentieth biggest city in the country. Birmingham is second, and London third. The quietest towns and cities are all beside the sea: Scunthorpe, the third quietest, Paignton, the second quietest, and Torquay, the quietest — or, perhaps we should say, the least noisy of all.

These values may all seem very bunched, but decibels are a logarithmic index. Thus, Chelmsford, 10 decibels louder than Torquay, is in fact *10 times louder* than Torquay; Newcastle, 10 decibels louder than Chelmsford, is *100 times louder* than Torquay. The traffic noise in Torquay is equivalent to listening to a normal conversation; the traffic noise in Newcastle is equivalent to having a loud alarm clock constantly ringing in your ears.

Admittedly, these readings were taken during rush-hour periods, but in city centres, it seems, rush hours are spreading across much of the day. Noise of this magnitude can have serious effects on health: indeed, they can be quite as serious as the effects of air pollution. Professor Prasher had this to say:

'Noise pollution in towns and cities is a growing problem and can have a serious long-term impact on health and well-being. Noise can raise our stress levels and associated hormone

1	Newcastle	80.4	15	Norwich	75.9	29	Bury St Edmunds	72.3
2	Birmingham	79.1	16	Bristol	75.8	30	Ipswich	71.9
3	London	78.5	16	Blackpool	75.8	31	York	71.5
4	Darlington	78.3	18	Croydon	75.5	32	Eastbourne	70.8
4	Doncaster	78.3	19	Swindon	75.2	33	Oxford	70.7
6	Gillingham	77.8	20	Exeter	74.6	34	Chelmsford	70.3
6	Leeds	77.8	21	Coventry	74.5	35	Reading	69.8
8	Leicester	77.5	22	Brighton	74.3	35	Cambridge	69.8
8	Liverpool	77.5	23	Carlisle	74.2	37	Colchester	68.1
10	Stoke	77.4	24	Sunderland	73.8	38	Folkestone	66.8
11	Manchester	77.3	25	Plymouth	73.6	39	Scunthorpe	66.4
12	Sheffield	76.3	26	Southampton	72.5	40	Paignton	65.7
13	Nottingham	76.2	27	Cheltenham	72.4	41	Torquay	60.2
14	Bournemouth	76.0	27	Lincoln	72.4			

Source: Widex Noise Report

levels. It can disturb sleep and increase the risk of heart disease and, if the noise is loud enough, it can lead to permanent hearing impairment and tinnitus.'

Nine million people in the UK have some form of hearing impairment, according to Pauline Loriggio of Hearing Concern — and once hearing has been lost, it can rarely be got back. This is not the least of reasons why we should act to reduce traffic levels in our towns and cities.

Adapted from Lucy Bannerman, 'Listen up, the traffic noise may damage your health', *The Times*, 2 February 2007, and from letters to the *Guardian*, 3 February 2007

Business and industry

Heritage conservation

Text B   Artefacts and their owners

The British Museum was established in 1753, in the early years of the British empire. Exhibits were imported from all over the world in the course of a programme of what might charitably be called preservation and, less charitably, pillaging.

The most famous of these exhibits were the so-called Elgin Marbles. Lord Thomas Elgin removed the carvings from the Acropolis in Athens in 1801–03, and sold most of them (some were lost at sea) to the British Museum, in 1816. Was this daylight robbery? Or were the Marbles saved from the neglect to which other Athenian masterpieces were subject? The argument about who can be said to *own* the Elgin Marbles, and where they should be *shown*, has rumbled on for generations. Now that Athens has modern museum facilities and Greece is an EU partner, it may be that a solution is at hand, whereby the Marbles are exhibited in an extension of the British Museum, in Athens.

In 2006 the British Museum lent 140 African exhibits to an African museum for the first time. They all came from East Africa originally. Now, as never before, Africans will be able to view their own heritage, in one place: the Nairobi base of the National Museums of Kenya. The director

general of these museums, Omar Farah, would like the exhibits repatriated to East Africa on a permanent basis. By contrast, it is the view of Neil McGregor, the director of the British Museum, that 'Repatriation is yesterday's question.' It is no longer true that objects need be kept in one place. 'The British Museum was set up in order that the collection might be studied by the world to advance knowledge worldwide. With recent advances in packing and transport we can make a reality of that ideal of the Enlightenment.'

What would be truly enlightened, according to many Africans, would be to make reparation for the decades of looting by restoring the artefacts to their rightful owners. One such is the 'iconic Festae Mask, a potent symbol of pan-Africanism', held 'captive within the vaults of the British Museum', according to Toyin Agbetu.

This is one artefact in one museum. Arguments about ownership and access are likely to rumble on for a while yet.

Adapted from Charlotte Higgins, 'British Museum insists that "repatriation is yesterday's question"', *Guardian*, 13 April 2006, and a letter by Toyin Agbetu, *Guardian*, 21 April 2007

Arts and media

New media

Text C   **A life on the internet**

We have become accustomed to 'reality' television, where we watch edited extracts of the house-bound lives of a number of young unknowns, or selected 'celebrities'. Justin.tv is a website that gives us the unedited record of the 24-hours-per-day life of just one self-selected 'housemate', Justin Kan.

Justin is 23 years old. He lives in a San Francisco apartment, and he wears a camera strapped to the side of his head. We therefore see exactly what Justin sees, the people he speaks to, the television programmes that he watches, the internet sites that he surfs, and the view that he has of the world outside — until he takes the camera off and turns it on himself, as he does, for example, when he is asleep.

Kan, a graduate of Yale University, was having a conversation with a friend one day when it occurred to him that others might be interested in listening to what they were saying. He thought: 'Maybe I should broadcast my life 24/7 over the internet. I put the idea to people and they looked at me as if to say "Why would you do that?" But since it started people have been e-mailing to say it's the best idea ever, so I feel kind of vindicated. You can literally live your entire life with me, and I love that.'

Whether or not anyone actually does live their lives with Justin Kan, neither Justin nor his producer and three technicians can tell. Beyond

saying that 'tens of thousands' of viewers every day log on to his site, Justin is cagey about precise audience figures. It is enough for him that he is kept busy replying to e-mail messages, and keeping in touch with visitors to the site's chatrooms, from countries all over the world.

How does Justin Kan make a living out of putting himself on 24-hour display like this? He hangs advertisements on the walls of his flat, and points his camera at them from time to time; and every time he uses a product, viewers 'use' it at second hand. Advertising of this sort can sustain one man's enterprise. It is questionable whether it would fund his ambition to strap cameras to hundreds of other people in the same way.

Adapted from David Smith, 'Share my life on the internet, 24 hours a day,' *Observer*, 1 April 2007

Beliefs and values

Transmission of norms and values

Text D

Moral by nature?

It used to be thought, in the Christian West, that — thanks to Adam and Eve — we were born evil. Only by faith or by good works might we be saved. God and the Devil were engaged in a cosmic struggle to claim our 'souls', and direct us towards heaven or hell.

The idea that original sin was passed on down the generations went out of fashion in the twentieth century. If we did wrong, it was because of where and how we were brought up: it was because of our nurture, not our nature. Psychologists, sociologists and moral philosophers largely agreed that it was our

environment (family attachments, economic circumstances, education) that conditioned us to be moral or immoral, virtuous or vicious.

More recently, there has been a swing back to the view that a moral sense might be 'hard-wired' into us. By analogy with Noam Chomsky's theory that we are born with a predisposition to learn language — a universal grammar — it is now proposed that a universal moral grammar is innate. Professor Marc Hauser of Harvard, for example, has advanced this theory in a recent book: *Moral Minds: How Nature Designed Our Universal Sense of Right and Wrong*. He found that when he presented a moral dilemma to large numbers of people — not moral philosophers — they all, intuitively, came up with the same response: they all refused to do certain harm to one individual, even if that harm might save the lives of a number of others. Not only was the response the same, it was immediate. This suggests, according to Hauser's theory, that our moral sense is intuitive; that it is genetically embedded in human nature.

What do we make, then, of fundamental disagreements about whether meat eating, euthanasia, abortion, gay adoption, stem-cell research, child labour, circumcision, capital punishment, sorcery, incest, fabulous wealth, holy war, burning coal and arranged marriage are morally right or wrong? What do we make of the variations in moral attitude from place to place and from time to time — sometimes (as in the case of homosexuality) quite a short time?

The universal moral grammar is a 'toolkit for building a variety of different moral systems as distinct from one in particular. The grammar or set of principles is fixed, but the output is limitless within a range of logical possibilities,' Hauser says. 'We may be as perplexed by another community's moral system as we are by their language' — but we do all have a capacity to learn language, to talk, just as we do to play and to walk.

Adapted from Joe Joseph, 'Are we born with a sense of what is right?', *The Times*, 1 February 2007

Society and politics

Social change

Source E — Faith schools

City academies are schools that are partly state-funded, and partly funded by business sponsors or voluntary bodies. The individual or sponsoring body putting up the cash has the power to determine the composition of the governing body and the content of the teaching curriculum.

Of the first 100 city academies to be established, 42 were 'faith schools'. The Church of England sponsored 15 of them, and the Roman Catholic Church sponsored four. Seven were sponsored by the United Learning Trust, an Anglican charity linked to the United Church; and four were sponsored by the Oasis Trust, a charity founded by television presenter and Baptist minister, the Revd Steve Chalke. The remainder were the protégés of assorted Christian businessmen and founders of charitable trusts.

Two teachers' organisations, at their 2006 annual conferences, raised concerns about these schools. The Association of Teachers and Lecturers (ATL), in Gateshead, and the National Union of Teachers (NUT), in Torquay, both called for an end to state funding of any further faith schools. Indeed the NUT, Britain's biggest teachers' union, went further: it wanted an end to state funding of faith schools, full stop.

The worry of the ATL was that yet more faith schools would threaten social integration and be 'fertile ground for religious and ethnic conflicts'. Andy Ballard from Somerset spoke for many when he said: 'Schools should focus on teaching kids to be decent human beings. They should take pupils of all faiths and of none in equal measure.'

Elizabeth Green from Wiltshire, on the other hand, said what the spokesman for the Department for Education and Skills later echoed: 'Faith schools have a place in our society and all parents should have the right to choose one for their child if they should so wish.'

Adapted from Richard Gardner 'Faith schools are "at odds with reason," says chaplain', *Independent*, 12 April 2006

Skills

Text A will always be a text of some 450–500 words, together with a table of numerical data, or a diagram of some sort, depending on the subject matter of the text.

The compulsory question based on Text A has this in common with questions on Assessment Unit 1, at AS: that cues are provided as a basic scaffolding for the response. Here, though, the cues are not phrases suggesting issues that might be considered; they are generally single words — three or four of them — defining subject approaches that should be taken. Thus candidates might be asked a question, for example, about consumer debt, or civil disobedience, or artistic tastes, from the following points of view (or others):

- historical
- scientific
- social
- political
- economic
- moral

A good, comprehensive response would normally require that a candidate consider the overall question in each of the three, or four, listed dimensions.

The question may also be, in effect, two questions rather than just one. For example:

- What do you think should be done...and why?
- Should we give access to...and how?
- Why do we...in this way? Might there be better ways?

Text A in this unit addresses (and answers in the negative) the question: **Has technology improved our quality of life?**

Here is the sort of question that might be asked:

> **Q1** If technology is the cause of much urban noise, might it offer some solution to the problem?
>
> For what:
> - social
> - political
> - economic
>
> reasons might it do so, or not?

You have an hour or so in which to present an answer to this question, so you have time to take it to pieces. The first sub-question to ask is:

(i) What technological means might there be of reducing urban noise?

Before answering this question, we need to ask whether there are *social* reasons why any of these solutions might not be adopted. (There are plenty of obvious

Congestion in London, the third noisiest city in Britain

social/public health reasons why they *should* be.) You might come up with the following thoughts:

- People like the convenience of commuting by car.
- They are less keen to use public transport, particularly after dark.
- Urban dwellers have become accustomed to noise.
- They do not realise the effects of the noise on their health until much later.
- Most people live and work in conurbations.

Are there separate *political* reasons why the solutions might not be adopted?

- Most of us drive, so there are no votes in antagonising motorists.
- It would take a bold government to introduce such measures against a long-term trend of commuting to work in urban areas.

Finally, what are the *economic* reasons that might inhibit the adoption of these technological solutions?

- Almost all the solutions are very costly (such as electric engines or anti-noise road surfaces), and the costs would fall on vehicle owners and taxpayers.
- There are few jobs in Paignton and Torquay; we would risk damaging the economy if we intervened in cities in the upper half of the list.

The weight of evidence is *against* the use of technology, perhaps, on the face of it, but there are several good reasons why we may have no choice but to look to technology to solve the problem.

(ii) Why might we have to exploit technology to solve the problem?

We now have the ingredients of a response: the answer to question (i) might supply us with our 'A' case; for our 'B' case, we might look at each of the three sets of reasons why technology might *not* offer a solution. Our conclusion will be that — notwithstanding the difficulties — we may have to turn to technology for a solution.

You will receive credit for any relevant, meaningful reference you make to a specific town or city with a particular problem, or to any solutions that you have heard or read about.

Text B answers, squarely, the question under 'Heritage conservation': **How might there be conflict between ownership of and access to cultural treasures?**

Text C, under 'New media', might be thought to answer either of the following questions: **What are the possibilities and what are the limits of the internet?** or

How democratising have these new [media] technologies been? Sharing Justin Kan's life can scarcely be called 'infotainment', so the fourth question is not really relevant.

A question based on both texts can only superficially reflect either or any of these questions. Here is one possibility:

> **Q2** Text B is about access to the world's treasures in one place; and Text C is about access by the world to the life and thoughts of one man in one place.
>
> How far might internet access be a solution to the problem that most people in the world can get to neither London nor Nairobi?

There is little that will be of much use in Text C, though one can imagine that:

- a guide with a camera strapped to his or her head might take us round a museum, commenting on exhibits
- internet 'visitors' to the museum might give a museum director useful feedback in the museum website's chatroom

The obvious relevant points that might be taken from Text B are that:

- an object that is necessarily kept in one museum, perhaps in one inaccessible place, can feature on several websites
- objects 'captive' in a museum's vaults can be made visible as never before, and to large numbers of 'visitors'

The real question here, of course, is whether looking at an exhibit on a screen can be any sort of substitute for looking at the exhibit in three dimensions. The answer must be, of course, that it cannot — but it is a lot better than not being able to see it at all. And even in a museum, sometimes an exhibit is so 'captive' in a glass case that you might almost as well be seeing it, close up, on a screen — and you would not have to squint at it or bend down to read the label.

Draft an 'S/A/B/C' response to Q2.

Text D has something to say in answer to the last two questions under 'Transmission of norms and values': **Are there moral values that transcend cultures?** and **How might we pass on these values?**

If we are to believe Professor Hauser, we are *born* with transcendent values. They are part of what makes us human; they are a product of natural selection. What we pass on are the values peculiar to our culture — and we do this passing on in the home and the school, in the course of primary and secondary socialisation.

Text E, under 'Social change', specifically relates to the question: **What are the chances of social integration or of disintegration?**

According to two of the large teaching unions, faith schools threaten social integration. Here, two values are in conflict: social cohesion and parental choice — both of them values espoused by government.

Here is a possible question 3:

> **Q3** Marc Hauser lays emphasis on our 'universal sense of right and wrong' (Text D); two teaching unions worry that faith schools might be 'fertile ground for religions and ethnic conflicts' (Text E).
>
> How might schools teach 'kids to be decent human beings'?

This question is about:

- whether there are ideals to which we remain committed
- whether they might be given institutional expression
- how values might be passed on
- the chances of social integration or disintegration
- how far — in schools — we are resistant or adaptable to change

It is not a direct question about 'faith schools', though students will want to express an opinion about these, and will be justified in doing so. It is about Andy Ballard's view that they are socially divisive, and Elizabeth Green's view that they seek to pass on ideals and values to which they are committed. Marc Hauser's idea about 'universal moral grammar' does not contradict either of them.

Are non-faith schools value-free or decency-free zones? Hardly. Quite apart from formal PSHE and citizenship classes, schools have always been communities with rules that define agreed standards of behaviour. You would do well to consider your own schooling and what it has done — or has tried to do — to make a decent human being of you.

Draft an 'S/A/B/C' response to Q3.

CHANGE
Example 2

Content

Educating for change

Text A   **A-level entries and A grades**

In 2006 22.8% of A-level candidates achieved an A grade; this was in a year in which the overall pass rate showed a twenty-fourth successive increase. This gives rise, each summer, to the complaint that A-levels are getting easier, and to difficulties faced by admissions tutors in selecting from among candidates with 'straight As'. It was said, in 2006, that as many as 10,000 candidates who were predicted to achieve top grades might be rejected by Oxford and Cambridge colleges.

Others would say that the success rate is less the result of 'dumbing down' than of the growing pressure on schools and colleges, and on students themselves, to succeed — and more help is given than ever before, by examining boards, by publishers and by teachers, to help them do so.

Maths, in particular, found itself in the spotlight in 2006. At the beginning of the decade, entries in Maths were worryingly low. It was perceived to be a more demanding subject than others and to be out of touch with the times. Ken Boston, chief executive of the Qualifications and Curriculum Authority (QCA), said: 'It was necessary to make changes to A-level Maths to encourage greater participation and progression on to higher education and

employment, and we hope that trend will continue. The changes came about after we listened to the views of the mathematics profession by giving students and teachers a more flexible and manageable A-level course.'

'More accessible' were the words of Ellie Johnson Searle, director of the Joint Council for Qualifications; 'in other words, easier' were the words of Alan Smithers, professor of education at the University of Buckingham. Maths entries were up by 5.8% in 2006, and by a gratifying 22.5% in Further Maths (from a much lower base). Of the nearly 56,000 entries in Maths, 43.5% scored a grade A, up by nearly 3% on the 2005 figure.

Chief executive of Mathematics in Education and Industry, Roger Porkess, insisted that there had been no dumbing down. 'These results are excellent news, and a step towards being able to run a competitive economy,' he said.

In the sciences there was less optimism about Physics and Chemistry: Physics showed a drop of 2.7% over the year, and of about 17% over the past decade. Chemistry has declined by 9.8% since 1991. Biology, however, has grown by 17.8% over the same period.

Similar concern was expressed about the trends in modern foreign languages: though

Subjects going up	% change from 2005	No. of entries 2006	Subjects going down	% change from 2005	No. of entries 2006
Further Maths	22.5	7,270	Business Studies	−0.2	30,648
Media/Film/TV	9.6	30,964	General Studies	−0.7	58,967
Modern languages	9.3	7,009	Geography	−0.9	32,522
Sport/PE	8.5	21,834	Economics	−1.0	17,455
Religious Studies	8.0	18,205	Physics	−2.7	27,368
Irish	7.5	329	Communication Studies	−2.9	2,114
Music	6.5	10,407	ICT	−4.5	14,208
Maths	5.8	55,982	Science subjects	−4.6	4,209
Psychology	5.2	52,621	Home Economics	−8.3	1,087
German	5.1	6,204	Computing	−13.9	6,233

Source: Joint Council for Qualifications

there was some increase in entries for German and Spanish, and a slight increase in French, the numbers of candidates for German have dropped by 42% since 1997, and those for French have dropped by 47%. There was a rise of 9.3% in the entries for modern languages overall in 2006, but this was almost wholly accounted for by entries in Russian, Portuguese, Punjabi and Chinese.

It remains to be seen what the effects will be of a toughening up of A-levels from 2009 onwards, the introduction of more 'stretching' questions and the likelihood of an A* grade.

Adapted from articles by Matthew Taylor and Rebecca Smithers, *Guardian*, 17 and 18 August 2006

Science and technology

The nature of science

Text B   The 'real' world

Common sense has always suggested that how we see the world is how the world is; that there is a direct — indeed, one-to-one — correspondence between the reality of the world and our sense of it. We hear, touch, see, smell and taste things as they actually are.

This is what has made science such a successful arena of human activity: scientists have observed conjunctions of phenomena, connections between phenomena, and developed ideas of a cause and effect kind; they have put their ideas to the test, over and over again, to the point where it could be said that their ideas had been confirmed or negated. Over time, science has accumulated a vast bank of findings that we have come to call facts; and the truth of those facts has been vindicated by the technology that is the product of science — technology that manifestly *works*.

This is, as it were, the absolute view: reality is out there, and science maps it, and logs it, in telescopic and microscopic detail. The relativist view is that reality is socially constructed; that 'facts' are the outcomes of theories, and that theories are embedded in a particular culture — in this case, western, liberal, academic culture. Scientists cannot claim to be giving us objective truth; the most they can claim is that they are presenting us with an effective description of

how things work, and one that succeeds in delivering goods and services and economic growth.

It is true, of course, that none of us *sees* the world as it *really* is: we perceive it — and optical illusions demonstrate to us how we can be deceived by what we think we see. The relativist would say: if we cannot judge with accuracy that two parallelograms that look different in size and shape simply because they have been artfully arranged on the page are, in fact, identical, what chance do we have of being objective when it comes to developing theories about race, gender, the pathology of violence, social structures and other highly charged matters that scientists turn their attention to? The scientist would probably reply that, just as we can be deceived by an optical illusion, so we can be *un*deceived when the mechanisms of the illusion are explained to us, in terms that people from all cultures would understand.

Adapted from ideas in Pinker, S. (2002) *The Blank Slate*, Allen Lane

Beliefs and values

Changing patterns of religious belief

Pope John Paul II

> Text C   **St John Paul II**

Cardinal Wojtila of Cracow, in Poland, was elected to the papacy, as John Paul II, in 1978. As Pope, he created more saints than all his papal predecessors put together. His successor, Cardinal Ratzinger, Pope Benedict XVI, announced that he would not create saints in such numbers.

When John Paul II died in April 2005, many mourners at his funeral carried banners demanding SANTO SUBITO! — 'Saint straight away!' — and his champion, Father Slawomir Oder, claimed that many Polish Catholics in particular already thought of John Paul as a saint. The new pope bowed to this pressure and waived the rule that the process of beatification and — ultimately — canonisation could not begin until at least 5 years after the death of the individual concerned.

To be set on the road to sainthood, the individual has to have led a virtuous, even heroic life. To be beatified — to be called the Blessed John Paul, for example — he must have been directly or indirectly responsible for a cure from beyond the grave (or, rather, from heaven), by having responded to prayers. It must have been a cure, furthermore, that was beyond the powers of mere doctors to achieve. Sainthood is conferred only after a second such miracle has been officially attested to.

The Vatican was already examining the evidence for one miracle, involving a French nun suffering from Parkinson's disease (as John Paul himself did) — when she prayed to the dead pope, she was cured — when news of a second was received. This involved an anonymous man sufferering from incurable lung cancer, in southern Italy. His wife prayed to the dead John Paul and he appeared to her in a dream, assuring her that her husband would be rid of the cancer. To the astonishment of his doctors, a 'marked improvement' in his condition was noted some days later. Within weeks he was a fit man again, and Mgr Gerardo Pierro, Archbishop of Salerno, declared what had happened a miracle.

John Paul II is not just on the road to sainthood, it seems he is in the fast lane.

Adapted from Richard Owen, 'Vatican studies John Paul "miracle"', *The Times*, 4 November 2006

Business and industry

Economic growth

Text D   **Going green**

Concern is often expressed by business that measures taken to protect the environment may have a negative impact on economic growth. There is growing evidence that if we *don't* take measures to protect the environment, the impact on the global economy will be a lot worse. Indeed, action to counteract climate change could have very beneficial effects on the economy, perhaps particularly in the UK.

- According to an EU-funded study, if the UK government were to invest in renewable energy, as many as 200,000 jobs might be created in this country.
- Evidence of this is provided by the solar-energy industry in Germany: turnover in the industry has increased by a factor of 10 in 6 years, and now stands at an annual 3.7 billion euros. No fewer than 42,500 employees now work in

production, distribution and installation roles.

- Switzerland, Finland and Sweden are among the world's highest-performing economies, and these countries are famous for their commitment to green solutions. Sweden aims to end its reliance on oil by 2020.
- If small and medium-sized businesses had taken simple energy-efficiency measures in the summer of 2006, they could have saved £570 million, according to the Carbon Trust, and over £1 billion in the course of a year.
- Thousands of jobs could be created in recycling and waste management, and in insulating the 6 million homes that do not have proper loft insulation and the 9 million homes without cavity-wall insulation.
- Business often overstates the cost of environmental regulation: the motor industry, for example, predicted that it would cost between £400 and £600 to fit a catalytic converter to each new vehicle; in fact, it cost about £40.

There are signs that business may be coming round to the view that environmental regulation might be good for the economy. The Corporate Leaders Group on Climate Change is actually asking the government for such regulation so that it can persuade its share-holders and boards to make the necessary investments up front.

Adapted from David Timms, 'Embracing change', *Earth Matters* (Friends of the Earth), spring 2007

Arts and media

Changing aesthetic criteria

Text E **The beautiful, the sour and the absurd**

Martin White is a dairy hygiene inspector employed by Teignbridge Council environmental health department, in Devon. He also calls himself — or is called — an artist. In 2006 he bought 5,000 litres of fresh milk, worth £1,200, and poured it into two huge vats.

This quickly curdled in the heat of June, turning rancid and green. *Spilt Milk*, as Mr White called his installation, was part of a farm arts project mounted in redundant buildings at Middle Rocombe Farm, Stokeinteignhead, and funded in part by the Arts Council.

The artist said of it: 'I wanted to give an insight into how beautiful milk is, and show how even such a wholesome foodstuff can transform into a toxic substance over time.'

American artists Seth Price and Kelley Walker have reproduced footage of the attempted assassination of Ronald Reagan. The stills are hidden behind a wall at Modern Art Oxford — a wall covered with logos and graffiti — and the video version plays out the president's near-death experience again and again on a small screen. They have downloaded Caravaggio's head of Goliath, and copied it endlessly, to evoke terrorist execution videos.

Antony Gormley, having scattered casts of his own naked body about the beach at Crosby, has now had 31 of them winched into place on the tops of London buildings, and on Waterloo Bridge, in what might be called the ultimate ego-trip. His first London exhibition, at the Hayward Gallery, includes a giant, transparent box, full of fog.

It was never the case that an artwork had to be beautiful to be respected, if it added something to our understanding of the world about us; but why should we be bullied into accepting an exhibit as an artwork that is merely silly?

Adapted from articles by Simon de Bruxelles, *The Times*, 1 June 2006, and Laura Cumming, *Observer*, 6 May 2007

Skills

You will be aware that controversy erupts every year about whether examinations are getting easier: whether the fact that more candidates 'pass' means that standards are dropping, or whether the increase in the number of A grades means that standards are rising. There are no easy answers that will draw down the curtain on the debate; it is a matter of fact, though, that examinations have been designed over the years for a variety of reasons, to perform a variety of functions. Any examination can 'fail' three-quarters of candidates if that is what it is intended to do; equally, it can measure the understanding and competencies judged to be necessary for further study or employment and be designed to 'pass' the majority of school-leavers.

Text A goes some way towards answering the first question under 'Educating for change' in the specification: **Does the curriculum keep up with social and political change?**

The A-level system has been in existence now for half a century, but subjects have multiplied in number, and the content and style of questioning have evolved. Teaching and learning priorities have also changed over time.

The text also has something to say about the second indicative question: **Does the education system prepare students for occupational change?** A-level Maths evidently needed to change; only time will tell whether the change was for the better.

Text A could also be used to answer the question: **In what ways is society resistant or adaptable to change?** Numerous proposals to reform A-levels have been proposed and then dismissed over the years. Which of the following groups have resisted change:

- teachers?
- employers?
- university admissions tutors?
- politicians on either the right or left wing?
- media commentators?

All of them, perhaps, have resisted change at one time or another.

Here is a possible question based on Text A:

> **Q1** Why might it be desirable to reform the A-level system for:
> - political
> - economic
> - educational
>
> reasons, and why might it be undesirable for these or other reasons?

It is necessary first to consider why it might be desirable to reform A-levels for each of the three reasons. It is not necessary to consider why it might be desirable *and* why it might be undesirable for each of the three reasons, in six rather laborious steps.

(i) Why might a political party propose a reform of the A-level system?

Some of the reasons for reforming A-levels that might be called *political* have — naturally enough — an economic or educational dimension. Making Maths A-level more 'accessible', for example, meant (at least in 2006) that more students were entered for it. This, according to Roger Porkess, means that there will be more A-level mathematicians feeding through into higher education, and so into industry — and this will be good for the economy.

One can imagine that similar calls for change might come from physicists and chemists in industry, and from employers in the global economy on the lookout for linguists.

A further *economic* reason for reforming the A-level system is that it is expensive to run. An entry for one student, for one (6-unit) A-level subject, costs a school or college in the region of £72.60 (2007 prices, at £12.10 per assessment unit). When we consider that a student may be entered for three A-levels, at £217.80, it can be seen that the examinations budget for all candidates, across the country, is huge — indeed, it may be bigger than the budget for teaching and learning resources.

(ii) What specifically *educational* reasons might there be for reforming the A-level system?

What one teacher, student, parent, admissions tutor, employer or politician might regard as a desirable aim or reform, another might reject as thoroughly undesirable. In general, any group might *not* welcome A-level reform because:

- There have been too many reforms already.
- There is no consensus as to how they should be reformed.
- The A-level system is tried and tested, and has been found to work.
- Reform always ends up costing more than the system in place.

There is, obviously, quite a lot of useful information in Text A — and credit would be given for drawing on the data in the table as well as on information in the text; but this is a topic that also cries out for reflection on first-hand experience.

The nature of science and the scientific method has always been a topic in General Studies. Text B addresses the first two questions under 'The nature of science': **What do we mean by science and the scientific method?** and **What do we mean by scientific objectivity?**

Pinker defends scientific objectivity against those who say that truth — even scientific truth — is relative to a particular culture in time and place. He would, of course, concede that there is a difference between a hard physical fact about an electric motor, and a soft psychological fact about motivation.

In Text C, we are presented with another sort of 'fact' altogether. Here, perception is all, and what is said to be 'real' is attested to not by any scientific method, but in defiance of science. If the question that it addresses is: **What changes have traditional religions undergone?** the answer seems to be — in the case of the Roman Catholic Church — very little. Looking at the fourth indicative question, is this a case of **religious fundamentalism**? And if so, is it a **cause for concern**?

Here is a question that might be based on Texts B and C:

> **Q2** In Text B it is suggested that technology is evidence of the success of science; in Text C, the Vatican is said to be examining evidence for the claim that the late Pope has worked miracles.
>
> Might it be that scientists take too narrow a view of what counts as evidence?

Your position 'A' might well be that science (or, perhaps, the 'public understanding of science') views the possibility of miracles with some scepticism. Certainly, if miracles were possible — if prayers to a dead person really could affect the biology and chemistry of the body — many scientific principles would have to be looked at again. It may be that some physicists would look askance at a sociologist's 'evidence' for a link between suicide and the decline of religion, or a psychologist's evidence for environmental influences on intelligence. There are still those who wonder whether the social sciences are sciences at all.

Your position 'B' might then be that scientists *have to* define evidence rather narrowly: that facts are only facts because the effects of *X* on *Y* can be demonstrated, repeated and measured rather precisely, and be integrated into what is known already. That science *does* make technology possible is impressive. You might give your own examples of such technology.

Draft an 'S/A/B/C' response to Q2.

Action to protect the environment involves regulation and costs. Business has tended to resist green measures in the past, arguing that they would hold back economic growth. Text D argues that they need do nothing of the kind; on the contrary, there could be many economic benefits from environmentally friendly policies. The text asks us to consider three of the questions on the specification:

- How do we define economic growth?
- Is economic growth [i.e. the old sort of economic growth based on rapid exploitation of natural resources] sustainable?
- How might we cope with retrenchment? [i.e. with lower levels of old-style economic growth].

Text E addresses the question born of public mystification: 'but is it art?' When anything can be art, the question we should really be asking, perhaps, is: 'is it good art or bad art?' However, art critics have not always been helpful when it comes to deciding what the standards might be for judging whether an artwork is 'good' or not.

Text E addresses the following questions under 'Changing aesthetic criteria': Can we be objective about beauty and ugliness? and How otherwise have tastes in art changed?

Here is a question that loosely unites the two sources:

> **Q3** It makes economic sense to go green, according to Text D; Text E, in part, is about an artwork that went green in a quite literal sense.
>
> What effects might climate change be having on our attitudes to what is good and bad?

'Good' and 'bad' are very loose terms, of course: but they carry the sense here of the opposites 'wise/unwise', 'acceptable/unacceptable', even (because the words have come to have a moral meaning) 'sustainable/unsustainable'.

Both texts can be drawn on to answer Q3 — perhaps Text D more than Text E (though there might be legitimate disgust at the waste of 5,000 litres of fresh milk). As always, on all four papers, credit will be given for using relevant source material from elsewhere.

Draft an 'S/A/B/C' response to Q3.

Content

Arts and media

Visions of the past and future

Text A — **Apologising for slavery**

After 20 years of campaigning, William Wilberforce succeeded in getting the UK parliament to debate 'A Bill for the Abolition of the Slave Trade', on 2 January 1807. It had been hard going: there had been considerable resistance to it, particularly in the House of Lords; but Wilberforce (with, successively, Pitt's, Fox's and now Prime Minister Grenville's support) had assembled a sufficient number of members sympathetic to abolition, so that, on 23 February, the motion carried the day by 283 votes to 16. On 25 March the bill became law.

There was a good deal of disagreement in March 2007 about how the bicentenary of the end of the slave trade (but not yet of slavery) should be commemorated. It was right and proper that Wilberforce's own memory should be celebrated, particularly in Hull, his parliamentary constituency; but there was some annoyance, in the black community in particular, that by celebrating Wilberforce the country was being too ready to congratulate itself on a good deed, when it should be hanging its head in shame. After all, a great deal of money had flowed into Britain from the slave trade — Liverpool's prosperity was largely founded on it. Among the beneficiaries of the trade, as one writer to the *Observer* noted, were 'the shackle

manufacturers of the West Midlands, the City banks, the Church of England, the royal family, landed gentry and Oxbridge colleges'.

The Church of England, in the persons of the Archbishops of Canterbury and York and several bishops, called on Prime Minister Blair to apologise for all the harm that was done to the slaves themselves, and for a trade that has poisoned relations between whites and blacks ever since. Tony Blair did not offer a formal apology on behalf of the state, though he did call the trade 'a profoundly inhuman enterprise', and he said the bicentenary of its abolition offered an 'opportunity to express our sorrow that it happened'.

Ken Livingstone, Mayor of London, did issue an apology, however, 'in recognition of the capital's role in the brutal enslavement of millions of Africans and the persistent racism, inequality and discrimination that was produced as a consequence'. He also supported the move for an annual memorial day, using the model of the Holocaust Memorial Day, to ensure that future generations will not forget the great evil that was done.

There was criticism of Tony Blair for not having apologised, in the press and elsewhere, and there was criticism of Ken Livingstone for having done so. The mayor could not apologise on behalf of all Londoners, it was said, because London is a multiracial city. How could Bangladeshis, Somalis and indeed West Indians be said to share the collective guilt? How can any of us, 200 years later, be said to have anything to apologise for, and to whom would such an apology properly be made? A gesture of this sort would be a distraction from people working in slave conditions today: 12.4 million of them, according to one United Nations estimate.

Region of Africa	Number of slaves accounted for	%
Senegambia (Senegal/Gambia)	497,000	4.7
Upper Guinea (Guinea, Sierra Leone)	411,200	4.0
Windward Coast (Liberia, Ivory Coast)	183,200	1.8
Gold Coast (Ghana)	1,035,600	10.1
Bight of Benin (Nigeria)	2,016,200	19.7
Bight of Biafra (Cameroon, Gabon)	1,463,700	14.3
West Central (Angola, Zaire)	4,179,500	40.8
South East (Mozambique)	470,000	4.6
Total	10,256,400	100.0

Adapted from Oliver Warner, *William Wilberforce and His Times*, Batsford, 1962 and letters to the *Observer*, 1 April 2007

Science and technology

Public understanding of science

Text B   Celebrity scientists

In a speech in Oxford, Tony Blair admitted to having been a 'refusenik' at school, where science was concerned. He now realised the importance of science, and scientists, to our long-term future. At the same time, he realised how vital it was to face down opponents who distorted the facts, whose thinking was emotional rather than rational.

He recalled the bruising controversies over the MMR vaccine, the use of animals in experiments, stem-cell research, genetically modified crops and nuclear energy. Part of the problem, he felt, was that the public had not been engaged in the debate about these issues early enough, with the result that misconceptions took hold.

These misconceptions, Blair said, were 'often

born of the most outrageous distortion of fact by campaigners who, in accusing others of a lack of scruple, show precious little of it themselves'.

Science is the best guarantee against journalistic scepticism and public prejudice. It was science, after all, that defeated the campaign against the MMR vaccine — *better* science than that on which the campaigners relied.

Blair went on: 'We need our young people today to embrace science enthusiastically, to realise that challenges like climate change can only be beaten by motivated and dedicated scientists, and to understand that a career in science today is not a life all spent in a laboratory, but has the best business and job prospects the modern world can offer.

'In the nineteenth century, working civil engineers like Isambard Kingdom Brunel were national figures, not for writing about science, but for what they achieved.

'We need our scientists today to be as celebrated and famous as our sportsmen and women, our actors, our business entrepreneurs. Scientists are stars too. This is Britain's path to the future, lit by the brilliant light of science.'

George Osborne, shadow chancellor of the exchequer, pointed out that it was during Blair's decade in power that science had been 'driven out of our schools and universities'.

Adapted from Philip Webster, 'We need celebrity scientists to inspire young people, says Blair', *The Times*, 4 November 2006

Business and industry

Trends in consumerism

Text C   **Shopping around**

We hold on to our worn jeans, childhood soft toys, burnt spatulas and oven-gloves, and we would not be parted from our first paperbacks and vinyl records, yet we discard electrical equipment as we might used ballpoint pens.

It is reckoned that the average UK household owns 25 electrical products: of these, five are thrown away every year. We discard a hair-dryer after about 3 years; a mobile phone lasts about 18 months; and a piece of DIY equipment — an electric drill or sander — might be abandoned after one weekend's intensive use.

What are the causes of this prodigality with electrical goods? One is the fact that they are 'black boxes', cheaper to replace than to repair. Another is the fact that prices have been dropping fast: televisions, vacuum cleaners and DVD players, for example, cost 45% less now than they did a decade ago; and the price of personal computers has dropped by a staggering 93% over the same period. Products are designed to be obsolete after a short time, and advertising persuades us that we need new ones.

'People do like the idea of developing long-term relationships with their possessions,' says Tim Cooper of Sheffield Hallam University; 'it is just that they have been prevented from doing so by industry, which is geared to stimulating a continuous sense of need for change in order to sell more and more.'

The consequence is that we are creating more and more waste. Two million computers are thrown away each year, contributing to a 1 million tonne mountain of discarded electrical appliances that is growing by 5% per year. In the UK, we throw away more consumer products, more speedily, than any other country in Europe — and the UK was the last country in Europe to implement the EU Waste Electrical and Electronic Equipment (WEEE) directive, obliging manufacturers to recycle waste products. This will be a mammoth task, and it will be consumers who will pay for it. Perhaps this will give us an incentive to hold on to our mobile phones and hair-dryers for a little longer than we have done in the past.

Adapted from Lois Rogers, 'Consumer adultery — the new British vice', *New Statesman*, 5 February 2007

Society and politics

Political reform

Text D   Grass roots politics

People say: 'politicians are all the same', 'they're all in it for themselves'; and they refrain from voting in greater numbers. The police inquiry into 'money for peerages' further convinces people that politics is a corrupt business, and that *loadsamoney* is the route to power.

What the inquiry really showed, though, was how all the political parties at central government level have become increasingly dependent on seven-figure gifts and soft loans from sympathetic tycoons. There is nothing new about political donations — the Conservative Party has always been reliant on big business for its funding, just as the Labour Party has always been reliant on the trade unions. What is new is the need for bigger sums of money at a time when shareholders and trade unionists are less willing to subscribe, and when parties at the local level are running out of members.

It is at the local level where what we call the 'democratic deficit' is most in evidence. General elections have to be fought in the constituencies. Leaflets have to be printed and distributed; party offices have to be manned and equipped with phone lines and IT facilities; meeting halls and loudspeaker vans have to be booked…How is all this paid for?

A new pressure group, *Unlock Democracy*, advocates state funding for political parties; a cap on donations to address the perception of corruption; and tax relief on small donations. These are not exciting proposals, but something must be done to revive political activity at the grass roots. This can't be done — and democracy can't be done — on the cheap.

Adapted from James Graham and Alexandra Runswick, *Party Funding: Supporting the Grassroots*, at
www.unlockdemocracy.org.uk/wp-content/uploads/2007/03/party-funding-book.pdf

Beliefs and values

The decline of ideology

Text E   **A crisis of uncertainty**

'Ideology' has been defined in various ways: it might be anything between a particular *point of view* and a *total commitment* to a way of life. The political systems of the twentieth century were ideologies: communism, fascism, socialism, liberalism, conservatism; the great religions are also ideologies of a sort.

Nietzsche declared that 'God is dead', and that truth is defined by those in power. In so saying, he foreshadowed postmodernism, whose philosopher-spokesmen — Derrida, Foucault, Rorty — spoke out against ideologies that pretended to know The Truth. The postmodern denial of certainty appeared to carry the implication that 'anything goes': there is no Truth; there is only your truth and my truth.

Where there is no true and false, there is no right and wrong; where there was moral conviction, there is now moral relativism: *we* don't discriminate against women, but if *you* want to, that's your business. It is not only the Roman Catholic Church that has railed against moral relativism — even the UK Ministry of Defence has expressed anxiety about the trend. It fears that the moral vacuum that relativism leaves will be filled by more rigid belief systems, whether this be religious orthodoxy or political ideology. Liberals, in other words, may be playing into the hands of the radicals. By denying the possibility of certainty, objectivity and truth, liberal intellectuals succeed in making liberalism deeply unattractive in comparison with the certainties of fundamentalism. Even democracy — government by opinion poll — may privilege what is fashionable over what is right.

We are rightly suspicious of dogmatic, narrow-minded ideology, but we should not oppose this with an empty relativism. We would be untrue to our own liberal positions (hard won, most of them) if we did not challenge wrong done in the name of ideologies old and new. To the extent that wrongdoing is relativised, relativism is partly to blame for that wrongdoing.

Adapted from Julian Baggini 'This is what the clash of civilisations is really about', *Guardian*, 14 April 2007

Skills

If we do not (or did not) like history as a school subject, we tend to think of it as a bank of serial facts: names, dates, battles, treaties, Acts of Parliament, inventions and — in this case — numbers of slaves exported from regions of Africa. History is too often presented to us as a cut-and-dried, fully documented record: something done and finished with.

Woodcut showing slaves being unloaded from a British slave ship

History is not like that at all, of course. Just as art is what artists say it is, so history is what historians say it is. History needs facts (or it is prehistory), but facts are only the beginning; history is the marshalling, selection and *interpretation* of facts. That interpretation must be faithful to the facts; it must take probability as near to certainty as possible; and it must accord with what we know already, or present convincing evidence for *reinterpretation* of what we thought we knew.

Text A addresses the first two questions under the heading 'Visions of the past and future' — especially the second: **How and why do ideas about the past undergo change?**

Here is a rephrasing of this question in more specific terms:

(i) **Why might we have changed our minds, and therefore might history have had to be rewritten, where slavery is concerned?**

Part of your answer to the above question might feed into your answer to Q1:

> **Q1** Why might it be a good idea for the heads of states that have committed wrongs in the past to apologise for those wrongs in the present?
>
> Consider why it might be a good idea for:
> - historical
> - political
> - moral
>
> reasons, and why it might *not* always be a good idea.

It is fairly obvious why it might be a good idea for *political* reasons:
- An apology removes a bone of contention between two states, or two peoples within a state; it clears the air (e.g. the Truth and Reconciliation Commission in South Africa).
- It allows the parties involved to 'move on', in a more positive spirit.

It is also fairly obvious why it might be a good idea from a *moral* point of view:
- It might serve as a declaration that the evil will not be repeated (e.g. Holocaust Memorial Day is a kind of annual expression of disgust at the Holocaust, and a reassurance that anti-Semitism is a thing of the past).
- It acts as a kind of moral cleansing or purgative, an act of confession or contrition. It enables people to start again, on a 'clean slate'.

Perhaps it is less obvious why there might be *historical* reasons for issuing an apology.

(ii) Why might it be worthwhile for *historical* reasons, for leaders to apologise for what their forebears have done?

A couple of reasons are given in Text A for its *not* always being a good thing for an apology to be made for what has happened in the past:
- The event(s) apologised for might be too long ago, and might (in the long term) have had some good consequences (e.g. should the Italian government have to apologise for the invasion of Britain by the Romans, in CE43?).
- The event(s) might be too recent, and too near the emotional and political surface (e.g. Sinn Féin might not be able to apologise for the killings of Protestants in Northern Ireland without handing the Unionists a political advantage and a 'moral victory' at the end of 30 years of 'troubles').

Well-chosen examples, as ever, will be what make for a good answer to Q1. Three have already been given:

- post-apartheid South Africa
- Nazi genocide (Jews, gypsies etc.)
- Catholic–Protestant/Nationalist–Unionist conflict in Northern Ireland

Other relevant examples might be:

- US military action in Vietnam or Iraq
- Sudanese treatment of black Africans in Darfur
- Sunni–Shia conflict in Iraq
- Serb oppression in Croatia, Bosnia and Kosovo
- Russian oppression in Chechnya
- ETA killings in Spain
- British injustice towards the Maoris of New Zealand and Australian aborigines

We saw, in Example 2, Text A on pages 196–97, that Physics and Chemistry have suffered a reduction in the number of candidates at A-level; science and engineering subjects at university level have also had problems recruiting students, over a long period. Are these subjects perceived to be harder than subjects like Psychology and Media Studies? Or do the sciences have an image problem? The very existence of a body like Women Into Science and Engineering (WISE) testifies to the long-term difficulty of enticing female students to study these subjects at university level.

Clearly, Tony Blair thought it vital that the general public understands what scientists are up to, in the interests of informed debate; but he particularly wanted to emphasise the attractiveness of science to young people. Elsewhere in his speech (Text B), he said: 'Science today abounds both with noble causes and with glittering prizes: reach out for them.'

Text B most obviously has to do with the question: **How might scientific findings be more effectively communicated to the public?** Blair evidently believed that one way was to make 'celebrities' of them. Richard Dawkins might be said to be something of a celebrity, and much was made by the media of Stephen Hawking's first experience of zero-gravity travel in April 2007.

Text C most obviously answers the question: **How aware are we of the need for sustainability in our patterns of consumption?** The answer seems to be — at least, in regard to electrical and electronic gadgets — that we are far from being aware of the need.

> **Q2** Text B is about a certain resistance to science, while Text C is about an enthusiasm for technology.
>
> Why is it important for the public to understand what scientists do?

The way in which the question is framed suggests that it *is* important for us to know what scientists do — and, perhaps, the point is beyond dispute. Your position 'A', then, will be that it is not important; your position 'B', that it is.

One does not have to know much about science to use a DVD player; nor does one need to know precisely what scientists do when they research the potential of stem cells — the potential benefits of such research speak for themselves. There is plenty of evidence in both texts, however (and plenty more from elsewhere) that ignorance of science may not be bliss.

Draft an 'S/A/B/C' response to Q2.

Text D addresses the first and third questions under 'Political reform': Why does the need for reform arise? and What reforms of the political system appear still to be called for?

The reform called for in the text concerns party funding, and it arises from what is referred to as the 'democratic deficit' (the fact that fewer and fewer people are joining political parties or voting for them), and from the risks attached to relying on individual donors with deep pockets.

Text E is about ideology; about postmodern scepticism towards ideologies; and about the dangers of falling back on an empty relativism. It answers the question under the heading 'The decline of ideology': Is it wise to be suspicious of ideologies? with a qualified 'yes'; with a 'yes...but'.

Are there ideals to which we remain committed? The answer to this question may well be 'yes'. Baggini commits himself to saying, elsewhere in his article, that discrimination against women, homosexuals and ethnic minorities is wrong; it is a 'falsehood', not only here in the UK, but 'anywhere else in the world'. Commitment to liberal values, to what we call an 'open society', is an ideology of a sort.

> **Q3** Democracy may be in decline at the 'grass roots' (Text D), and it may be associated with the belief that 'anything goes' (Text E).
>
> Might the real 'democratic deficit' be that the political parties no longer seem to have firm beliefs about what it is 'right' to do?

This may look rather philosophical, but it is actually a practical question. When one party was committed to keeping things as they were in the interests of the 'establishment', and the other was committed to change in the interests of the labouring poor, an election might have generated some interest, even passion — and it might have been easy to choose between them.

Now, if one party were in favour of meeting the challenge of climate change, and the other were in favour of doing nothing, again, the choice would be easy. But it is not like that. The question is not *whether* to:

- reduce carbon emissions
- improve state education
- maximise access to healthcare
- ease congestion on the roads
- protect the natural environment
- house the homeless

It is a question of *how* to do these things.

Your position 'A' might be that *democracy* does not matter very much; we live in a *technocracy* now, where government is just a question of making things work well. There is some 'truth' in this. Your position 'B' might then be that we do not need *ideology*, but we do need a commitment to *principles*. If the parties share the same principles, perhaps proportional representation and coalition government should be tried.

Draft an 'S/A/B/C' response to Q3.

Content

Business and industry

Economic growth

Text A   **Ecological debt**

We like to think, in the UK, that we stand on our own feet; that we 'pull our weight' in the world, and punch above it. We did draw largely on our own resources in the Second World War (as long as we were able to break the German blockade of our shipping). Even in 1961, we could have been self-reliant until 9 July in any one year.

However, in the present day:

- We could survive on our own resources in the UK only up to 16 April.
- If all other countries consumed resources at the same rate as we do in the UK, we would need the resources of 3.1 planets.

If everyone in the world consumed resources at the rate of the USA, we would need 5.3 planets. Nevertheless, the USA could survive on its own resources until 24 June.

Of 13 countries in the EU, the UK is one of the least self-sufficient, with the Netherlands the least self-sufficient of all. The most self-sufficient is Slovakia: the Slovaks could last out until 11 November, because they are still able to satisfy most of their own food needs and consume relatively little.

Andrew Simms, of the New Economics Foundation, said: 'Our rising interdependence with the wider world is a fact and doesn't have to be a bad thing. But at the moment, the UK is abusing its place in the international scheme of things and setting a standard that is fundamentally unsustainable and cannot be copied without disastrous consequences.'

In 1987 the world ceased to be able to meet the resource demands we make of it on 19 December. In 2000, it was 1 November. In April 2006, it was 23 October; by October

Date in 2006 until which selected countries could have been self-reliant	
2 March	Netherlands
3 March	Japan
13 April	Italy
16 April	UK
29 April	Greece
1 May	Spain
6 May	Switzerland
13 May	Portugal
29 May	Germany
24 June	USA
24 July	Czech Republic
27 July	France
2 August	Hungary
5 August	Poland
17 August	Denmark
27 September	Turkey
1 October	Austria
23 October	The world in general
11 November	Slovakia

of the same year, it was reported that the date had edged even earlier — the world went into ecological debt on 9 October.

Because the economically developed countries live way beyond the world's means, they deprive the less economically developed of the land, food and water resources that they need if they are to raise their standard of living above the misery level.

Our economy depends on forests, oceans, agricultural land — and the resources that these provide are being exhausted.

Fredrik Erixon, director of the European Centre for International Political Economy, is sceptical about the use of the word 'debt', since it implies a creditor who can lend spare resources — but, of course, there is no such creditor.

Besides, says Erixon, technological advances in the past have brought about a more effective use of resources, which has enabled economic growth to be sustained.

Adapted from Larry Elliott, 'Easter Sunday — the day we start living off the rest of the world', *Guardian*, 15 April 2006, and BBC News (online), 9 October 2006

Society and politics

Social change

Text B   Childhood in Britain

In February 2007 Unicef published its report: *Child Poverty in Perspective: An Overview of Child Well-being in Rich Countries*. It evaluated the experience of children and young people in 21 countries, on six dimensions:

- material well-being
- health and safety
- education
- peer and family relationships
- behaviours and risks
- subjective well-being

Of the 21 countries, the Netherlands came top, with an average ranking across all dimensions of 4.2; and the UK came bottom, with an average ranking of 18.2. The UK came bottom in three out of the six dimensions: peer and family relationships, behaviours and risks, and subjective well-being.

It had been known for some time that underage sex and the rate of teenage pregnancies are a particular problem in the UK; but that young people in the UK should suffer a greater number of unhappy relationships with their family and peers than young people elsewhere did come as something of a surprise. Fewer than half of the UK's 11–15-year-olds said they found their peers 'kind and helpful'.

Admittedly, the Unicef findings were based on existing data, collected in different ways, in different languages and at different times in the 21 countries; nevertheless, as Bob Reitemeier, chief executive of the Children's Society, put it: 'Unicef's report is a wake-up call to the fact that, despite being a rich country, the UK is failing children and young people in a number of crucial ways.'

The government is committed to halving child

poverty by 2010, and claims that 700,000 fewer children are now living in relative poverty than in 1998/99. The number of children living in absolute poverty has already been halved.

Colette Marshall, UK director of Save the Children, said that £4.5 billion of extra money would be needed if the government was to meet its 2010 target.

Adapted from Jonathan Brown, 'Britain's children: unhappy, neglected and poorly educated', *Independent*, 14 February 2007

Beliefs and values

Transmission of norms and values

Text C   The bookseller of Kabul

Åsne Seierstad is an award-winning Norwegian journalist. In the spring of 2002, she spent 4 months in the household of a bookseller and his family, in Kabul, Afghanistan. Subsequently, she wrote about her experience in what proved to be an 'international bestseller': *The Bookseller of Kabul* (Virago, 2004).

Sultan Khan (not his real name) was an Afghan patriot who dedicated himself to passing on the jewels of the literature and culture of his people. He had built up a stock of books over time, only to have them destroyed by the Russian communists, who invaded the country in 1979. He restocked when the Russians left, but the Mujahedeen — the warlords' militias — looted his shops. Then, when the fundamentalist Taliban came to power, his shelves were ransacked all over again, and all the books to which the extremists took exception were burnt. With Hamid Karzai in power in Kabul, and the Taliban on the run, Sultan Khan began dealing and selling books again. He even had plans to set up a bookshop, lecture room and library in a disused cinema in Kabul.

Though he journeyed to Pakistan and Iran and he spoke English, Khan was no cosmopolitan liberal. On the contrary, he was determined to keep faith with traditions of the most conservative kind: in middle age, he took a second, teenage wife; his mother, wives and sisters ate apart from the men, and wore the head-to-toe burka on the few occasions that they left the house to go to the bazaar and the hammam. If the girls received any education at all, they were not permitted to seek employment as teachers; and everyone in the household, including Khan's brothers and sons, was required to obey him in everything. His sons would man his shops, whatever other ambitions they might have nursed; and when his brothers crossed him, Khan drove them from the house.

Girls were married young to older, well-connected relatives, whatever their own wishes — and when they became pregnant by their husbands, they prayed for sons.

Seierstad paid homage to Khan for the hospitality that she received, but, she said, 'I have rarely been as angry as I was with the Khan family. The same thing was continually provoking me: the manner in which men treated women. The belief in man's superiority was so ingrained that it was seldom questioned.'

Arts and media

New media

Text D — The gospel according to Google

Google™

First there were individual computers running software packages; then there were edited pages of text uploaded to a server; then there was the internet that gave open access to all these web pages; and then there were search engines, like Google, that offered users a clear pathway through what would otherwise have been a tangled web.

Google was founded in 1998 in a garage; now the California company is acknowledged to be the biggest media company on Earth. Just as the big retail giants (Tesco, ASDA, Sainsbury's and Morrisons) account for 74% of the grocery trade in Britain, so the big search engines (Google, Yahoo!, Microsoft, Ask Jeeves and others) are the way into the web for eight out of every ten users. It was thought in the early days that users would dispense with these guides, navigating their own way about the web but the opposite has happened. As websites have multiplied, so users have needed a powerful tool to separate the wheat from the chaff.

Identifying sites is one thing; evaluating them is another. Of four great libraries, out of whose book-stocks Google is digitising 15 million books (Harvard, Stanford, the New York Public Library and Oxford), three are in the USA — and, of course, the language of these books is English. This is one more cultural affront to the French and others whose languages are judged to be — and are, therefore, made — less 'user-friendly'.

Two other forms of evaluation are likely to be still more controversial. Google is planning not merely to present users with an array of, for example, news stories; it aims to rank-order those news stories according to whether they are judged — by Google's own statistical criteria — to be reliable and accurate. How reliable and accurate a story is reckoned to be will depend on the size of the source, on its 'hit rate' and news coverage.

Not only will the *source* of the stories be assessed, users' own online behaviour may be logged, also. Thus, the 'search profiles' of individual users, and of users in the mass, will act as another sort of sieve, so that what is customarily sought out will be what is automatically sorted out for users, in what Google supposes to be their own interest.

Just as the big retailers base their shelving policy on what the tills tell them customers buy most, so we may find that our *choice* of websites is being constrained, effectively by what web-users worldwide habitually choose. Google's motto is: 'don't be evil'. Is this a licence to tell users what is good?

Adapted from Owen Gibson, 'Coming soon: Googling the truth', *Guardian*, 18 June 2005

Science and technology

The nature of science

Text E   The re-emergence of creationism

The law banning the teaching of evolution in Tennessee schools was repealed only in 1967. John T. Scopes, a Tennessee biology teacher, had fallen foul of this law, most famously, in 1925 for teaching Darwinian theory. Fundamentalists in the USA have persisted in their attempts to have creationism taught, at least alongside Darwinism, as an alternative interpretation.

The school board in Dover, Pennsylvania, ruled in 2004 that before Darwinism was taught in biology, the following statements should be read to high-school students: 'Because Darwin's theory is a theory, it continues to be tested as new evidence is discovered. The theory is not a fact. Gaps in the theory exist for which there is no evidence. Intelligent design is an explanation of the origin of life that differs from Darwin's view.'

Students were to be referred to a book, *Of Pandas and People*, in which it is argued that nature is so complex that it can only have been designed by an intelligent being.

In 2005 the school-board members were voted out of office, and a federal judge ruled that the board had violated the American constitution, in that it had sought to 'promote religion in the public school classroom'.

In 2006 concern was expressed by teachers in the UK about creationist teaching in the three

Anti-Evolution League protest, 1925

academies sponsored by the Vardy Foundation. Car-dealer Sir Peter Vardy, one of a number of sponsors of new 'faith schools', is an avowed creationist.

The *Independent* took up the cudgels in an editorial: 'Creationism, or "intelligent design" as its more subtle proponents now prefer to promote it, should have no place in the teaching of science. It is a belief with no relationship to facts or proof through empirical enquiry.'

Teachers should be permitted to present the case for intelligent design in Religious Studies, said the *Independent*, but 'what you should not be permitted to do is to teach this belief as a self-evident explanation of human evolution in the biology class. It is the antithesis of science.'

Adapted from Harry Mount, 'Keep the divine out of biology lessons', *Daily Telegraph*, 21 December 2005, and an editorial in the *Independent*, 12 April 2006

Skills

It is not necessary, of course, for a country to be self-sufficient in all resources, as long as there is international trade. When that trade was interrupted in the Second World War, people dug up their lawns and planted seedlings for food crops, or they were allotted parcels of land (allotments) on which to grow food, under the slogan: 'Dig for victory'.

In peacetime, we have imported bacon from Denmark, lamb from New Zealand, oil from Saudi Arabia and oranges from Spain, and we have paid for these goods by selling English-language textbooks, Land Rovers and financial services.

It is necessary, though, for the world to be self-sufficient, because it is the only one we have got. We are taking out of it, as it were, more than we are putting back — and there are more and more of us doing it at an increasingly fast rate.

Second World War poster promoting self sufficiency

Erixon's point in Text A, that technological advance enables us to use resources more effectively, responds to the fourth question under 'The nature of science': **How strong is our faith in the 'technological fix'?**

However, Text A mostly centres on the possibilities and limitations of economic growth, and on the question under 'Economic growth': **Is economic growth sustainable?**

Andrew Simms, speaking of the UK, claims that we are setting a standard that is 'fundamentally unsustainable'; Fredrik Erixon, speaking of the world as a whole, claims that growth can be sustained.

Here is an example of the sort of question that might be asked in connection with Text A:

Q1 Is (near) self-sufficiency, on the Slovak model, a goal that it would be wise for the UK to adopt?

Why might this be difficult for:
- economic
- political
- ethical

reasons, or even — for whatever reason — undesirable?

Perhaps the first step is to consider whether it would be wise/desirable for the UK to try to be self-sufficient.

(i) **Copy and complete a table like the one below, listing reasons *for* trying to achieve self-sufficiency and reasons *against* doing so:**

Reasons for	Reasons against

It is only necessary to give broad-brush reasons at this stage — but in outlining them, we can begin to identify some of the things we might say in each of the three dimensions: economic, political and ethical.

We are told everything we need to know about the 'Slovak model' in the text: the Slovaks (5,439,448 of them in July 2006) produce most of the food that they need themselves, and they are modest in what they consume.

There are some fairly obvious reasons why it would be difficult on *economic* grounds for us to live like the Slovaks:
- We have moved further away from being an agricultural economy.
- We have exploited almost all the potential agricultural land at our disposal by building houses, roads, playing fields etc. on much available land.
- The UK has a much bigger population to support than Slovakia, working in the secondary and tertiary sectors.

Political difficulties also suggest themselves:
- It would not be politically easy to shift economic growth into reverse.
- Policies designed to encourage people to live more simply would not be vote-winners (unless the external threat were dire and immediate).

- It would not be easy to disentangle ourselves from trade relationships around the world.

(ii) **What *ethical* reasons might there be for adopting the goal of self-sufficiency or not? (You might have given more than one in the table, in answer to question (i).)**

Q1 as it stands is a simplistic, even naïve question; realism would suggest that self-sufficiency is not an option for the UK — but the question does concentrate the mind. We may yet have to think the unthinkable.

Text B is about the 2007 Unicef report on child well-being, which gave rise to much soul searching in the UK. Shadow chancellor George Osborne pointed the finger at chancellor (not then prime minister) Gordon Brown. This was a portrait of 'Brown's Britain', he said. Text B states a problem in relation to the question (under the heading 'Social change' on the specification): **What changes in society might we hope to see brought about?**

An end to child poverty is obviously one such change. When poverty is defined as living on less than half the national income, and when one considers that the average is pushed up by a small minority of people earning six- and seven-figure incomes, it is evident that there will be more child poverty in countries (like the UK and the USA) where there is a large disparity between high salaries and low wages. Poverty is relative.

Another social change that is thought to be responsible for adversely affecting child well-being is family break-up. What chance is there of reducing the number of failed marriages in the UK?

Text C is about two aspects of the 'Transmission of norms and values' in answer to the question: **How might we pass on these values?** The text suggests two ways of doing this: by ensuring the survival of cultural artefacts, and by living those values in the home. Khan's values were not shared by Åsne Seierstad: she would have liked to see a major change in the social norms and values of Kabul.

Q2 The UK is perceived to have been 'failing children and young people' (Text B); Seierstad was angry with the 'manner in which men treated women' in Afghanistan (Text C).

How might the sort of social change we want to see be brought about?

This is a big, open question (most questions on this paper are), but it is also a practical one.

Some of the gender issues referred to in Text C may apply to the UK, but much of our focus will be on the issues raised in Text B. Here is, perhaps, a case where positions 'A' and 'B' do not oppose each other: they are stages in the argument. Thus, position 'A' might be a statement of the 'problem', and position 'B' the outline of a 'solution'.

Draft an 'S/A/B/C' response to Q2.

Text D is dated, but it is not out of date. It still suggests some answers to the question under 'New media': **What are the possibilities and what are the limits of the internet?**

The possibilities are clear to anyone who has conducted an internet search. Limits suggested in the text are that:
- There is a pronounced American bias.
- Non-English-speakers are relatively disadvantaged.
- Google may not be the best judge of the reliability and accuracy of sources.
- The choice of websites may be constrained, arbitrarily.

Text E has something to say in answer to the question under 'Changing patterns of religious belief': **Why might religious fundamentalism be a cause for concern?** However, it has also been chosen for what it says about 'The nature of science', and specifically in answer to the question: **What do we mean by science and scientific method?** A point is also made in relation to: **How 'scientific' can other disciplines be, and should they seek to be?**

It is suggested that in Religious Studies it is perfectly permissible to put creationism forward as one possible interpretation of the beginnings of the world and of life — as long as it is made clear that Religious Studies is a subset of cultural studies, or the history of ideas. There is no 'science' in the Book of Genesis, and there is no room for religious faith in the science laboratory.

>   **Q3** Concern is expressed in Text D that Google may not only be identifying websites, but evaluating them as well; and Text E is about whether there is room for religious interpretation in science lessons.
>
> We prize 'freedom of information'; might the freedom to *interpret* this information be at risk?

The texts contain good material to start with, and our position 'A' might well pick up certain of the concerns expressed, that:

- Search engines may limit our choice of websites by directing us to those considered to be 'reliable and accurate' by other users — by an artificial sieving process.
- School sponsors might use the curriculum as a platform for their own views (or might think that a scientific interpretation has been privileged over one that is faith based).

We will probably want to say in the main ('B') part of our response, though, that there has always been room for interpretation, and that there is probably *more* room now, in an open society, than ever before. As long as the information is out there, we will find subversive, anti-monopolistic ways of interpreting it.

Draft an 'S/A/B/C' response to Q3.

CHANGE
Example 5

Content

Changing patterns of religious belief

| Text A | The waning of religious belief |

It might be the sight of young Muslim radicals on our television screens; or of Sunnis and Shiites bombing each other in Iraq; or it might be still-fresh memories of Catholic–Protestant tensions in Northern Ireland. Whatever the reason behind it, of 1,006 adults sampled by telephone in December 2006, 82% agreed that religion is a cause of division and tension. Only 16% of respondents disagreed with the statement.

It used to be commonplace to claim (perhaps without thinking what it meant) that Britain is a Christian country, just as it used to be commonplace to write 'Church of England' against 'Religion' on an official form. Now, only 17% of adults would call Britain a Christian country, while 62% agreed with the description of it as 'a religious country of many faiths'. (What the remaining 20% of the sample would call it is not recorded.)

Just one-third of those sampled described themselves as religious, against the nearly two-thirds (63%) who said they were not — and, interestingly, those who said they were not religious included more than half of those who claimed to be Christians. It is, apparently, more acceptable to call oneself a Christian (as in being baptised or married in a Christian church) than to call oneself religious. Being 'religious' seems to imply actually going to church, praying and so on. It is fair to add that there is a gender difference where describing oneself as religious is concerned: 37% of women would call themselves religious, against 29% of men.

Of Christians, only 13% claimed to attend a religious service on a weekly basis, while among those of other religions the figure rose to 29%.

A spokesman for the Church of England had this to say: 'You have to bear in mind how society has changed. It's more difficult to go to church now than it was. Communities are displaced, people work longer hours — it's harder to fit it in. It doesn't alter the fact that the Church of England will get a million people in church every Sunday, which is larger than any other gathering in the country.'

Roman Catholics might counter-claim that since Poland joined the EU in May 2004, and young Poles flocked to Britain in their thousands, Catholic church pews have been filling fast. A church that was having to amalgamate parishes is now having some difficulty recruiting priests. Francis Davis, director of a Catholic institute in Cambridge, said: 'It is the Catholic community's biggest opportunity and challenge. In terms of its own life, this is a huge opportunity. They are bringing new energy, new life, and new resources and networks into the Catholic community.

'The challenge is in the mutual lack of understanding, not only between the local population and the new arrivals, but within the Polish community, between those who came because of communism and the young economic migrants. There are 35,000 in the Southampton area alone — more than was expected for the whole country.'

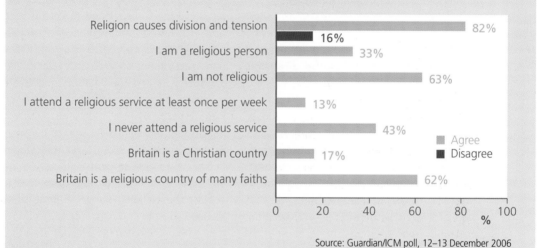

Source: Guardian/ICM poll, 12–13 December 2006

Adapted from articles by Julian Glover, Alexander Topping and Stephen Bates, *Guardian*, 23 December 2006

Society and politics

Educating for change

Text B   Social class and 'league tables'

The old '11+' examination was supposed to be a measure of intelligence and of the potential to benefit either from a grammar school education or a secondary-modern school education. In fact, it proved to be a rather blunt measure of social class. Children from middle-class homes, in general, went to grammar schools and children from working-class homes went to the secondary moderns.

The '11+' passed into history as an element of government policy in 1965. The comprehensive school was to be for all children, irrespective of their 'intelligence' or social-class background. Many middle-class parents were content with 'good' comprehensives (often those that had been grammar schools); some moved into the catchment areas of 'better' comprehensives, or of surviving grammars; and some forwent luxuries to send their children to independent schools.

Conservative governments set great store by parental choice of schools. They introduced grant-maintained schools and city academies; they set National Curriculum tests at key stages; and they obliged schools to publish the results of these tests, so that the schools might be set in rank order, or in 'league tables'. (It may be that it was newspapers that borrowed this metaphor from the sports pages, and not the government — but, whoever first used it, the name has stuck.)

The 'league tables' survived under New Labour. It was recognised, though, that certain schools were high up in the tables for no better reason than that they recruited high-ability children in the first place. Schools whose intake was working class might not do so well, yet their students did better in public exams than they might have been expected to. These schools 'added value' to students, it was said — taking a metaphor, this time, from the City pages. So,

'value-added league tables' were introduced, in which some schools found that they had been promoted, and others that they had been relegated.

It would appear, from findings published in 2006, however, that even these 'value-added' tables fail to capture what it is that distinguished a 'good' school from a 'not-so-good' school. London University professors Webber (at University College) and Butler (at King's) have discovered that — more than 40 years on — what still influences whether a school does well or not so well, in exam terms, is whether it is a predominantly 'middle-class' or 'working-class' school. The UK population was divided, by postcode, into 61 socio-economic groups: 476,000 11-year-old students, and 482,000 15-year-old students (almost 1 million students altogether) were assigned to the 61 groups and matched against the National Pupil Database of test results, at 11 and 15, respectively. This matching process demonstrated that — to put it bluntly — the more 'middle class' a student is, the better he or she does at school; and the more 'middle class' a school is, the better test results it achieves. No matter how dynamic the headteacher, no matter what the ICT facilities, no matter whether it is called a school, a college or an academy, what really seems to count for 'league table' purposes is whether the parents of its students did well at school, are in skilled, professional occupations, own their houses in 'nice' neighbourhoods, read and take an informed interest in the world.

Adapted from Matthew Taylor, 'It's official: class matters', *Guardian*, 28 February 2006

Business and industry

Heritage conservation

Text C   **Listed buildings**

You have probably heard it said that something is a 'listed' building. What does this mean? What *list* is the building on, and why? It means that the building is considered important enough, for historical or architectural reasons, to be protected against demolition, or insensitive alteration or extension.

Anyone can make a recommendation that a building or buildings be listed. It is one of the responsibilities of English Heritage to consider the recommendation, and — if it endorses it — to pass it to the secretary of state for culture, media and sport. The owners of the building are consulted about listing, and are fully informed about what the consequences are.

A listed building cannot be altered or extended without permission, either externally or internally. This means that an owner may not change doors or windows, paint brickwork, remove cement rendering, or add satellite dishes, burglar alarms, aerials, roof-lights or dormer windows without consent; nor may an owner remove or construct internal walls, or remove or cover old fireplaces, panelling or staircases without the permission of the local authority.

A repair that restores a damaged feature to its original state is unlikely to need consent; but, if in doubt, the owner of a listed building should

Corel

take advice from an architect who is experienced in listed-building cases, then seek the consent of the conservation officer of the local council. If the building is a particularly important one, it may be that the conservation officer would consult with English Heritage. A change to a building of national significance would probably merit the attention of the secretary of state.

Demolition of, or structural alteration to, a listed building without consent is a criminal offence and can carry heavy penalties, not the least of which might be that the owner is required to restore the building to its original condition.

Listed buildings — not stately homes, but unusual, characterful, well-designed, eccentric, familiar buildings with historical associations — may add much to a townscape. We owe it to the next generation to pass them on intact.

Adapted from **www.english-heritage.org.uk/server/show/conWebDoc.2422** (accessed 16 May 2007)

Science and technology

The idea of progress in science and technology

Text D — The concept of progress

The ancient Greek understanding of time was of a never-ending cycle of ages, or aeons. Organic nature lived, died and regenerated itself in repeating patterns. Pythagoras was a thinker who believed in what we now call reincarnation, or the migration of the soul from one life to another. If there was 'progress', it consisted in the soul's achieving harmony with the universe.

Ancient Jewish thinking was more linear: Jewish history, as represented in the Old Testament, was about the working out of God's purpose in the salvation of his chosen people.

Christians saw history in a similar way: the difference here was that the Messiah had come, and that in what remained of time before he returned, souls would be gathered up and paradise lost be regained.

It was one of the lessons of the Renaissance that if there was to be progress it would be man who would make it. Harnessing nature, the accumulation of scientific knowledge, political equality and human freedom would make for improvement of the human condition. Francis Bacon and René Descartes were pioneers of the view that nature is a vast machine whose workings are open to our growing understanding.

It was this vision — that technology was about realising human possibilities by mastering nature — that gave rise to a destructive, exploitative, man-against-nature concept of progress. Now we see things more holistically: we think of nature in constant flux, as a complex, multi-state system; as a play in which human beings are actors rather than authors or producers; as a self-regulating biosphere of interactivity and feedback loops.

Our techno-systems must interlock with eco-systems to ensure that all we do is sustainable. If we learn to manage sustainable development over the long term, in Pythagorean harmony with nature, then we shall make progress indeed.

Adapted from www.unesco.org/most/esscgaspar.doc

Arts and media

Visions of the past and future

Text E — Future hype

More than 30 years ago, Alvin Toffler's *Future Shock* was a bestseller that shocked and appalled with its vision of runaway technology. Everyone was convinced that technological development (like the population explosion and resource depletion) would be *exponential*. Linear or arithmetic change is steady and predictable; the curve of exponential change starts out slowly, but then rockets upwards to the near-vertical. It was predicted that technology would advance so far and so fast that it would be beyond society's power to control it. Such predictions were made about robots (and not only in the science-fiction literature); and more recently they have been made about nano-technology.

As Danish physicist Niels Bohr said, though: 'Prediction is very difficult — especially about the future.'

Bob Seidensticker has written a book — *Future Hype* — that sets out to challenge Toffler's vision. Technological development simply does not work like that, he says: ideas germinate over time; technological applications are developed; they peak; they settle; and they are superseded.

Seidensticker worked at a number of computer companies, including — for 8 years — Microsoft. It was there that he began researching technology change, and came to the conclusion that it does *not* develop by leaps and bounds.

He points to speed limits on roads, which have reached an effective maximum; to manned space flight that stalled after the moon landings; and to supersonic commercial aeroplane flight that died with the elegant, doomed Concorde. More controversially, perhaps, he cites nuclear power as a technology that has hit the ceiling.

Most of today's issues in technology, he says, have been around for a long time, and they will be around for a while yet. We must not be beguiled by the concurrent rapid growth of computer memory and the miniaturisation of computers into supposing that this is typical. Besides, it will not last: there is only so much data storage that anyone might need; and how much smaller would we want our mobile phones to be?

'Tomorrow,' says Seidensticker, 'will look more like today than most predictions would lead us to believe.'

Adapted from a review by P. D. Smith, *Guardian*, 24 June 2006

Skills

Many surveys have charted the decline in church attendance, not least those conducted by the Church of England itself. Methodists, Baptists and United Reformed churches have all experienced reductions in numbers. Certain 'Alpha' groups and Pentecostal churches buck the trend for a while — and Text A testifies to an increase in numbers attending Roman Catholic services. How temporary or permanent this resurgence proves to be remains to be seen.

Some people say that the UK is an increasingly secular country. Others say this is not the case. They point to the growing numbers of followers of other faiths; the readiness of many to call themselves 'spiritual', rather than religious, or specifically

Christian; the ordinary, non-churchgoers who were touched, spiritually, by the death of Diana, and the growth in numbers of 'faith' schools.

Is religious belief a part of being human? Religious believers would think so; and it always seems to have been so in the past. But if we ask the question of Christianity: **What changes have traditional religious undergone?** it would have to be acknowledged that there are fewer church-going Christians than there were — or, at least, that institutional Christianity has not been able to count on the sort of automatic allegiance, particularly of young people, that it once commanded.

Attendance has declined in Church of England services

(i) Why do you think this is?

> **Q1** There is a connection, but there is a difference, between *attending a place of worship* and *being religious*.
>
> It may not matter much that fewer people go to services of worship; how much would it matter, from
> - cultural
> - psychological
> - moral
>
> points of view, if religious belief declined in the UK — or disappeared entirely?

There is no second question here, because the first is quite substantial enough.

It may be your view — if you are not religious — that it would not matter at all if there were a decline in religious belief. You might even take the view that the less religious belief there is, the better. If this is the case, you would give your reasons for this view in position 'B'.

Consider, though, whether there might not be some *cultural* loss if there were no churches, synagogues or temples — no religious expression of any kind.

(ii) **What might be lost to UK culture by the decline, or even the disappearance, of religious belief?**

Under the *psychological* effects of a loss of religious belief, one might bear in mind that:

- Some people may rely for their social bonds on the group dynamics of religious services, study groups or social activities affliliated to the church, mosque, synagogue or temple.
- They may derive comfort from their beliefs, from the rituals associated with them, and from prayer to a higher being, whether this be God/Allah, or an agent (the Pope, or a priest, imam or rabbi).

Under the *moral* effects of a loss of religious belief, some people might say that 'if you don't believe in God you could do anything'. Some believe that:

- Our moral and legal codes are rooted in the teachings of the Bible and of Jewish, Christian and Muslim interpretations of 'The Book', successively.
- Fear of hell and hope of heaven — God's anger or approval respectively — are the ultimate sanctions of our moral behaviour.

If you are a believer, you might want to incorporate some of the above thoughts in your position 'B'; if you are not a believer, you ought not to discount them altogether.

Text B is something of an overview: a looking back to see how we got to where we are now. The research findings were the focus of the Matthew Taylor article. It may be that 'working class' and 'middle class' are terms less familiar now than they were, so it might be as well to give some broad-brush descriptions:

You were considered to be 'middle class' if:	You were considered to be 'working class' if:
Your parents had been to 'good' schools	Your parents had been to secondary-modern schools
One or both parents were in professional or white-collar jobs	One or both parents were in manual, unskilled, blue-collar jobs
The family lived in its own (mortgaged) house	The family lived in rented accommodation, or a council house
The house was in a 'leafy' neighbourhood of privately owned houses	The house or flat was on an estate, or on an urban street
There were books at home and a support for education	There were no books at home or any cultural activity

The specification question that is most obviously addressed here is: **In what ways is society resistant or adaptable to change?** It seems that, whatever attempts have been made to ensure equality of opportunity in the school system, and to break down social-class barriers, educational *outcomes* are the direct result of social-class *inputs*.

Text C offers some ideas in response to the first two questions under 'Heritage conservation': **What do we mean by 'heritage'?** and **How might conservation differ from preservation?** Here, heritage seems to mean fine (not necessarily very old) buildings of the sort that we would miss if they were pulled down or remodelled — good, noble, honest, familiar landmarks. It seems to be the intention of English Heritage to *preserve* listed buildings in a state as close to their original as possible. *Conservation* would imply that to adapt them to modern purposes would be perfectly in order.

> **Q2** In spite of the educational policies of different governments, schools seem to be much the same as they were (Text B); it is the very intention of English Heritage that listed buildings remain as they were (Text C).
>
> How far can it be said that we tend to resist change?

The question could be answered either way: much will depend on the nature of the examples/illustrations chosen whether the answer 'Yes, we are' or 'No, we aren't' is the more persuasive.

So as not to echo the texts too much, it would probably be wiser to refer to the texts in position 'A', and then to exemplify in position 'B' the case for our being prepared to embrace change.

Draft an 'S/A/B/C' response to Q2.

Text D could be used to respond to the question: **What do we mean by 'progress'?** under the heading 'The idea of progress in science and technology', while Text E responds both to the question, under the same subheading: **What do we expect from science and technology in the future?** and to the third question under 'Visions of the past and future': **Do the media present us with credible visions of the future?**

Scientists themselves, of course, have collaborated in presenting a vision of the future that invites us to wonder. Up to 10 million viewers used to tune in to Raymond Baxter's *Tomorrow's World* on the BBC, between 1965 and 1977; but science-fiction writers, and directors of films like *Star Wars, 2001: A Space Odyssey* and *The Day after*

Tomorrow have run on ahead of the evidence. Seidensticker's view is that Toffler did much the same.

> **Q3** Text D makes the point that 'progress' in the past has been destructive; and Text E pours cold water on the idea that technology advances by 'leaps and bounds'.
>
> Could technology play a smaller part in the future than we might have thought?

As Bohr said: 'Prediction is very difficult.' Even so, both texts might serve to instruct us in a certain scepticism: we might want to argue that we should rein in technology; that we should not hope for a 'technological fix'.

On the other hand — though we may not be going into space any time soon — we still need to develop the technologies that will help us to adapt to changing conditions, such as:

- water desalination
- effective solar heating
- drought-resistant GM food crops
- tidal-energy stations

Draft an 'S/A/B/C' response to Q3.